I Never Knew That
ABOUT
WALES

Christopher Winn has been a freelance writer and trivia collector for over twenty years. He has worked with Terry Wogan and Jonathan Ross, and sets quiz questions for television as well as for the *Daily Mail* and *Daily Telegraph*. He is the author of the bestselling *I Never Knew That About England*. Books in the same series cover Ireland, Scotland, Wales, London, Yorkshire, the Lake District and New York, and he has written further books on the River Thames and Royal Britain. He is also the Associate Producer for a TV series by ITV about Great Britain. He is married to artist Mai Osawa, who illustrates all the books in the series.

Christopher Winn

I Never Knew That ABOUT WALES

ILLUSTRATIONS
BY
Mai Osawa

EBURY
PRESS

5 7 9 10 8 6 4

Ebury Press, an imprint of Ebury Publishing,
20 Vauxhall Bridge Road,
London SW1V 2SA

Ebury Press is part of the Penguin Random House group of companies whose addresses can be found at global.penguinrandomhouse.com

First published by Ebury Press in 2007
This edition published by Ebury Press in 2015

www.eburypublishing.co.uk

A CIP catalogue record for this book is available from the British Library

ISBN 9781785031021

Typeset by Palimpsest Book Production Limited,
Falkirk, Stirlingshire
Printed and bound by Clays Ltd, Elcograf S.p.A.

Penguin Random House is committed to a sustainable future for our business, our readers and our planet. This book is made from Forest Stewardship Council® certified paper.

For Esther

Contents

Preface ix
Map of Wales x
Counties of Wales xi

ANGLESEY 1
BRECONSHIRE 16
CAERNARFONSHIRE ... 30
CARDIGANSHIRE 48
CARMARTHENSHIRE ... 59
DENBIGHSHIRE 69
FLINTSHIRE 83
GLAMORGAN 94
MERIONETH 114
MONMOUTHSHIRE 125
MONTGOMERYSHIRE .. 138
PEMBROKESHIRE 147
RADNORSHIRE 164

Gazetteer 175
Index of People 180
Index of Places 188

Conwy Castle, Caernarfonshire

Preface

Wales may be small in size but her influence is mighty. She is an ancient civilisation with Europe's oldest language and earliest seats of learning. Her collection of castles is the finest in the world and speaks of a rich and turbulent history. Wales gave us Britain's greatest Royal dynasty, the Tudors. A Welshman gave his name to America, Richard ap Meryk, who became Sheriff of Bristol and sponsored the Cabot brothers in their voyages of discovery to the New World.

Wales is the Land of Song and Poetry and brings the peoples of the world together in friendly competition. Her music soars around the globe and her musicians and actors mesmerise and win awards with their passion and their range.

Wales was the world's first industrial nation. Her coal and iron and back-breaking toil drove the Industrial Revolution and built the modern world. Her people fought for social justice, for dignity and for fairness.

The beauties of Wales, her wild mountains and moorlands, lacustrine valleys and glorious coastlines, inspired the Picturesque movement, the first landscape painters, and the first Area of Outstanding Natural Beauty.

For all this, Wales does not strut or boast or preen, but quietly nurtures her plentiful treasures behind mountains or in deep valleys. She is full of surprises, constantly delighting the traveller with the unexpected, one moment vast, magnificent panoramas, stately cathedrals and castles and giant monuments of industry, then tiny, exquisite chapels, ancient burial grounds, cottages, waterfalls, green woods and dales.

In Wales there is nowhere that is not wondrous, nowhere that fails to amaze and charm, nowhere that does not bring forth the exclamation 'I never knew that!'

Wales is like nowhere else.

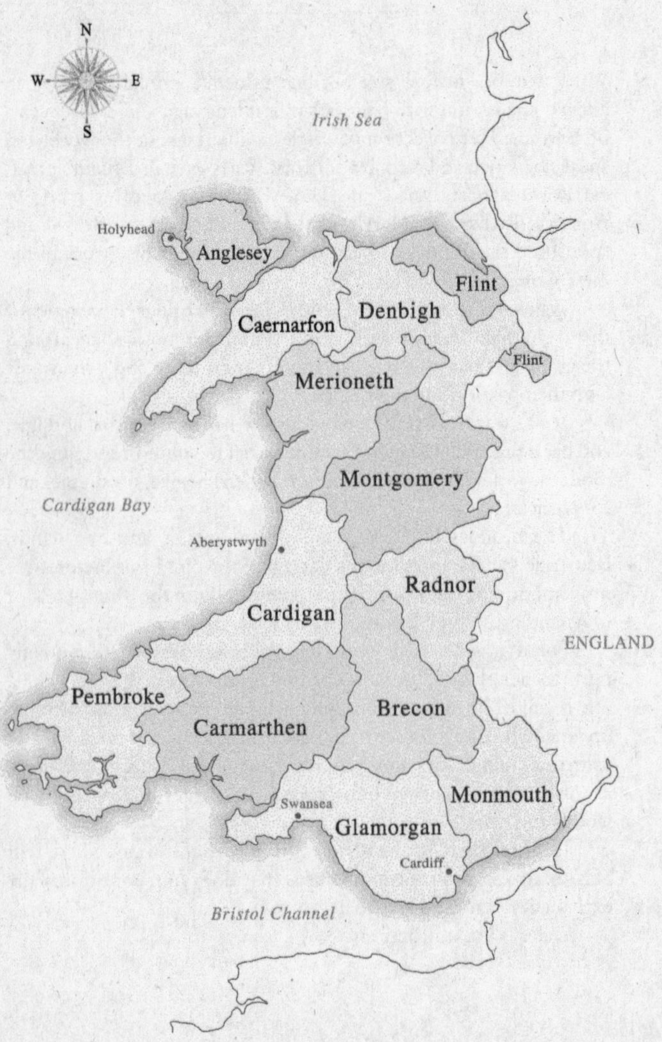
N
W
E
S
Irish Sea
Holyhead
Anglesey
Flint
Denbigh
Caernarfon
Flint
Merioneth
Montgomery
Cardigan Bay
Aberystwyth
Radnor
Cardigan
ENGLAND
Pembroke
Brecon
Carmarthen
Monmouth
Swansea
Glamorgan
Cardiff
Bristol Channel

The Counties of Wales

I have organised *I Never Knew That About Wales* into the 13 traditional counties that existed from medieval times until the lamentable local government reorganisation in 1974.

Glamorgan and Pembrokeshire have both been distinctive areas from ancient days, while Anglesey, Caernarfonshire, Cardiganshire, Carmarthenshire, Flintshire and Merioneth were created by the Statute of Rhuddlan in 1284. The other 5 counties of Denbighshire, Montgomeryshire, Radnorshire, Breconshire and Monmouthshire were established out of the Marcher fiefdoms by the Law in Wales Act of 1535, which abolished the powers of the Lordships of the Marches.

While the post-1974 county names reflect some of the old Welsh kingdoms, their physical boundaries do not always equate to those of the original territories, which were, in any case, somewhat fluid. Nor do the modern counties take account of old loyalties and identities. The traditional counties, on the other hand, were quite deliberately determined by the ancient divisions of the country, are the most settled and long lasting of all the divisions of Wales, and form the backdrop, in terms of both time and flavour, to most of the stories in this book.

ANGLESEY

(YNYS MON)

COUNTY TOWN: BEAUMARIS

St Tysilio's Chapel and the Menai Bridge, the world's first large-scale suspension bridge

Menai Strait

Bridging the Divide

For as long as anyone can remember, the island of Anglesey has been separated from the mainland by its own very effective moat, the MENAI STRAIT, 12 miles (19 km) of surging tides, treacherous sandbanks and whirling currents, 600 ft (180 m) across at its narrowest point. Today, according to the European Union, Anglesey no longer qualifies as an island, thanks to the success of two unique bridges.

Menai Bridge

The MENAI BRIDGE, designed by Thomas Telford and opened on 30 January 1826, was THE FIRST SUSPENSION BRIDGE IN THE WORLD CONSTRUCTED TO TAKE HEAVY TRAFFIC. At the time it was built it was THE LONGEST BRIDGE IN THE WORLD, 1,265 ft (386 m) in length, with a main span of 579 ft (176 m) hung from wrought-iron chains and suspended 100 ft (30 m) above the high tide mark, allowing plenty of room for ships to pass

underneath. In 1839, the deck of the bridge was damaged by strong gales, and it has been replaced twice, once in 1893, and most recently in 1940 with a steel deck.

As well as being an engineering wonder, the Menai Bridge is utterly beautiful. When seen from the A4080 viewing point to the west, it looks like an integral part of the landscape, the graceful lines of the bridge blending seamlessly with the undulating shapes of the Snowdonia mountains behind.

On the Anglesey side, on a little promontory below the bridge, there is a reminder of the times when it was not so easy to reach the island. A small 14th-century church sits on the site of a chapel founded in AD 630 by St Tysilio, where travellers could rest and pray, or give thanks, for a safe crossing.

Britannia Bridge

A little to the west is the BRITANNIA BRIDGE, opened in 1850 to carry the Chester to Holyhead railway across the Menai Strait. Designed by Robert Stephenson, son of railway pioneer George Stephenson, this was THE FIRST MAJOR TUBULAR BRIDGE IN THE WORLD. It consisted of two wrought-iron tubes of 479 ft (146 m) in length, along with two additional spans of 230 ft (70 m), set 100 ft (30 m) above the water and supported on limestone piers.

Originally, it was intended to hang the tubes from chains, rather in the manner of Telford's Menai suspension bridge but, in testing, the tubes proved immensely strong and quite capable of bearing the weight of the trains on their own. The holes from which the chains were to be slung can be seen at the top of the piers.

In 1970, a couple of local boys exploring the tubes dropped a burning torch and set fire to the bridge, which had to be closed for four years. It was reconstructed without the tubes, using a conventional arch structure, an option made possible by the fact that clearance was no longer needed for large ships to pass underneath. In 1980, a road deck was opened above the railway, and this now carries the A55 across to Anglesey. The monumental stone lions that guarded the original bridge still stand sentinel at each end.

As their famous bridges stand side by side across the Menai Strait, so Thomas Telford and Robert Stephenson rest side by side in Westminster Abbey.

Marquess of Anglesey

The best view of the two bridges is from the top of the 90 ft (27 m) high marble column built on the edge of his estate, in 1816, to commemorate the

1ST MARQUESS OF ANGLESEY, second in command to the Duke of Wellington at the Battle of Waterloo. The climb up 115 rickety steps is rewarded with one of the great views of the world, taking in the whole of Anglesey, the Menai Strait, the mountains of Snowdonia as well as the distant hills of the Lleyn Peninsula. To stand before this stupendous panorama, protected from the drop merely by a thin iron railing, with the wind buffeting the column and threatening at any moment to pluck you from the flimsy platform, is a truly exhilarating experience.

Sharing the view from the top of the column is a bronze statue of Henry Paget, the 1st Marquess of Anglesey, added in 1860. At Waterloo, while seated on his horse beside the Duke of Wellington, the Marquess, or the Earl of Uxbridge as he then was, had his leg shattered by a canon shell, an uncomfortable experience which caused him to exclaim, 'By God, Sir, I've lost my leg!'

'By God, Sir, so you have!' replied the Duke, before resuming his examination of the battlefield through his telescope.

Later that same day Lord Uxbridge had the remains of his leg amputated, and on his return to London he was advanced to the Marquessate of Anglesey and given a wooden leg. He went on to have 18 children and 73 grandchildren and lived to the noble age of 86. His wooden leg, THE FIRST ARTICULATED WOODEN LEG EVER MADE, can be seen in the Military Museum at PLAS NEWYDD, the Marquess of Anglesey's elegant 18th-century home on the banks of the Menai Strait. The house, designed by James Wyatt, is now owned by the National Trust, and the Dining Room contains THE LARGEST PAINTING EVER COMPLETED BY REX WHISTLER, a panoramic 'mural', 58 ft (18 m) wide, painted on to a single piece of canvas.

Beaumaris

'Beaumaris is second to none'
GEORGE BORROW

The coastal road to BEAUMARIS from Menai Bridge is one of the most attractive in the whole of Britain. It winds and dips past elegant villas that gaze out across the water towards the dark green of Snowdonia, and there are tantalising glimpses of glittering blue sea through the trees.

Arriving in Beaumaris itself is no disappointment. The woods and the vistas open out in spectacular fashion on to the 'beau marais' or 'beautiful marsh' that gives the town its name. The Great Orme looms on the horizon, while yachts and pleasure boats bob up and down against the lowering black backdrop of the cliffs at Penmaenmawr on the mainland. Two miles (3.2 km) across the water is the Lavan sandbank, from where ferries and mail packets once crossed to Beaumaris, with passengers and mail for Holyhead and Ireland.

There is a genteel, undeniably 'English' feel to Beaumaris, which is hardly surprising since, at the end of the 13th century, the native Welsh inhabitants of the original village, called Llanfaes, were forcibly moved across the island to start again at Newborough, freeing up space and material for King Edward's new castle.

On the seafront of Beaumaris, a short pier and a huge expanse of smooth green lawn, laid down on land reclaimed from the marshes in 1832, are overlooked by a dignified mix of elegant Georgian houses and impressive Victorian terraces. The latter were built by Joseph Hansom, of Hansom Cab fame, who also was responsible for the 'model' town GAOL of 1829, a shining example of a progressive and humane Victorian prison system. There were separate cells for women and children, each cell had running water, and you can still see the drunkards' cell, the soundproof isolation room, the whipping room and THE ONLY TREADWHEEL IN BRITAIN STILL IN ITS ORIGINAL POSITION. There is also an intriguing crank that was used as a particularly cruel and mind-numbing punishment, with a prisoner's meals being dependent on the number of turns completed – 2,000 for breakfast, 3,000 for supper and so on.

Apparently, no one ever escaped from Beaumaris Gaol. In 1862, the last inmate of the gaol to hang, a man called Richard Rowlands, put a curse on the nearby church clock as he went to the scaffold, vowing that the four faces would never again show the same time. And, indeed, until the clock was given an overhaul in 1980, each face displayed a slightly different time.

Beaumaris was Anglesey's first county town. It was also an administrative and legal centre, and the restored Jacobean COURTHOUSE, established in 1614 and still in use as a magistrate's court, is THE OLDEST COURTHOUSE IN WALES and ONE OF THE LONGEST-SERVING COURTROOMS IN BRITAIN. When used for assizes, it was THE ONLY COURTROOM IN BRITAIN WHERE THE JURY SAT HIGHER THAN THE JUDGE.

In the porch of ST MARY'S CHURCH, which dates from

Old Courthouse

the early 14th century, is the stone coffin of JOAN (1195–1237), daughter of King John, brought here from Llanfaes Priory at the Dissolution of the Monasteries in the 16th century. She was married to Llywelyn the Great and was known in Wales as 'Siwan'.

At the entrance to the coach yard of the 15th-century YE OLD BULL'S HEAD INN is THE LARGEST SIMPLE-HINGED DOOR IN BRITAIN, 13 ft (3.96 m) high and 11 ft (3.35 m) wide.

Beaumaris Castle

Just Perfect

If a modern computer was asked to design a perfect medieval fortress it would undoubtedly come up with BEAUMARIS CASTLE, considered to be THE MOST TECHNICALLY AND ARCHITECTURALLY PERFECT EXAMPLE OF A CONCENTRIC CASTLE IN EUROPE. The work of James of St George from Savoy, it was begun in 1295, the last of the iron ring of fortresses built by Edward I to contain the mountainous kingdom of Gwynedd. Beaumaris's role was to guard the northern approach to the Menai Strait.

Partly because it was never fully completed, owing to a lack of funds, and partly because of its low-lying position, Beaumaris Castle is a less spectacular sight than King Edward's other castles. More beautiful than intimidating in its inconspicuous position at one end of the main street, it complements rather than dominates the town. However, further examination reveals the remarkable strength and ingenuity of the design.

For anyone attempting to capture the castle, there are some 14 obstacles to overcome. The first line of defence is a deep moat, connected to the sea by a short canal, and at high tide supply boats could sail right up to the castle walls, protected by guns sited on a raised platform on the 'Gunner's Walk'. An iron mooring ring where the boats would tie up can still be seen hanging from the wall.

The next defence is an eight-sided curtain wall punctuated with 16 drum towers and two gates. The main gate in the south wall, protected by 'murder holes' through which boiling oil could be poured, is set slightly off centre, so that anyone who succeeded in getting through the gateway would have to execute a sharp right and left before setting about the barbican, all the while under fire from above.

The walls of the huge inner ward, 16 ft (5 m) thick and over 40 ft (12 m) high, are riddled with narrow passageways that cry out to be explored, and hidden away in one of the massive inner towers is the castle's jewel, an exquisite vaulted chapel.

Beaumaris Castle is a World Heritage Site.

Penmon

Doves and Peace

Almost as far east as you can go on Anglesey, at PENMON ('end of Mon'), there is a picturesque collection of medieval buildings, the ruins of a 13th-century refectory and a 16th-century domestic house, grouped around a beautiful Norman church. A cell was established in this lonely but lovely spot by a monk called St Seiriol, in the 6th century, and this later became an Augustinian priory. The remnants of St Seiriol's Well, where the original priory stood, can be found a short step away from the present church, itself begun in the 12th century.

Added to, and restored, at various times, Penmon today has a very special atmosphere. The church, which still retains its original Norman tower and pyramid cap, is approached through the small garden courtyard of the Prior's House. Once inside, if you turn right you find yourself in 18th-century grandeur. Turn left, under a glorious Norman arch, and you are in the bare beauty of the 12th century, with crooked walls and delicate stone arcading. It is quite startling to find such superb Norman architecture in this isolated place and, just to add to the wonder, there are two finely sculptured Celtic crosses set up in the south transept which were brought in from the fields outside.

Across the road is a huge square dovecote, put up in 1600 by the local landowner, Sir Richard Bulkeley, to house up to 1,000 birds. Inside is an extraordinary stone pillar with projecting stones that provide a ladder giving access to the nests.

Nearby is a disused quarry that provided stone for Beaumaris Castle and the pillars of the Menai and Britannia bridges.

Puffin Island

A Tasty Morsel

From Penmon, a short, bumpy toll road leads to Anglesey's eastern tip at Black Point, where there is a lighthouse and an old lifeboat station. A melancholy bell tolls a warning from the rocks in the middle of the treacherous waters that separate the point from Ynys Seiriol (Seiriol's Island), once known as Priestholm. St Seiriol had a sanctuary on the island, and some scant 6th-century remains can still be seen. He also had a chapel on the mainland at Penmaenmawr, and would travel between the two along a secret sand bank, now vanished beneath the waves of Conwy Bay.

The island is better known today as PUFFIN ISLAND, from the large colony of puffins that once nested there. In the 18th and 19th centuries the colony was almost eradicated by rats and by a food fad of the time – pickled puffin was considered a tasty delicacy.

Moelfre

Gold Bullion and Gold Medals

MOELFRE is a small village of pastel-painted stone cottages that tumble down to a pebble beach and tiny harbour popular with fisherfolk and yachtsmen. It sits on a rocky headland that has caught out many an unwary vessel rounding Anglesey on its way to or from Liverpool. The Moelfre lifeboat has been involved in countless rescue missions over the last 200 years, most famously in October 1859 when the steam clipper *Royal Charter* foundered on rocks just to the north, during a fierce storm. The lifeboat crew managed to save 39 lives before the ship broke up, but some 460 men, women and children perished. The ship was returning to Liverpool from the Australian Gold Rush with a cargo of gold, much of which is thought still to be on board the wreck. Frequent efforts have been made to try and recover the haul, allegedly to no avail, although Customs Officers still keep a beady eye on the village for any signs of unexplained extravagance amongst the local inhabitants. The bodies of most of those who drowned are buried at Llanallgo, a little way inland, and there is a memorial on the headland.

Exactly one hundred years later, almost to the day, the Moelfre lifeboat crew saved the eight-man crew of the coaster *Hindlea*, which had hit rocks below the coastguard station, a rescue that earned RICHARD EVANS, the lifeboat coxswain, his second Royal National Lifeboat Institution gold medal.

Further north, on the cliff top at PORT LYNAS there used to be a semaphore station, part of a system which, in good weather, could relay messages from Holyhead to Liverpool in under a minute. Today ships bound for Merseyside stop here to take on board a pilot to steer them safely into port.

Amlwch

Copper Capital

AMLWCH, an attractive little town on Anglesey's north coast, is THE MOST NORTHERLY TOWN IN WALES and, for much of the 18th and 19th centuries, was THE COPPER CAPITAL OF THE WORLD as well as THE RICHEST PORT IN WALES.

The source of its wealth, PARYS MOUNTAIN, sits scarred and lifeless just outside the town, a barren, dusty place riven with pits and craters like some sore on Anglesey's fair face. Evidence has been found that suggests copper was mined here some 4,000 years ago in the Bronze Age, making Parys one of THE EARLIEST MINES IN BRITAIN. And it was copper that brought the Romans to Anglesey. In the 1760s mining started up once again on a small scale and expanded to meet the growing demand for copper until, by the end of the 18th century, Parys Mountain was THE WORLD'S BIGGEST PRODUCER OF COPPER and the site of THE LARGEST OPEN-CAST COPPER MINE IN THE WORLD. The copper was of such a high grade that the Parys Mine Company minted its own coins known as 'Amlwch Pennies', stamped with a Druid's head on the front and its initials, PMC, on the back. These are now highly sought-after collector's items.

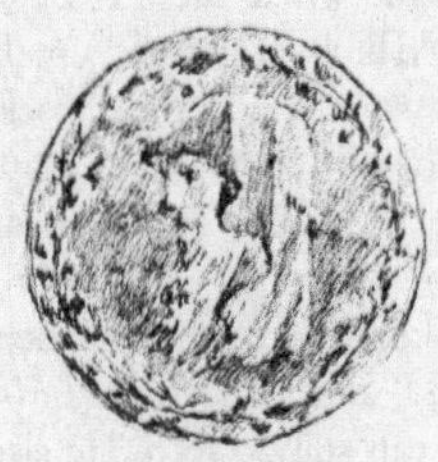

Today, the eerie pink and orange landscape can be explored with the help of a guide. Highlights include the remains of an engine house that once sheltered one of the earliest Cornish beam engines in Britain, and a brown lake full of sulphuric acid at the bottom of the derelict open-cast mine. The unearthly location has also attracted many film and TV companies. Parys Mountain has starred in the BBC television series of *Doctor Who* and films such as *Mortal Kombat, The Annihilation* in 1997 and *Infestation* in 2005.

Amlwch, in the meantime, has settled down to become a quiet seaside town popular with holiday-makers. The harbour that once sent copper around the world now bustles instead with pleasure craft and yachts.

The town's dry dock was created by enlarging a natural inlet and is thought to be THE ONLY DRY DOCK OF ITS KIND IN BRITAIN.

At Bull Bay is the unique church of OUR LADY, STAR OF THE SEA, built in the 1930s in the shape of an upturned boat by an Italian, G. Rinvolucri, a former prisoner of war.

Holyhead

(Caergybi)

End of the Road

The largest town in the county of Anglesey, HOLYHEAD is not actually on the island of Anglesey but rather on Holy Island, which stands just off the north-west coast of Anglesey. Its origins are Roman, and the present-day St Cybi's parish church stands within the thick, 16 ft (5 m) high walls of a 3rd-century Roman fort. In the 5th century, a Celtic monk, St Cybi, built a monastic cell within the protection of these walls, where the existing church now stands. Dating mainly from the time of the Tudors, the church was restored by Sir George Gilbert Scott in the 19th century, and contains some superb stained-glass windows by William Morris and Edward Burne-Jones.

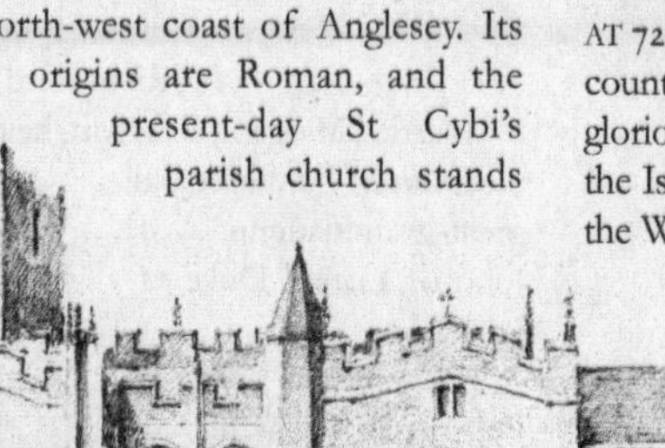

ADMIRALTY ARCH was erected in 1821 to commemorate the visit of George IV and to mark the end of Thomas Telford's road from London, now the A5. The railway arrived shortly afterwards, cementing Holyhead's position as THE PRINCIPAL BRITISH TERMINAL FOR THE CROSSING TO IRELAND.

Holyhead's North Breakwater, designed by James Meadow and completed in 1873, is THE LONGEST BREAKWATER IN BRITAIN. It is 1½ miles (2.4 km) long, shelters 700 acres (283 ha) of water, and took 30 years to build.

To the west is HOLYHEAD MOUNTAIN, AT 720 ft (219 m) the highest point in the county of Anglesey. At the top, as well as glorious views of Anglesey, Snowdonia, the Isle of Man and even, on a clear day, the Wicklow Mountains in Ireland, there are the remains of a hill fort and some ancient hut settlements. A little further west, 410 steps lead down from a car park to SOUTH STACK, a tiny islet linked to Holy Island by a metal footbridge,

Admiralty Arch

and crowned with a lighthouse built in 1809. The slow climb back up is rewarded with close views of the numerous sea birds nesting on the steep cliffs.

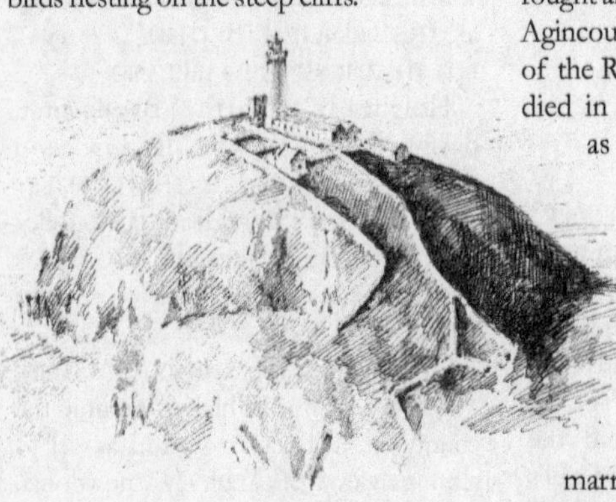

South Stack

Penmynydd

Cradle of a Dynasty

In the 13th century, Ednyfed Fychan, Lord Steward to Llywelyn the Great, was granted the lands around Penmynydd as a reward for his services. In 1385 his descendant, OWAIN AP MAREDUDD AP TUDUR, was born at Plas Penmynydd, in the original house on the site. Owain ap Tudur, the 'Rose of Mona', fought alongside Henry V at the Battle of Agincourt in 1415 and was made head of the Royal Household. After Henry V died in 1422, Owain, by now known as Owen Tudor, and Henry's widow Catherine de Valois, daughter of the French King Charles VI, fell in love and secretly married. They had three sons, Edmund, Jasper and Owen. Edmund became Earl of Richmond and married Margaret Beaufort, heiress to the Duke of Somerset and great-granddaughter of John of Gaunt, Duke of Lancaster.

Their son, born at Pembroke Castle in 1457 (*see* Pembrokeshire), ascended the throne of England in 1485 as Henry VII, exactly 100 years after his grandfather was born at Penmynydd, finally fulfilling Merlin the Wizard's prophecy that a man from Anglesey would one day sit upon the English throne.

In a chapel of the village church of St Gredifael are the grand alabaster tombs of Henry VII's great-grand-uncle Gronw Fychan ap Tudur and his wife Myfanwy. Over the years pilgrims have removed bits of the tombs in the belief that they are bestowed with healing powers. There is also a colourful stained-glass window illustrating the royal regalia of the English throne, the Tudor rose and the portcullis of the Beaufort family. Lettering in Welsh around the window translates as 'unity is as a rose on a river bank and a house of steel on a mountain top'. Ty Dur, or Tudor, is Welsh for house of steel.

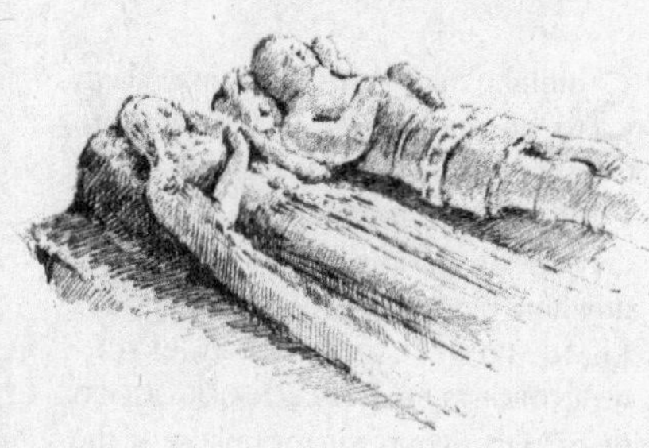

Aberffraw

Lost Splendour

Ten miles (16 km) away on Anglesey's west coast an old grey stone, single-arch packhorse bridge leads into the little fishing village of ABERFFRAW, ancient capital of the Kings of Gwynedd. Celtic Britain was ruled from here for hundreds of years, from not long after the Romans left until the time of Llywelyn the Last and Edward I. Today, little remains to show of the glittering royal court except an arch in the church of St Bueno said to come from the palace of the Princes.

Nearby, beneath the nave of the church at LLANGADWALADR, lies CADFAN, ruler of Gwynedd between AD 616 and 625. His tombstone bears the Latin inscription *sapientisimus opinateimus omnium regum* – 'wisest and most renowned of all kings', and lays claim to being THE OLDEST ROYAL TOMBSTONE IN BRITAIN. The village is named after Cadfan's grandson Cadwaladr, king of Gwynedd who died of the plague in 664.

A little to the north is another survivor from Aberffraw's glory days, the tiny island church of ST CWYFAN'S, founded in AD 605 and reached only at low tide, via a causeway. Set in the sea against a backdrop of mountains, this must be one of the most ravishing locations for a church anywhere in Britain. Despite its remoteness, occasional services are still held here.

St Cwyfan's

Newborough

Sand Dunes and the Island of Love

The village of NEWBOROUGH was founded at the end of the 13th century by the displaced inhabitants of Llanfaes, moved here by Edward I to make way for his castle at Beaumaris. South of the village is one of the largest areas of sand dunes on the west coast of Britain. In 1992 parts of the lost royal palace of Llys Rhosyr were discovered beneath the sand, and new sections are slowly being uncovered every year.

Beyond the dunes, a walk along the vast, windswept beach leads to YNYS LLANDDWYN, the island where ST DWYNWEN, patron saint of lovers, made her sanctuary. On her feast day, 25 January, the lonely island becomes a place of pilgrimage for courting couples. It can be reached, with difficulty, by those determined enough to brave the elements and clamber across the rocks at low tide. It is exalting to sit upon this bare, romantic outcrop, with the sea breeze blowing in your face and the wide expanse of sand at your back, gazing across the wild, white-capped waves to the distant grey coastline of Lleyn.

Llanfair PG

Long Stop

Shinjuku Station in Tokyo may claim to be the world's busiest station. Clapham Junction may claim to be Europe's busiest station. But for sheer density of people in a small space, nowhere beats the station at Anglesey's LLANFAIRPWLLGWYNGYLLGOGERYCH-WYRNDROBWLLLLANTYSILIOGOGOGOCH or 'St Mary's church in the hollow of the

white
hazel near a rapid
whirlpool and the church of
St Tysilio of the red cave'.

Turn off the quiet, nondescript high street of what the locals and the Post Office call Llanfair PG, into the station car park, and you enter a frenetic, parallel world. Vast double-decker coaches buck and hiss as they disgorge their loads by the thousand. The air is thick with the curses of strong men who wave their fists while bumping and scraping their paintwork, as they battle for any parking space that becomes available. Children and tourists yap excitedly, beaming with anticipation.

But surely the people who come here are not just dense in quantity, but also in intellect, for few trains stop here and there is absolutely nothing to see. Except a name – with 58 letters, THE LONGEST PLACE NAME IN EUROPE. THE LONGEST NAME FOR A RAILWAY STATION IN THE WORLD, possibly (*see* Merioneth). And now THE LONGEST, VALID, SINGLE-WORD INTERNET DOMAIN NAME IN THE WORLD. And a brilliant hoax.

In the middle of the 19th century, a local cobbler, looking to drum up some trade, alighted on the idea of combining the name of the village with that of neighbouring Llantysiliogogogoch to create the longest station name in the world. It worked to perfection and, ever since, the station has been one of the most popular tourist attractions in Wales. Today the real station is almost deserted as the throng patronises the modern, purpose-built visitor centre next door, where you can be issued with THE LONGEST PLATFORM TICKET IN THE WORLD and purchase sung musical versions of the name, guides to its pronunciation in every language, and postcards of the station sign.

The name Llanfairpwllgwyngyll-gogerychwyrndrobwllllantysiliogogogoch was used in the 1968 film *Barbarella*, starring Jane Fonda, as the password for the headquarters of the resistance leader Dildano (played by David Hemmings).

Llanfairpwllgwyngyllgogerychwyrn-drobwllllantysiliogogogoch is twinned with the Dutch town of d'Ee.

BORN IN ANGLESEY

GLENYS KINNOCK, Member of the European Parliament and wife of the former Labour Party leader Neil Kinnock, was born in Holyhead in 1944.

DAWN ROMA FRENCH, comedienne and actress, best known as one half of the French and Saunders comedy duo, and as the Vicar of Dibley in the BBC television situation comedy of that name. She was born in Holyhead, where her father was stationed with the RAF, on 11 October 1957. She is married to comedian Lenny Henry.

ALED JONES, singer and television presenter, was born in Llandegfan, near Beaumaris, on 29 December 1970.

BURIED IN ANGLESEY

SIR PATRICK ABERCROMBIE (1879–1957), town planner and co-founder, in 1926, of the Council for the Protection of Rural England. He came up with the idea of green belts around cities to limit their expansion. He is buried in the churchyard at Rhoscolyn on Holy Island, where he had a retirement home.

ROBERT EVERETT (1902–42), winner of the 1929 Grand National on Gregalach at odds of 100–1. In the Second World War he became a fighter pilot and was killed when his Hurricane crashed in January 1942. He is buried in the churchyard at Llanddona, just north of Beaumaris.

Well, I never knew this ABOUT ANGLESEY

Anglesey is THE FIFTH LARGEST ISLAND OFF THE COAST OF BRITAIN and THE LARGEST ISLAND OFF THE COAST OF BRITAIN OUTSIDE SCOTLAND.

Anglesey has A GREATER CONCENTRATION OF PREHISTORIC REMAINS THAN ANYWHERE ELSE IN WALES. Perhaps the best preserved of these is BRYN CELLI DDU, a fine chambered burial mound near Plas Newydd which dates from around 2000 BC. Another Neolithic burial chamber, BARCLODIAD Y GAWRES, can be found on the cliffs north of Aberffraw. This contains THE MOST EXTENSIVE COLLECTION OF STONE AGE WALL PAINTINGS IN WALES. The construction of both these burial places, as well as the chevron and spiral shapes carved on to the stones inside, are similar to those of the celebrated passage graves in the Boyne valley of Ireland, such as Newgrange.

Thanks to its abundant wheatfields, which for a long time fed the people of Wales, Anglesey has always been known to the Welsh as MON MAM CYMRU, the 'Mother of Wales'. It was the wheatfields, as well as the rich copper deposits at Amlwch, which drew the Romans here and encouraged them to take on the fearsome Druids, who had withdrawn to Yns Mon and made it their headquarters after being driven off the mainland. Under the command of Suetonius, the Romans crossed the sands at Newborough in AD 61 and slaughtered the Druids, who stood amongst the trees brandishing fiery torches and screaming terrible curses in a courageous but forlorn show of defiance.

Built in 1716, the lighthouse on the SKERRIES, off the north-west coast of Anglesey, was THE LAST PRIVATE LIGHTHOUSE IN BRITAIN. Control passed to Trinity House in 1841.

The A5114, which runs for less than 2 miles (3.2 km) between Llangefni and the A5, is THE SHORTEST 'A' ROAD IN BRITAIN.

Just outside Llanfair PG is a distinctive octagonal building, one of three surviving tollhouses on the A5 between Llanfair PG and Holyhead. The last toll was charged here in 1895, and the road was THE LAST PUBLIC TOLL ROAD IN BRITAIN, until a congestion charge began to be levied on traffic entering Durham in 2002.

THE FIRST EVER MEETING OF THE WOMEN'S INSTITUTE HELD IN EUROPE took place in a house in Llanfair PG in 1915. The Women's Institute originated in Canada.

In July 1663, Holyhead was the finishing line for THE WORLD'S FIRST OFFICIAL SEA-GOING OPEN YACHT RACE, when the world's first catamaran, Sir William Petty's *Experiment,* beat the Dublin Packet in a race from to Holyhead from Dublin.

Opened in Holyhead in 1949, HOLYHEAD COUNTY SECONDARY was BRITAIN'S FIRST COMPREHENSIVE SCHOOL.

The WYLFA NUCLEAR POWER STATION, on Anglesey's north coast, is THE LARGEST CAPACITY MAGNOX STATION IN BRITAIN, with an output of some 980 megawatts. Its two Magnox reactors are THE LARGEST OF THEIR TYPE IN THE WORLD. The plant was begun in 1963 and first generated electricity in 1971. Today Wylfa supplies over 40 per cent of Wales's electricity needs. It is due to be decommissioned in 2010, but discussions are under way on whether to build a new nuclear power station on the site.

BRECONSHIRE

(SIR BRYCHEINIOG)

COUNTY TOWN: BRECON

Brecon Cathedral, home to Britain's largest Norman font

Brecon

(Aberhonddu)

Home for Heroes

Ancient Britons, Romans and Normans, each have left their calling cards at BRECON. The huge Iron Age hill fort of PEN-Y-CRUG, on a hill just to the north of the present town, has a circumference of 1,650 ft (503 m) and ramparts 18 ft (5.5 m) high. A little to the west is BRECON Y GAER, THE LARGEST ROMAN FORT OF ITS TYPE IN WALES. Remains of the castle, begun in 1093 by the Norman baron Bernard de Neufmarche, can be found in the Bishop's Palace gardens and in the garden of the Castle Hotel.

Brecon sits in its own green bowl of hills, where three rivers meet, the Usk, the Tarrell and the Honddu, and where all ways converge, mountain, valley and road. Cut off from the rest of the world by the Black Mountains and the Brecon Beacons, it has the aspect of a Welsh agricultural market town, yet feels like an English cathedral city. At the centre

of the town, traffic swirls around St Mary's parish church, while narrow streets and passageways lined with Jacobean shop fronts dive down to the river or straggle up the hill.

Once it dawns that St Mary's is not the cathedral, it is but a short steep walk up the hill, past the massive battlemented wall of the medieval priory close, to the attractive lich-gate leading into the cathedral close.

Cathedral
The 'Church of St John the Evangelist Without the Walls' was founded sometime after 1093, as a Benedictine monastery, by Bernard de Neufmarche's confessor, a monk from Battle Abbey in Sussex. All that remains from the original Norman structure is the magnificent font, elaborately carved with extraordinary birds and beasts. The present building, most of which dates from the 13th and 14th centuries, is 205 ft (62 m) in length, solid and well-proportioned. The chancel, dating from 1201, is one of the most sublime examples of Early English architecture to be found in any British cathedral.

In the baptistry can be found THE BIGGEST CRESSET STONE IN BRITAIN, with 30 cups. A cresset stone is an ancient form of lighting, a large stone slab with a number of chambers scooped out of it, in which to put candles.

The elegant five-lancet east window commemorates the officers and men of the 24TH REGIMENT (SOUTH WALES BORDERERS) who lost their lives in the Zulu War of 1879. In the Havard Chapel on the north side of the chancel, now the Regimental Chapel of the South Wales Borderers (since amalgamated into the Royal Regiment of Wales), there hangs the Queen's Colour of the 1st Battalion 24th Regiment. This was recovered after the Battle of Isandlhwana, having been gallantly defended by Lieutenants Melvill and Coghill at the cost of their own lives. Each was awarded a posthumous Victoria Cross in 1907.

South Wales Borderers

The barracks of the South Wales Borderers is down in the town. The museum houses mementoes of their heroic defence of the British supply base at Rorke's Drift in January 1879, when 104 men held off 4,500 Zulu warriors for more than 12 hours, until relieved at seven o'clock in the morning. Eleven Victoria Crosses were won at Rorke's Drift, including seven for men of the 'Old 24th', THE LARGEST NUMBER OF VCs EVER AWARDED TO A SINGLE REGIMENT FOR ONE ACTION. The classic film *Zulu*, that tells the story of the battle, was made in 1964 and starred Michael Caine and Stanley Baker.

A noted occupant of the delightful Prior's House beside the cathedral was SIR JOHN PRICE (1502–55), church commissioner for Wales and the man given responsibility for dissolving the monasteries in Wales in 1537. He was the author, in 1547, of THE FIRST BOOK TO BE PRINTED IN WELSH, *Yn y Lhyvyr hwnn*, an instruction manual for the Welsh priesthood.

Another Price from Brecon, DR HUGH PRICE, founded Jesus College, Oxford, in 1571, primarily for students from Wales. The college still maintains strong links with Wales.

THE FIRST OFFICIAL WELSH SETTLER IN AMERICA, HOWELL POWELL, was from Brecon. He left for the state of Virginia in 1642.

SARAH SIDDONS (1755–1831), regarded as the greatest actress of her day, was born Sarah Kemble in the Shoulder of Mutton Inn, now the Sarah Siddons, on Brecon High Street. The inn sign is a reproduction of a portrait of the actress by Gainsborough. Sarah's brother Charles Kemble (1775–1854), an equally famous actor in his day, was also born in Brecon.

Cilmery

The Last Prince

The name of the pub in CILMERY gives a clue to the significance of this little village on the River Irfon, to the west of Builth Wells. It is called the Prince Llewelyn, in honour of LLYWELYN AP GRUFFUDD, THE LAST WELSH-BORN PRINCE OF WALES, who was killed in a skirmish here in 1282.

No one really knows what happened, but somehow Llywelyn became separated from his men and was run through by an English soldier, who stumbled upon him in woods down by the river. According to some sources, the soldier at first failed to realise whom he had killed, until he rummaged through Llywelyn's clothes and came across some precious items, including a leather pouch with some splinters of wood inside it. This was recognised by the priest who came to bless the body as one of the great treasures of Gwynedd, fragments of the True Cross, known as the Cross of Gneth. Whether this tale is true or not, the Cross of Gneth ended up in the English treasury, and was given by Edward III to be displayed in St George's Chapel at Windsor Castle. It did not survive the Reformation.

A 15 ft (4.6 m) high monument of Caernarfonshire granite has been erected near the spot, encircled by 13 oak trees planted in 1952 to represent the 13 historic Welsh counties.

Llanwrtyd Wells

(Llanwrtud)

Smallest Town?

Nobody has yet been able to disprove the claim of LLANWRTYD WELLS, population 700, to be THE SMALLEST TOWN IN BRITAIN. It is indisputably the home of the annual WORLD BOG SNORKELLING CHAMPIONSHIPS, held in August, whereby competitors must race for two lengths of a 180 ft (55 m) cutting through the peat bog, wearing flippers and a snorkel – but without using normal swimming strokes. Other competitions held in the town include the Man versus Horse race in May and the Real Ale Wobble – which can happen at any time.

The well at Llanwrtyd is THE MOST SULPHUROUS IN WALES and was publicised by the historian Theophilus Evans (1693–1767), when he wrote about how the waters had cured his scurvy.

SOSPAN FOCH (Little Saucepan), the Welsh rugby anthem (*see* Carmarthenshire), was composed by Talog Williams and the Revd D.M. Davies while they were staying in Llanwrtyd Wells in 1895.

Trefeca

Strawberry Hills

TREFECA must have come as quite a surprise to anyone strolling through the green foothills of the Black Mountains, north-west of Brecon, in the middle of the 18th century. HOWELL HARRIS, leader of the great Methodist Revival in Wales, was born here in 1714, and later in life he extended and redesigned the property in pure 'Strawberry Hill' Gothick style, as a home for his 'family' of followers.

It all began on Palm Sunday in 1735, in St Gwendoline's Church at Talgarth, just up the road. 'I felt suddenly my heart melting within me like wax before a fire, with love to God my Saviour.' This experience spurred Harris on to become a preacher, and he went off to travel many hundreds of miles through Wales on foot, preaching in the open air to vast crowds.

In 1752 he withdrew to his home at Trefeca and founded his 'Connexion', a self-sufficient religious community, part monastic, part co-operative. They looked after themselves and shared everything, while all practising different crafts and trades, in what John Wesley called a 'little paradise'. Life was actually pretty tough, with everyone rising at 4 a.m. and working, either in the fields or in the workshops, until 11 p.m., stopping only to pray three times a day. In the main communal room an all-seeing eye was painted on the ceiling, and there were spy-holes through which Harris could keep an eye on his flock.

Amongst other things, Harris was an innovative agriculturalist, who introduced the turnip to Wales and co-founded the BRECONSHIRE AGRICULTURAL SOCIETY, THE FIRST OF ITS KIND IN WALES. He also pioneered new printing methods with his Trefeca Press, and many of the pamphlets and religious tracts he printed can be seen in the fascinating museum dedicated to his life, housed in the memorial chapel. Although his bombastic ways upset many, his funeral at St Gwendoline's in 1773 was attended by over 20,000 people. Inside the church there is a huge, black, commemorative tablet near the communion table, marking his burial place, which attracts its fair share of pilgrims even now.

Still in use as a retreat, Trefeca is now a Lay Training Centre for the Presbyterian Church of Wales. Unfortunately, much of Harris's Strawberry Hill confection has been subsumed over the years into a bland block of unimaginative white buildings, but the quiet atmosphere and the silence amidst the surrounding hills is wonderfully restful.

Craig-y-Nos

Queen of Song

The fairytale pinnacles and turrets of neo-Gothic CRAIG-Y-NOS CASTLE nestle in a remote and ravishing valley beneath the bare slopes of Fforest Fawr, south-west of Brecon. Built by Thomas Wyatt in 1840 for Captain Rhys Powell, CRAIG-Y-NOS, or 'Rock of the Night', became a magnet for European society as the home for 40 years of the singer ADELINA PATTI (1843–1919), described by Verdi as 'the finest soprano of her age'. The Queen of Song came to live in the Land of Song in 1878, with her lover and future husband the tenor Ernesto Nicolini. She was drawn by the pure mountain air, the dramatic scenery, and the opportunity to create her own private musical kingdom, where she could rest and recharge after her exhausting tours of the opera houses and salons of the world.

Born in Madrid, the fourth of six children, to a Sicilian father and an Italian mother both involved in opera, Adelina soon began to beguile with her clear, pure voice. At the age of 19 she sang 'Home Sweet Home' at the White House and reduced Abraham Lincoln and his wife to tears – they were in mourning for their son, who had just died of typhoid. 'Home Sweet Home' became her most requested song. She performed before all the crowned heads of Europe, including the Kaiser, the Tsar and Queen Victoria, sang at Rossini's funeral, married Napoleon III's equerry, and became one of the world's richest women – for one

performance of *La Traviata* in Boston she was paid $5,000, more or less what she paid for Craig-y-Nos.

Adelina Patti was a generous and popular chatelaine. She would arrive at Craig-y-Nos rather like Queen Victoria arriving at Balmoral, travelling in her own special train to the tiny station at Penwyllt, and being borne along to the castle down a private road lined with cheering crowds. She lavished a fortune on the estate, laying out gardens and installing all the latest technology – Craig-y-Nos was ONE OF THE FIRST PRIVATE HOUSES IN BRITAIN TO HAVE ELECTRICITY.

On 19 June 1886, most of South Wales turned out to see her marry Ernesto Nicolini at the tiny St Cynog's Church in the nearby village of Ystradgynlais. Afterwards, at the reception, over 100 local people enjoyed dinner in the castle's banqueting hall, there were fireworks and dancing until dawn, and a giant bonfire was lit on the mountainside above.

They all came to see Patti at Craig-y-Nos – the Crown Prince of Sweden, Prince Henry of Battenberg, the Prince of Wales, (later Edward VII), and, in 1891, Baron Julius Reuter, the founder of Reuter's News Agency, who officiated at the opening of her new private theatre, modelled on the Theatre Royal Drury Lane. The theatre is still used today for opera and remains one of the most perfect examples of a state-of-the-art working Victorian theatre surviving in Britain.

Adelina Patti died in 1919 at Craig-y-Nos and is buried close to Rossini in the Père Lachaise cemetery in Paris.

Cave Country

Deep Thoughts

Dan-yr-Ogof

The southern fringe of the Brecon Beacons National Park is renowned for its limestone caves, and Craig-y-Nos sits right in the middle of some of the best caving country in Britain. The caves of DAN-YR-OGOF at the National Showcaves Centre to the north are 'BRITAIN'S LARGEST AND LONGEST SHOWCAVES', and are family friendly with lighting, concrete steps and handholds. They were first properly explored in 1912, and so far over 10 miles (16 km) of caverns have been discovered. Weddings are held in the vast Cathedral Cave. In the Bone Cave 42 human skeletons were found.

Ogof Ffynnon Ddu

Further south, towards Abercraf, and for more experienced cavers only, is OGOF FFYNNON DDU, at 1,010 ft (308 m) THE DEEPEST CAVE IN BRITAIN, and the third longest, with over 30 miles (48 km) of passages.

Maen Madoc

A little to the east, running in a dead straight line from near the village of Coelbren towards Ystradfellte, there is a remarkably untouched stretch of Roman road, dating from around AD 74, when the Romans conquered Wales. It crosses the bare exposed moorlands of Fforest Fawr, passing on the way a 9 ft (2.7 m) high standing stone called MAEN MADOC, which bears an incomplete

Latin inscription that translates as '... of Drevacus, son of Justus. He lies here'.

Porth-yr-Ogof

PORTH-YR-OGOF, meaning 'gateway to the cave', lies south of the mountain hamlet of Ystradfellte, and is THE LARGEST CAVE ENTRANCE IN WALES, one of the largest in Britain. Once inside there are some 2 miles (3.2 km) of caves to explore, and Porth-yr-Ogof remains very popular with cavers, despite the fact that the cave system here has claimed more lives than any other cave in Britain, with ten deaths in 50 years.

Sgwd y Eira

This area of Breconshire is also known as waterfall country, and at SGWD Y EIRA, the 'Waterfall of Snow', just to the south of Porth-yr-Ogof, you can follow a path behind the falls, an exhilarating experience.

Chartist Cave

Travelling east, beyond the Brecon Mountain Railway, to the east of Garn Fawr on Mynydd Llangynidr, is the CHARTIST CAVE, where Chartist meetings were held and weapons were stockpiled prior to the march on Newport in November 1839 (*see* Monmouthshire). The entrance has crumbled somewhat and access is difficult.

Mynydd Llangatwg

Further east, underneath MYNYDD LLANGATWG, south of Crickhowell, is THE LARGEST CAVE SYSTEM IN EUROPE, discovered in 1960 by students from the University of Wales. It can be accessed from Llangattock.

Shakespeare's Cave

South of Mynydd Llangatwg, in CLYDACH GORGE, there is a FAIRY GLEN and SHAKESPEARE'S CAVE, which has led many to speculate that this is where William Shakespeare wrote *A Midsummer Night's Dream.* Certainly the wild and mystical atmosphere here can inspire fantastical visions of fairies and star-crossed lovers. It is believed that Shakespeare came to explore the gorge while staying with friends at Trebarriad House, north of Brecon. The house in which the Bard stayed was subsequently replaced with a quite exceptionally beautiful Jacobean mansion that has been recently restored.

Trebarriad House

Crickhowell

The Heights of Fame

Framed by the Abergavenny Sugar Loaf and the dramatic Table Mountain, Crickhowell is one of the most delightful small market towns in Wales. The 17th-century bridge across the River Usk here is THE LONGEST STONE BRIDGE IN WALES. A pleasant diversion is trying to solve the conundrum of Crickhowell Bridge – seen from the eastern end it has 13 arches, but seen from the western end it only has 12.

Just outside Crickhowell, to the west, is a fine Georgian house called GWERNDALE, now a hotel, where SIR GEORGE EVEREST (1790–1866) was born. He was appointed Surveyor-General of India in 1830, and the pioneering triangulation methods he developed for his work were used by his successor, Andrew Waugh, in 1852 to calculate the height of the highest mountain in the world. In tribute to Sir George Everest, 'that illustrious master of geographical research', as Waugh described him, the world's highest peak was given the name MT EVEREST.

High in the hills behind Crickhowell, on a slope above the valley of the Grwyne Fawr, is one of those heavenly places that you can only find in Wales. Slumbering peacefully at the end of a steep mountain track, embowered in its own patch of green churchyard, bedecked with flowers and unbelievable views, is the little church of PARTRISHOW, no more than a tumble of stones, huddled up against the wind. A little stream burbles nearby, and a spring. Stone seats run along the church wall facing a tall, wonderfully preserved preaching cross. As the door of the church swings open it is hard not to gasp at the treasures revealed. An unpainted screen and balustrade of Irish oak, exquisitely carved with dragons and vines, that served as a 15th-century storybook for a congregation long gone. A font with an inscription that dates it to circa 1055, and, behind it, the medieval hermit's cell belonging to St Ishow. There is also an early mural of a Doom figure on the west wall.

It must be the isolation that has protected these wonders from the

Reformation, from Cromwell's soldiers, from vandals. Partrishow is hard to find but even more difficult to leave.

Llangoed Hall

The White Palace

On the banks of the River Wye between Builth Wells and Brecon is LLANGOED HALL, thought to be built on the site of the fabled White Palace, home of the first Welsh Parliament in the early 6th century. In AD 560 the palace was passed over to the See of Llandaff by Prince Iddon, who wished to earn forgiveness for his wrongdoings, and it evolved into an Episcopal Grange. By 1632 the Grange had become dilapidated, and a splendid pile was then built from the ruins for Sir Henry Williams, whose coat of arms can be found above the surviving Jacobean porch.

In 1880 the house was won in a game of poker by a John Macnamara, and then, in 1912, the new owner Sir Archibald Christie asked Clough Williams-Ellis to redesign and extend the property. This was Clough Williams-Ellis's first major commission and shows many of the characteristics and tricks he would later use to great effect when designing his masterpiece at Portmeirion (*see* Merioneth). Llangoed Hall eventually fell into a terrible state of neglect and was rescued from demolition in the 1980s by SIR BERNARD ASHLEY, who turned it into a country house hotel to showcase his wife's Laura Ashley Fabrics.

Capel-y-Ffin

Borderline Behaviour

The narrow road along the Vale of Ewyas from Abergavenny to Hay-on-Wye, past Llanthony Priory and up over Hay Bluff, is one of the most gorgeous roads in Britain. About 4 miles (6.4 km) west of Llanthony, just as you cross the border from Monmouthshire into Breconshire, lies the tiny community of CAPEL-Y-FFIN, which means 'chapel on the border'. There is a beautiful little chapel of ease here, white, with a crooked, wooden belfry, surrounded by ancient yew trees. Just off the road is a small group of Italianate buildings with a statue of Jesus outside. This is 'Llanthony Tertia', a Benedictine monastery founded in 1870 by an Anglican priest, Joseph Leycester Lyne, known as Father Ignatius. He had wanted to buy the original Llanthony Priory ruins but was thwarted, and so he decided to build his own retreat, where he lived in contented seclusion with a small community of like-minded fellows. The buildings were never completed, and when Father Ignatius

Eric Gill only stayed at Capel-y-Ffin for four years from 1924 until 1928, but a good deal of his best work was accomplished here, so the solitude and invigorating air must have been great inspiration. In his autobiography, much of which he wrote here, Gill recalls his days at Capel-y-Ffin as the happiest time of his life, and he returned frequently to visit his daughter Betty, who stayed on with her family. Examples of his calligraphy can be found on gravestones in the monastery and in the burial ground of the little white chapel. The monastery is privately owned but the remains of Father Ignatius's unfinished church can be explored.

died in 1908 the monks of Caldey Island, near Tenby, took over the monastery.

In 1924 the eccentric sculptor and artist ERIC GILL (1882–1940) bought the crumbling monastery buildings and moved to Capel-y-Ffin with some of his exotic retinue of animals, family and craftsmen, from their commune at Ditchling in Sussex. They lived as self-sufficiently as they could, growing their own food and making their own furniture. It was while living at Capel-y-Ffin that Gill designed what he is perhaps best remembered for, apart from his controversial life-style, the classic GILL SANS typeface. Acknowledged as THE FIRST BRITISH MODERNIST TYPE DESIGN, Gill Sans was used on the covers of pre-war Penguin books, and by British Railways, and was chosen for the BBC logo in 1997. Amongst his major sculptures are *Ariel* and *Prospero* on Broadcasting House in London's Portland Place, the *East Wind* sculpture over the entrance to St James's Park underground station, and the *Stations of the Cross* in Westminster Cathedral.

Hay-on-Wye

(Y Gelli Gandryll)

Books, Books and More Books

Hay-on-Wye revels in its claim to be THE SECOND-HAND BOOK CAPITAL OF THE WORLD. It is, however, no idle boast, for this small border town has 38 bookshops and was THE WORLD'S FIRST BOOK TOWN – there are now some 60 Book Towns across the world and the number is growing all the time.

It was all started by RICHARD BOOTH in 1961 when he opened his first bookshop in Hay, which soon grew into EUROPE'S LARGEST SECOND-HAND BOOKSHOP. His motto was that 'you buy

books from all over the world and your customers come from all over the world'. In the 1970s he came up with the idea of a Book Town and whipped up a lot of publicity on April Fool's Day in 1977 by declaring Hay-on-Wye an independent kingdom, and proclaiming himself King of Hay.

In 1988, the first Hay Literary Festival was held and this has since grown into one of Europe's premier literary occasions, attracting 100,000 visitors and top writers to the town. The star speaker in 2002 was former US President Bill Clinton.

Books aside, Hay is a fascinating ancient town clustered around a Norman castle, on one of the most beautiful stretches of the River Wye. It is full of tempting narrow streets, half-timbered houses, cosy pubs and restaurants and a slightly musty, intellectual, other-worldly atmosphere that is highly seductive.

Well, I never knew this
ABOUT
BRECONSHIRE

The 520 sq. mile (1,346 sq. km) BRECON BEACONS NATIONAL PARK, established in 1957, is the newest National Park in Wales. Today, Wales's three National Parks and five Areas of Outstanding Natural Beauty cover 23 per cent of the country.

At 2,906 ft (886 m) PEN Y FAN in the Brecon Beacons is THE HIGHEST POINT IN SOUTHERN BRITAIN.

BRYNMAWR, on the southern slopes of Mynydd Llangattock, is 1,350 ft (411 m) above sea level, THE HIGHEST TOWN IN WALES.

BUILTH WELLS claims to possess the only Post Office that was opened in Britain during the short reign of Edward VIII.

Beside the A40 near Halfway, equidistant from Trecastle and Llandovery, is one of the first drink driving warning signs, a striking obelisk known as the 'COACHMAN'S CAUTIONARY'. It commemorates a disaster which took place in 1835 when a stagecoach full of passengers, with a drunk driver at the reins, careered over the edge and rolled down the hill into the river.

HEOL SENNI, a tiny village south of Sennybridge, was the birthplace of the RT REVD W.T. HAVARD, THE ONLY BISHOP TO PLAY RUGBY FOR WALES. He was capped in 1919, before going on to become Bishop of St Asaph.

On 14 December 2000, the WELSH WHISKY COMPANY began producing whisky in the pretty village of PENDERYN on the Glamorgan border. This was the first whisky to be produced in Wales since the closure of the Frongoch distillery near Bala in 1894 – as a result of a 'chapel building' religious revival which encouraged temperance (*see* Merioneth). The design of the purpose-built new distillery at Penderyn is based on that of the old 19th-century distillery at Frongoch. In the early 18th century, there was a small distillery at Dale in Pembrokeshire, owned by Evan Williams, whose family emigrated to America and helped to found the Kentucky Whiskey industry. The new Welsh Whisky single malt is matured in Jack Daniels and Evan Williams casks – a fitting tribute to the Welsh pioneers of bourbon.

The BRECON MOUNTAIN RAILWAY which runs between Merthyr Tydfil and the Taf Fechan reservoir is the only one of Wales's 'Great Little Railways' located in South Wales.

LLANGORS LAKE, south-east of Brecon, is THE SECOND LARGEST NATURAL LAKE IN WALES.

The Iron Age hill fort of CASTELL DINAS, near Talgarth, occupies THE HIGHEST CASTLE SITE IN WALES, 1,476 ft (450 m) above sea level.

CAERNARFONSHIRE

(SIR CAERNARFON)

COUNTY TOWN: CAERNARFON

Caernarfon Castle, Constantinople in the West

Caernarfon Castle

Royal Spin

CAERNARFON CASTLE is the largest of Edward I's castles in Wales. It was designed to be not just a fortress but also a palace, and a seat of government as well. Begun in 1283, the castle took 50 years to build and, even then, was never finished.

The first impression of Caernarfon Castle is the sheer size of it. The entrance arches soar higher than a cathedral and the tall, grim walls darken the narrow streets below. Voices and footsteps echo in the shadows. You feel cold, cowed, conquered. If Caernarfon Castle has that effect now, then how much more awe and fear did it inspire 1,000 years ago?

But there is more to Caernarfon than simple brute power. There is subtle imagery at work here too. Edward built Caernarfon near the site of the Roman fort of Segontium, the remains of which can still be seen outside the town walls to the south. In AD 383, the commander of the Roman forces in

Britain, Magnus Maximus, who was married to the daughter of a Welsh prince, declared himself 'Caesar' and went out from Segontium accompanied by many Welsh warriors, to set himself up as Emperor of the West. Although Maximus was eventually defeated, the symbolism of Welsh princes fighting alongside Roman legions was not lost on Edward, and Caernarfon was designed to draw on that symbolism, showing Edward to be the natural successor of Roman imperial power. Each of the three mini turrets of Caernarfon's distinctive Eagle Tower bears a sculpture of a Roman eagle from Segontium.

The imagery goes deeper still. A strong element in Welsh legend is the belief that the Emperor Constantine (306–37) was born at Segontium, and the banded walls of Caernarfon Castle, lined with strips of dark sandstone and layers of decorative tiles, are deliberately reminiscent of the massive walls of Constantine's great city in the East, Constantinople, asserting Caernarfon as the Constantinople of the West. A masterpiece, not just of engineering, but of political propaganda.

Edward I even went so far as to make sure that his son, the future Edward II, was born at Caernarfon, in 1284, and was later proclaimed Prince of Wales, thus completing the illusion.

And it worked. Over 700 years later it is accepted almost without question that the eldest son of the reigning monarch should become Prince of Wales. In 1911, the 20th Prince of Wales, another Edward, assumed the title at Caernarfon, and the whole world watched on television as Prince Charles, eldest son of Elizabeth II, was invested as the 21st Prince of Wales in 1969.

Conwy

Perfect Medieval Town

CONWY IS THE MOST COMPLETE MEDIEVAL WALLED TOWN IN BRITAIN. Seen from the river with the mountains as a backdrop, the fantastic castle looms over the bustling rooftops of the town like a crouched lioness guarding her cubs. The castle was begun in 1283, the same year as Caernarfon, but unlike Caernarfon, it was finished in just four years. It is a real 'Boy's Own' castle, rugged and dour, a solid doorman relying on brute muscle to intimidate. And yet, while there is strength outwardly, there is also beauty within – the Chapel Royal inside the Chapel Tower is quite lovely

Three bridges lead across the river to the castle at the gate. The 1958 road bridge is ugly. Obviously no thought was given to how it might be made to enhance rather than ruin the view. Its chief misdemeanour is to hide Thomas Telford's graceful suspension bridge, built in 1822, with turreted piers at each end in deference to the great towers of the castle. This bridge was a mini prototype of Telford's 1826 Menai Bridge, 20 miles (32 km) to the west, and therefore not just beautiful to look at but of great historical significance. In 1965 the town council voted to demolish it, but thankfully the National Trust stepped in to save it, and you can now walk across it

forever, on payment of a small toll at the restored toll house.

Next to it runs Robert Stephenson's Tubular Railway Bridge of 1847, also a prototype for his Britannia Tubular Railway Bridge of 1850, across the Menai Strait. The Conwy bridge provides us with a good opportunity today to see what the Britannia Bridge looked like before the fire of 1970. At Conwy, trains still disappear into the tubes and re-emerge the other end like snakes from a hole. Stephenson, like Telford, made an effort to have his bridge blend in, by raising crenellated towers at each end.

All three bridges decant their traffic at the narrow town gate, and Conwy used to be a real bottleneck, but now cars are taken under the town in a tunnel, THE FIRST IMMERSED TUBE TUNNEL IN BRITAIN.

It is possible to walk virtually all the way around Conwy along the town walls. They are three-quarters of a mile (1.2 km) in length, include three gates and 21 towers, and were built as an integral part of the defences at the same time as the castle. Enclosed within the walls is a virtually unchanged medieval townscape of almost film set quality.

ABERCONWY HOUSE in Castle Street, a timber and stone merchant's dwelling

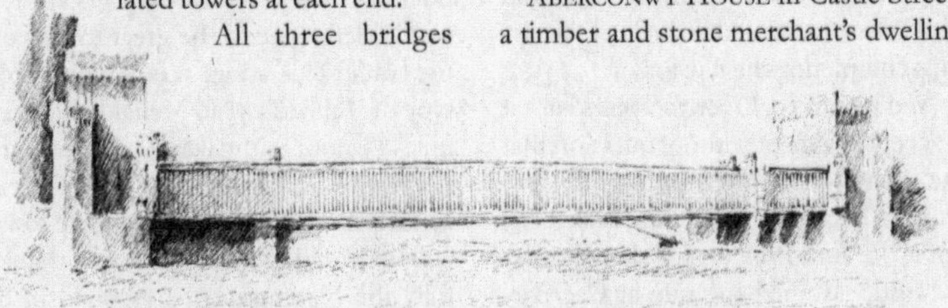

now run by the National Trust, dates from the 14th century and is THE OLDEST TOWN HOUSE IN WALES.

In the High Street is THE FINEST TOWN HOUSE IN WALES, PLAS MAWR, an Elizabethan mansion built around an inner courtyard, with a decorated stone facade and more than 50 mullioned windows. It was built for Robert Wynne, a rich merchant, in 1576, taken over by the Mostyns, and then given to the nation in 1991.

In sharp contrast, down on the quay is THE SMALLEST HOUSE IN BRITAIN, just 10 ft 2 inches (3.1 m) high and 6 ft (1.8 m) wide. It has only two rooms, and the last tenant was a fisherman who was 6 ft 3 inches (1.9 m) tall.

Bangor

Britain's Oldest Bishopric

BANGOR came into existence around AD 525, when a monk by the name of ST DEINIOL established a cell on the site, building a church and enclosing the small community with a type of wattle fence known as a 'bangor'. In AD 546, St Deiniol was officially granted the land by Maelgwn, King of Gwynedd, and the church became BRITAIN'S SECOND CATHEDRAL, after Whithorn in Scotland. The land around became THE FIRST TERRITORIAL DIOCESE IN BRITAIN, with St Deiniol as its first Bishop. Bangor is

now THE OLDEST CATHEDRAL STILL IN USE IN BRITAIN.

The first stone cathedral was begun by Bishop David in 1120, but destroyed by King John in 1210. The present building dates largely from the 13th century, and underwent a major restoration by Sir George Gilbert Scott, in the 1870s.

The grandfather of Llywelyn the Great, Owain Gwynedd, Prince of Gwynedd, who died in 1170, was buried at the High Altar of the Norman church, near where the Bishop's throne now stands.

Next to the former Bishop's Palace, now council offices, is a BIBLE GARDEN planted in 1962 by Tatham Whitehead, with every type of plant and tree mentioned in the Bible, or, at least, all those able to survive the Welsh climate. There are examples of the Fig Tree from the Garden of Eden, the Judas Tree on which Judas Iscariot hanged himself, and the Glastonbury Thorn, grown from the staff of Joseph of Arimathea.

For hundreds of years Bangor was no more than a village, and the old settlement gathered around the modest cathedral on the side of a valley still has the air of a small country town. In 1884, the University College of North Wales was founded across the valley, overlooking the Cathedral. Earlier in the 19th century, docks were built to cater for the booming slate industry and Bangor suddenly took on a commercial role, as well as becoming an important resort, with the introduction of the steam packet from Liverpool. In 1896, a pier was built, reaching 1,500 ft (457 m) out into the Menai Strait, THE SECOND LONGEST PIER IN WALES. The view from the end of the pier, which was restored in the 1980s, is tremendous, taking in the mountains, the boats passing through the strait, and the handsome houses of Anglesey with their gardens running down to the water's edge.

All this raucous activity, however, does not impinge one bit on the cloistered peace of the university and cathedral quarter, tucked away in its valley behind Bangor mountain. They seem like two completely different towns and it is this dichotomy that gives Bangor its special flavour.

In 1967, THE BEATLES came to stay in one of the university halls of residence, Neuadd Reichel, to meet Maharishi Mahesh Yogi, and it was while they were here that they learned of the suicide of their manager Brian Epstein.

Vaynol Park

If Walls had Ears

On the outskirts of Bangor, to the south-west, a 7-mile (11 km) long wall hides what was, until recently, the mysterious world of VAYNOL PARK. In 2005, the National Eisteddfod was held here, and every August Bank Holiday since the year 2000, Vaynol has been the home of Bangor-born BRYN TERFEL'S Faenol Festival which brings together top names from the world of opera, musicals and Welsh pop music, for a three-day open-air concert.

Before that, very little was known of what was behind the wall. To begin with, there are two Vaynol Halls: the rather unimaginative early 19th-century Vaynol New Hall, now a conference centre, and the utterly gorgeous but dilapidated Elizabethan Old Hall, one of the finest Tudor houses in Wales, which was featured on BBC2's first *Restoration* series.

The last private owner of the estate was Sir Michael Duff, 3rd Bt, who died in 1980. He and his wife Lady Caroline led rather colourful lives. Sir Michael was godfather to Princess Margaret's husband, Lord Snowdon, and Lady Caroline was the daughter of the 6th Marquess of Anglesey, from Plas Newydd. Amongst her very, very close friends were Prime Minister Anthony Eden and the artist Rex Whistler, whose murals of Snowdonia and the Menai Strait, as seen from Vaynol Park, can be seen today at Plas Newydd.

So hidden away and secret was Vaynol that politicians, society types, and Royalty could all come here and disappear without anyone knowing they were there. The Queen Mother, the Queen, Princess Margaret, Harold Macmillan and his family, all were able to let their hair down in complete confidence at Vaynol. Some 18 members of the Royal Family gathered there for the investiture of Prince Charles at Caernarfon in 1969.

Today much of the estate is open to the public. There are two viewing platforms by the sea and a folly built to rival the Marquess of Anglesey's Column across the Menai Strait.

Penrhyn Castle

Sugar and Slate

PENRHYN CASTLE, on the eastern outskirts of Bangor, was built for the Pennant family on profits from West Indian sugar and, as with Vaynol New Hall on the other side of Bangor, Welsh slate. Built by Thomas Hopper between

1820 and 1845, it is a monstrous place, fashioned like a Norman castle, the five-storey main tower a copy of the keep at Castle Hedingham in Essex. Inside, the castle, now owned by the National Trust, seems to go on for miles, with corridors and stairways and state rooms filled with Rembrandts, Canalettos and Gainsboroughs and heavy oak furniture. The Great Hall is simply cavernous, and the opulent Grand Staircase took ten years to build. One of the highlights is a huge four-poster bed made of slate, weighing over one ton and commissioned for the visit of Queen Victoria in 1859 – she apparently refused to sleep in it.

The extensive grounds include a Victorian walled garden and afford stupendous views out across the Menai Strait, north towards the Great Orme and south and west to the mountains.

Source of all this wealth, the Penrhyn Quarry at BETHESDA, 5 miles (8 km) inland to the south, is THE BIGGEST SLATE QUARRY IN THE WORLD, some 1,200 ft (366 m) deep, and still being worked today. In 1801, THE FIRST NARROW-GAUGE, HORSE-DRAWN RAILWAY IN WALES was laid between the quarry and Port Penrhyn at Bangor. The line closed in 1962, but two of the steam engines that were introduced in 1878 are now at work on the Ffestiniog Railway (*see* Merioneth).

Slate from here has been used for floors, roof tiles, furniture and headstones, not just in Wales but all over the world. As well as the unmistakable flat galleries carved out of the sides of the mountains, and the slag-heaps and vast, shining, grey slopes of broken slate, there are some intriguing monuments still to be seen of the Victorian heyday of the slate industry. Preserved at Penrhyn Quarry is a huge water balance incline, where platforms with water tanks underneath were used to haul slate out of the quarry by filling and emptying the tanks – the weight of an empty wagon with a full tank of water being sufficient to haul up a loaded wagon with an empty tank. Down at Port Penrhyn there is an original locomotive shed and a neat little circular lavatory.

Most of the Pennant family are buried in St Tegai's church in Llandygai, the estate village at the gates of Penrhyn Castle. A notable exception is Lord George Sholto Gordon Douglas-Pennant, 2nd Baron Penrhyn of Llandegai (1836–1907). He was a fierce opponent of the trade unions and ran the quarry like a feudal lord of old. This led to friction with his quarrymen, and a three-year lock-out lasting from 1900 to 1903, THE LONGEST INDUSTRIAL DISPUTE IN BRITISH HISTORY.

Llandudno

Naples of the North

LLANDUDNO is THE LARGEST SEASIDE RESORT IN WALES. Developed in the 1850s, it is elegant, Victorian and wonderfully unspoilt, and has the benefit of two fine beaches, the North Shore and the West Shore.

On the North Shore, grand white, pink and blue hotels overlook the Promenade, which follows the softly curving bay for 2 miles (3.2 km) between high headlands, the Great Orme and the Little Orme. Here is Sir John Betjeman's favourite pier, opened in 1878, at 2,295 ft (700 m) THE LONGEST PIER IN WALES, acres of iron lacework floating on the sea like a Byzantine palace.

Across the narrow neck of the Great Orme is the West Shore, miles of quiet sand at the mouth of the River Conwy, with fine views towards Conwy and Anglesey. In 1933 Lloyd George came here to unveil a statue of the White Rabbit from *Alice in Wonderland*, commemorating the many happy summer holidays that Alice Liddell, the model for Alice, spent here with her parents in the 1860s. At first they stayed at what is now the St Tudno Hotel, and then at Penmorfa, the house that Alice's father, the Very Revd Dr Henry Liddell, Dean of Christ Church, Oxford, had built for them as a holiday home. Whether the author of *Alice in Wonderland*, Lewis Carroll, actually visited Alice here is unproven, but looking out from Penmorfa across the wide expanse of sand, it is easy to imagine that it was here that the Walrus and the Carpenter 'wept like anything to see such quantities of sand . . .' Penmorfa, much extended, is now a hotel.

Between the North and West Shores, encompassed by the 5-mile (8 km) Marine Drive, is the GREAT ORME, Orme being a Norse word for sea ogre. This particular sea ogre, 679 ft (207 m) high, 1 mile (1.6 km) wide and 2 miles (3.2 km) long, is packed with superlatives, old and new. To start with, the view from the top is superlative, as are the many archaeological treasures to be found all over the headland. There is a neolithic burial chamber, an Iron Age fort, a medieval village, the Great Orme Long Huts and, most exciting of all, the GREAT ORME BRONZE AGE COPPER MINE, discovered in 1987 and THE ONLY BRONZE AGE COPPER MINE IN THE WORLD OPEN TO THE PUBLIC.

There are myriad ways to get to the top of the Great Orme. One way is to take the ornate GREAT ORME TRAMWAY, engineered in 1902, THE ONLY CABLE-

HAULED STREET TRAMWAY IN BRITAIN and one of only three surviving in the world, the others being in Lisbon and San Francisco.

Another way to the summit is via BRITAIN'S SECOND LONGEST CABLE CAR, the LLANDUDNO CABIN LIFT, completed in 1972 and just over 1 mile (1.6 km) long.

The cabin lift's lower station is situated on the eastern side of the Great Orme in a sheltered valley known as Happy Valley, given to Llandudno in 1887 by the 3rd Lord Mostyn, the local landowner, in celebration of Queen Victoria's Golden Jubilee. The Mostyn family are THE OLDEST LANDOWNING FAMILY IN WALES AFTER THE CROWN. There is a restored Victorian camera obscura of 1860 here, and a little higher up, THE LONGEST ARTIFICIAL SKI SLOPE IN BRITAIN, nearly 1,000 ft (300 m) long, built in 1987.

If you decide to climb to the top of the Great Orme on foot, look out for the wild goats, descendants of a pair given to Queen Victoria by the Shah of Persia, and donated to the Great Orme by Lord Mostyn.

Llandudno's lifeboat station is THE ONLY INSHORE LIFEBOAT STATION IN BRITAIN. It sits on the neck of the Great Orme, halfway between the North Shore and the West Shore, so that the lifeboats can be swiftly launched from their trailers off either shore.

Lleyn Peninsula – north

(Penrhyn Llyn)

Pilgrim's Way

The LLEYN PENINSULA recedes far out into the Irish sea mists, poised above the tear drop that is Bardsey Island, like a hand reaching out for a sweet. It is the most remote, secluded and mysterious part of Wales, more so even than Anglesey, for it is far less visited, was never fought over, and has no gold or copper or palaces to be won. What it does have is a desolate beauty, secret landscapes and simple monuments to the many pilgrims who trod the ancient route from Caernarfon to Aberdaron, and thence to Bardsey, Wales's most holy island.

First stop along the north coast road from Caernarfon is the shrine of ST BEUNO, considered to be the patron saint of North Wales. The 15th-century church here is huge and lavish, built with money from pilgrims on their way to Bardsey, and built on to the little chapel that covers the site of St Beuno's shrine. Pilgrims who slept here overnight would be cured of their epilepsy and rickets by drinking from the nearby St Beuno's Well next morning. In the churchyard is ONE OF ONLY TWO CELTIC SUNDIALS IN BRITAIN.

St Beuno's

The small harbour, built to ship slate from the surrounding hills, was abandoned for a while after the quarries closed, but now the settlement has been developed as a residential centre for learning the Welsh language. It can be reached by the steepest road I have ever driven, which snakes down through a brooding wood of dripping trees, before opening out on to two small sunlit rows of cottages, whose windows gaze across the sea to Celtic Ireland.

Tre'r Ceiri

The north coast of Lleyn is a bleak moonscape with few breaks in the cliffs. Visible for miles around is a mountain with three sharp peaks known as Yr Eifl, or the 'Fork', highest point on the Lleyn Peninsula. On the southern slope stands one of the great Iron Age forts of Wales, TRE'R CEIRI, 'town of the giants'. It was still lived in during Roman times and at 1,500 ft (457 m) up, is almost impossible to get to. This may explain why it is so well preserved, with evidence of some 150 huts and complete sections of high wall up to 15 ft (4.6 m) thick. If you can make the stiff climb the view is stupendous, with sea all around and, far, far below, the deep, dark valley of Nant Gwrtheyrn.

Nant Gwrtheyrn

NANT GWRTHEYRN is named after the 5th-century Celtic King Vortigern, who died here, maddened and alone after being dispossessed of his kingdom by the very Saxons he had invited in to protect him. There is a melancholy here that speaks of some tragedy, and maybe gives credence to the legend that Nant Gwrtheyrn was cursed, after the inhabitants of the little fishing community here refused hospitality to some monks travelling to Bardsey.

Pistyll

Westwards, at PISTYLL, sited below the road and sheltered by trees, is another St Beuno's Church built by pilgrims, 12th-century this time, also with a healing well. If you turn right inside the church gate and walk along the pathway, you will come to a low headstone almost hidden in the grass. This is the last resting-place of actor RUPERT DAVIES (1916–76), voted TV Actor of the Year in 1963 for his portrayal of pipe-smoking detective Maigret. On meeting Davies for the first time, Georges Simenon, Maigret's creator, exclaimed, 'At last, I have found the perfect Maigret!' For slightly younger viewers, Rupert Davies was the voice of Professor Ian McClaine (Mac) in the *Joe 90* puppet series. Pistyll was his holiday retreat.

Madryn Castle

Overlooked by the Iron Age hill fort of Garn Fadryn, midway between Nefyn and Abersoch, is a sturdy gatehouse that once guarded the entrance to the romantic 16th-century MADRYN CASTLE. The castle is no more, demolished in 1910, its

Rupert Davies

contents dispersed, its foundations now hard core for a caravan site. The name of Madryn did not die, however, for over on the other side of the world, on the coast of Patagonia, there is the town of Puerto Madryn. The owner of Madryn Castle, SIR THOMAS DUNCOMBE LOVE JONES-PARRY BT (1832–91) sailed to South America in 1862, accompanied by Caernarfon-born Lewis Jones, to investigate the feasibility of setting up a Welsh settlement there (*see* Bala, Merioneth). They named the bay where they first made landfall Porth Madryn, after Love Jones-Parry's ancestral home.

Whistling Sands

One of the few beaches on the rocky north coast of the Lleyn Peninsula is at PORTH OER, about 1 mile (1.6 km) north of Aberdaron. The cove is also known in English as Whistling Sands – at certain stages of the tide, the smooth white sand actually whistles or squeaks as you walk across it. The noise is caused by the unusually shaped grains rubbing together as they are compressed.

Bardsey Island

(Ynys Enlli)

Island of Saints

Seen from the 534 ft (162 m) high summit of Mynydd Mawr on the tip of Lleyn, against a backdrop of the great arc of Cardigan Bay, BARDSEY ISLAND looks deceptively small, and the waters between, calm and placid. The distinctive shape seems hunched up, its back turned against the mainland in disdain, the great 550 ft (168 m) high bulk of Mynydd Enlii concealing any view of the island's settlement, compounding the illusion. But this is one of the great holy sites of the Celtic world, the Iona of Wales.

A monastery was founded on Bardsey in AD 516 by St Cadfan, although long before that the island had been used as a sanctuary for Christians escaping the terrors of post-Roman Britain. The Welsh name for Bardsey, Ynys Enlli, means 'island of currents', and the treacherous waters of the Sound made the journey extremely perilous – three pilgrimages to Bardsey was considered the equal of one to Rome. Chapels and churches were set up on the mainland, where pilgrims could pray for safe passage across. Many came to die and be buried on Bardsey, and another name for the island is 'island of 20,000 saints'.

Although St Cadfan's monastery remained as one of the last bastions of Celtic Christianity for several hundred years, there is very little evidence left of it or of the 13th-century Augustinian abbey that replaced it. Part of a tower, some walls and plenty of Celtic crosses stand testament.

In the 19th century Bardsey was part of the Newborough estates and supported a population of some 100 crofters and fishermen and their families. Only one of the original crofts, Carreg Bach, is still there, the rest of the community having been rebuilt in the 1870s, with the chapel of 1875 the last building to be put up.

Today Bardsey is owned by the Bardsey Island Trust and it is possible to stay on the island in one of the farmhouses or cottages. Boat trips leave from Aberdaron and Pwllheli.

Bardsey possesses THE TALLEST SQUARE LIGHTHOUSE IN BRITAIN, 98 ft (30 m) high.

The colloquial term for a lavatory in Welsh, 'ty bach' or 'little house', came from the 'ty bach' in the garden on Bardsey.

An apple tree thought to have been growing in the island since the 14th century is the source of 'THE WORLD'S RAREST APPLE', the BARDSEY ISLAND APPLE. It was originally unique to Bardsey, but it is now possible to buy saplings from the tree.

Lleyn Peninsula – south
(Penrhyn Llyn)

Tourist Way

The south coast of the Lleyn Peninsula is much softer and gentler than the north, with sandy beaches and colourful fishing villages, attracting yachtsmen and holiday-makers.

Aberdaron

For many centuries the main embarkation point for Bardsey island was Aberdaron, consisting of a cluster of cottages, an old humpbacked bridge, a medieval resting house, Y Gegin Fawr, meaning 'the big kitchen', where you can still eat, and a huge church, almost on the beach and half buried in sand. Originally founded in the 5th century by St Hywyn, the church was greatly enlarged in the early 12th century, and a second nave added in the 15th century, to cope with the growing number of pilgrims. Lots of space inside, but the simple, single Norman doorway is tiny. To sit in the stillness of this lovely church at the far end of the world, where so many have come to pray for courage to face what lies ahead, listening to the waves lapping almost to the door, is a deeply moving experience. The 21st century seems very far away, as indeed it is, for Aberdaron lies FURTHER AWAY FROM A RAILWAY STATION THAN ANYWHERE ELSE IN ENGLAND AND WALES.

Plas yn Rhiw

Unexpected, and half hidden behind tumbling banks of shrubs and flowers, up on the hill above the turbulent bay that is Hell's Mouth, sits one of the most romantic little houses in Wales, PLAS YN RHIW. It was rescued from neglect in 1938 by the three Keating sisters, who restored the house and planted a magic garden in the woods with every plant and flower imaginable. A small stone manor

house dressed up as a country cottage, Plas yn Rhiw is mainly 16th century with Georgian additions. The views of Cardigan Bay are breathtaking, the polished stone floor in the main hall is the most gorgeous I have ever seen, and the gardens overflow with colour and bowers and secret walkways. It is hard to step back out into the real world.

Llanystumdwy

'The greatest Welshman which that unconquerable race has produced since the age of the Tudors'

WINSTON CHURCHILL ON DAVID LLOYD GEORGE

Even though he has been dead for more than 50 years, DAVID LLOYD GEORGE (1863–1945) still dominates the village of LLANYSTUMDWY, on the Lleyn Peninsula near Criccieth, as he dominated the world of politics in his lifetime. He was born in Manchester, the son of a Pembrokeshire schoolmaster, but came to live in Llanystumdwy with his uncle, Richard Lloyd, at the age of two, after his father died. HIGHGATE, the stone house he lived in for 15 years, stands opposite the village pub and has been restored to how it was when he was a boy. The comprehensive LLOYD GEORGE MUSEUM tells the story of his life, with the help of personal items such as a lock of his white hair, his pipes and walking sticks and his own copy of the Versailles Peace Treaty. His initials can be seen carved in the stonework of the bridge over the River Dwyfor, at the bottom of the village.

David Lloyd George, THE ONLY WELSH PRIME MINISTER OF GREAT BRITAIN, became an MP in 1890 and represented Caernarfon for 55 years. As Chancellor of the Exchequer between 1908 and 1911 he laid the foundations of the Welfare State, introducing the Old Age Pension and the National Insurance scheme. His 'People's Budget' of 1909 set out to tax the rich in order to help the poor and was blocked by the House of Lords. This resulted in the 1911 Parliament Act, restricting the powers of the Lords. His greatest political ally at the time was Winston Churchill and together they were known as the 'Heavenly Twins'.

Lloyd George became Prime Minister in 1916 and his policies helped to ensure victory in the First World War, albeit at a terrible price. He was instrumental in negotiating the ill-fated Treaty of Versailles alongside US President Woodrow Wilson and French Prime Minister Georges Clemenceau.

During his premiership, the 1918 Representation of the People Act gave the vote to women over 30, opening the way for women to achieve the same voting rights as men in 1928.

In 1921, Lloyd George forced through the Anglo-Irish Treaty, which saw the creation of the Irish Free State, while excluding the six counties of Ulster that became Northern Ireland.

He had his setbacks. In 1907, the greatest tragedy of his life happened when his beloved elder daughter Mair died at the age of 17. In 1913, his London home was blown up by militant suffragettes. And at the end of his Prime Ministerial career he was accused of corruption, for handing out peerages in return for contributions to party funds. This led to the 1925 Honours (Prevention of Abuses) Act.

Lloyd George had two nicknames, 'the Welsh Wizard', referring particularly to his skill as a wartime leader and negotiator, and 'the Goat', which referred to his reputation as a womaniser.

He is remembered for his brilliant oratory. After watching Lloyd George make a speech to a large crowd, photographer Alvin Coburn observed, 'He had them under his spell, as a conductor holds his orchestra, and he could do what he pleased with them.'

His trademark was his moustache – he was one of nine British Prime Ministers to sport a moustache. During a trip to Canada in 1899 he shaved it off, and on his return to the House of Commons, the Speaker failed to recognise him. He never shaved it off again.

His personal life was complicated. He had a constituency home in Criccieth called Brynawelon, on a hill overlooking the bay, where his wife Margaret lived. He also had a house in Churt in Surrey, where he lived much of the time with his secretary Frances Stevenson, by whom he had a daughter in 1929. He married Frances in 1943 after the death of his wife, to whom he had remained devoted, in 1941.

In 1944 he retired from politics, and returned home to Llanystumdwy, becoming Earl Lloyd George of Dwyfor and Viscount Gwynedd. He died in March the following year. He had already chosen the place where he wanted to be buried, pacing up and down during a family picnic beside the River Dwyfor until he found exactly the right spot. He then bought the land and had it consecrated.

He chose well. His grave is in a sublime location, under the trees above the River Dwyfor, just upstream from the bridge. His tombstone is the large grey boulder on which he used to sit beside the river and think, set in the middle of a small, oval lawn, reached through an iron gate and surrounded by a low wall of Welsh stone. It was designed by his friend Clough Williams-Ellis (*see* Merioneth) and is perfect.

Driving through the mountains of Snowdonia on his way to Caernarfon,

Lloyd George took the wrong turning and got himself lost. He stopped to ask where he was and was told, 'You're in a motor car.' Long afterwards he referred to this as the perfect kind of answer to a Parliamentary question – 'it's true, it's brief and it tells you absolutely nothing you don't already know!'

Gwydir Castle

America and Back

Idyllic GWYDIR CASTLE, a remarkable example of a 16th-century Tudor courtyard house, was built for the powerful Wynn family and vies with Plas Teg in Flintshire as THE MOST HAUNTED HOUSE IN WALES. Sir John Wynn (1553–1627) had a reputation as a ruthless tyrant, and was said to have seduced a servant girl and then murdered her and bricked her body up in one of the chimney breasts. Today the stench of her decomposing body can still be experienced in the passageway near the Great Hall. Sir John himself apparently lies under Swallow Falls at Betws-y-Coed, until the water has purified him of his evil deeds.

Gwydir Castle was badly damaged by fire in 1920 and caught the rapacious eye of newspaper baron William Randolph Hearst (immortalised by Orson Welles in *Citizen Kane*), who was touring Britain looking for artefacts to fill his castle at San Simeon in California. He snapped up the Jacobean wood-panelled dining-room from Gwydir and shipped it across the Atlantic, where it remained packed away in boxes. When Hearst died in 1956, the panels were bequeathed to the Metropolitan Museum in New York and put into storage. Meanwhile Gwydir gradually became derelict until rescued in 1994 by architect Peter Welford and his wife Judy Corbett, who retired from city life and set about restoring the house. They traced the dining-room to New York – oak fireplace, doorcase, panelling, gold and silver leather frieze – and negotiated to have it returned, the first time any of Hearst's collection had been repatriated. In 1998, the Prince of Wales officially reopened the dining-room at Gwydir, fully restored to its glorious best.

Mount Snowdon

(Yr Wyddfa)

High and Wet

At 3,560 ft (1,085 m) high, MT SNOWDON is THE HIGHEST MOUNTAIN IN ENGLAND AND WALES, the tallest of 15 peaks in Wales over 3,000 ft (914 m). The summit Mt Snowdon is THE WETTEST PLACE IN WALES, averaging 180 inches (4,570 mm) of rain every year.

Sir Edmund Hillary, the first man to climb Mt Everest, trained with his team on the slopes of Mt Snowdon before setting off for his triumphant ascent of the world's highest mountain in 1953.

The SNOWDON MOUNTAIN RAILWAY was built in 1896 and climbs 2,950 ft (900 m) over 5 miles (8 km), from Llanberis to a few yards short of the summit. It is THE ONLY RACK AND PINION RAILWAY IN BRITAIN.

Mt Snowdon is one of the traditional SEVEN WONDERS OF WALES.

Well, I never knew this ABOUT CAERNARFONSHIRE

T. E. LAWRENCE (1888–1935), better known as Lawrence of Arabia, was born in TREMADOG, at Snowdon Lodge, an undistinguished house on the southern approach to the town, opposite Capel Peniel.

BANGOR has THE LONGEST HIGH STREET IN WALES.

RAF LLANDWROG, now CAERNARFON AIR WORLD, is the home of THE FIRST RAF MOUNTAIN RESCUE SERVICE.

Wales's most celebrated harpist and composer DAFYDD Y GARREG WEN, who died in 1749 aged 29, is buried in an isolated country churchyard off the road at Pentrefelin near Criccieth, under a tombstone with a harp carved on it. THE VERY FIRST WELSH WORDS EVER HEARD ON THE BBC, in 1923, were sung to a tune that Dafydd composed on his deathbed, called after him 'Dafydd y Garreg Wen'.

GREENWOOD FOREST PARK, near Bangor, has THE LONGEST SLIDE IN WALES.

ABER FALLS at Abergwyngregyn, near Bangor, is THE LARGEST NATURAL WATERFALL IN WALES.

Set in the beautiful woodlands of the upper Conwy valley some 3 miles (5 km) south of Betws-y-coed, is TY MAWR, birthplace of BISHOP WILLIAM MORGAN (1545–1604) who, in 1588, completed the translation of the Bible from the original Hebrew and Greek into Welsh. The 16th-century stone farmhouse is run by the National Trust and contains a comprehensive collection of Bibles in Welsh and other languages.

The NATIONAL SLATE MUSEUM at Llanberis boasts THE LARGEST WORKING WATER-WHEEL IN MAINLAND BRITAIN.

DINORWIG POWER STATION sits nearly half a mile (0.8 m) deep inside Snowdonia's Elidir Mountain, near Llanberis, inside THE LARGEST MAN-MADE CAVERN IN EUROPE.

SWALLOW FALLS (Rhaeadr Ewynnol) at Betws-y-coed is THE MOST VISITED WATERFALL IN BRITAIN.

Betws-y-coed claims THE UGLIEST HOUSE IN WALES. The UGLY HOUSE is thought to be an example of a 'One Night House' (*see* Pembrokeshire).

The SNOWDONIA NATIONAL PARK is THE LARGEST PARK IN WALES. Opened in 1951, it covers an area of 838 sq. miles (2,170 sq. km).

While he went off hunting, Prince Llywelyn the Great left his dog, GELERT, to guard his baby son. On his return, the Prince found the dog covered in blood and no sign of the child. Enraged, he slew Gelert, only to discover the baby hidden under the bed, safe and sound, and a dead wolf lying nearby. Gelert had, in fact, saved the baby from the wolf. Distraught, Llywelyn buried Gelert in a magnificent grave down by the river, which is still there to this day. In 1802, a local hotel owner embellished this popular legend to attract customers, and the picturesque mountain village of BEDDGELERT (Gelert's Grave) has flourished ever since.

ALFRED BESTALL (1892–1986), one of the writers and illustrators of *Rupert Bear*, lived for a while in Beddgelert.

In the churchyard of ST CIAN'S AT LLANGIAN, near Abersoch on the Lleyn Peninsula, there is a stone pillar bearing a Latin inscription that reads, in three vertical lines, 'Meli Medici Fili Martini Iacit' – 'The body of Melus the Doctor, son of Martinus, lies here'. The stone was carved probably in the 5th century, and not only is it THE FIRST MENTION ANYWHERE IN WALES OF A DOCTOR, it is THE ONLY KNOWN RECORD OF A 'MEDICUS' ON ANY EARLY CHRISTIAN INSCRIPTION IN BRITAIN.

PLAID CYMRU, the Welsh nationalist party, was founded in PWLLHELI, on

5 August 1925, during the National Eisteddfod. Six members were present, and the immediate aim of the party was to gain recognition for the aspirations of the Welsh people, followed by self rule for Wales. In 1966, GWYNFOR EVANS became the first Plaid Cymru MP, winning the Carmarthen by-election.

THE OLDEST TREE IN WALES is the LLANGERNYW YEW in St Digain's Churchyard, Llangernyw, near Conwy. It is approximately 4,000 years old.

CARDIGANSHIRE

(CEREDIGION)

COUNTY TOWN: CARDIGAN

Strata Florida Abbey, the cultural and political heart of medieval Wales

Cardigan
(Aberteifi)

First Eisteddfod

The ancient borough of CARDIGAN is a compact maritime town of narrow streets, attractive, jumbling old houses of many colours, and a lovely five-arched bridge across the Teifi, which was built in 1726. It still has the air of a busy port, which it once was, until the river silted up and the railway arrived in the 19th century. There is a Cardigan in Nova Scotia, named by Welsh settlers in memory of the town from which they sailed to the New World.

The name Cardigan is an anglicised pronunciation of Ceredigion, the Welsh name for the county of Cardiganshire. Although Cardigan is close to the Welsh woollen trade, the woollen garment called a cardigan gets its name, not from the town, but from the 7th Earl of Cardigan, who led the Charge of the Light Brigade, and wore such a type of sweater beneath his uniform to keep out the cold.

The original Cardigan Castle was built in 1100, in wood, by the Norman knight Gilbert de Clare. In 1136, it was captured by Lord Rhys ap Gruffydd, who rebuilt it in stone. In 1176, Lord Rhys put on THE FIRST-EVER NATIONAL EISTEDDFOD at the castle.

The modern annual ROYAL NATIONAL EISTEDDFOD is the largest competitive music and poetry festival in Europe. It is conducted entirely in Welsh and is a celebration of Welsh language, art and culture. Eisteddfod means 'a gathering', and it evolved from ancient tournaments where musicians and poets would compete against each other for a 'chair' at a nobleman's table. Winners could be assured of regular employment from wealthy patrons.

The festival takes place at the beginning of August and lasts for eight days, attracting up to 6,000 competitors and 180,000 visitors. It is held in North or South Wales in alternate years to avoid regional bias.

The most prestigious prizes awarded at the National Eisteddfod are the Chair and the Crown, both for poetry. The Crown is given to the best free-metre poet, while the Chair is won by the best strict-metre poetry written in cynghanedd, which is a system of chiming that involves internal rhyme along with assonance and consonance.

The Eisteddfod at Cardigan Castle in 1176 is the first recorded occasion at which poets and musicians from all over Wales attended. In 1523 an Eisteddfod was held at Caerwys, which laid down some regulations, and in 1819, during an Eisteddfod at the Ivy Bush Hotel in Carmarthen, the first 'Gorsedd', or assembly of Druidical bards, took place at a festival. Since then the ritual Gorsedd of Bards has become an established part of the National Eisteddfod.

The first 'modern' National Eisteddfod, conducted as we recognise it today, was held in 1861, at Aberdare in Glamorgan. The National Eisteddfod Association was formed in 1880, charged with staging the annual event.

Aberystwyth

Welsh Centre

Aberystwyth is at the heart of Wales, set right at the centre between North and South, a capital in all but name. It is the largest town on Cardigan Bay, a University town, Book

Town and seaside resort. Being cut off from the rest of the world by mountains, Aberystwyth has had to fall back on its own resources and learn to survive by itself. There is a certain bloody-mindedness about Aberystwyth that is quite exhilarating.

The setting is stunning. A backdrop of steep green hills, a wide sweep of bay, stately but paint-peeling Edwardian guesthouses following a gently curving promenade. A walk from south to north along the Promenade and Marine Terrace takes you past some of the many faces of 'Aber'.

The Harbour

Now a bustling modern marina, this used to be one of Wales's busiest harbours for fishing and shipbuilding. It is fed by two rivers, the Ystwyth and the Rheidol, the latter acclaimed as THE 'STEEPEST' RIVER IN BRITAIN.

Aberystwyth Castle

Standing above the harbour on a rocky promontory are the scattered remnants of Aberystwyth Castle, begun in 1277 by Edward I to protect and subdue the walled settlement at its feet. It changed hands many times before Owain Glyndwr made it his base in 1404. In 1637, a mint was set up in the great hall to produce coins made with silver from the local mines. These were used to pay Charles I's soldiers during the Civil War, when Oliver Cromwell had control of the London mint. Cromwell duly slighted the castle in 1649. The mighty west gatehouse is particularly impressive.

Old College

Next to the castle is Aberystwyth's most striking and best-loved building, the Old College. Originally, there was a John Nash villa here called Castle House, built in 1790. When the railway arrived from Shrewsbury in the 1860s, the entrepreneur who had brought it to the town, Thomas Savin, purchased the villa and had it transformed into a grand Victorian Gothic hotel, in anticipation of a tourist boom. In an early example of the package tour, he offered special rates to anyone who booked a return railway ticket at Euston in London. He then sat back and waited for the guests to arrive. Alas, they never did, at least not enough to fill the huge hotel, which went bust, and in 1872 Savin sold up.

The beneficiaries were a collection of Welsh patriots who were looking for somewhere with size and prestige to locate Wales's first university. Savin's hotel was perfect and became home to THE FIRST UNIVERSITY

COLLEGE IN WALES. In 1896, the Prince of Wales, later Edward VII, visited Aberystwyth to be installed as THE FIRST CHANCELLOR OF THE UNIVERSITY OF WALES. The occasion also marked THE LAST EVER PUBLIC APPEARANCE BY FOUR-TIME PRIME MINISTER WILLIAM GLADSTONE.

In 1919, the FIRST DEPARTMENT OF INTERNATIONAL POLITICS ANYWHERE IN THE WORLD was established at the Old College in Aberystwyth.

The University has since moved to a new campus on Penglais Hill to the east of the town, and Old College now serves mainly as a museum and university administration centre.

It is an awe-inspiring building, with its solid *porte-cochère* entrance and a Tyrolean-style tower forming the southern extremity, complete with mosaic of Archimedes receiving the symbols of Science and Industry. Old College is completely out of character with the rest of the sea front, and yet it adds a glamourous quirkiness that somehow suits the personality of this extraordinary town.

Pier

Just past Old College is the pier, which marks the end of the Promenade and the start of Marine Terrace. Built in 1864, the pier used to extend 900 ft (274 m) out into the bay, but was swept off its spindly legs by a storm in 1938 and now just paddles at the water's edge.

Welsh Revival

The Welsh Language Society, Cymdeithas yr Iaith, has its headquarters on Marine Terrace, which gives credence to the story that it was here that the movement to save the Welsh language really began in 1963. The Society had been set up in that year in response to a radio lecture by Saunders Lewis in 1962, highlighting the disappearance of the Welsh language. A member caught wobbling along the sea front on his bicycle, with his girlfriend on the back, received a summons, which he ignored, as it was written only in English. The subsequent furore sparked further protests, notably at Trefechan Bridge in Aberystwyth on 23 February 1963, with members being imprisoned for non-payment of their fines. This in turn led to a nation-wide campaign which eventually won recognition for Welsh as an official language. Since then, all place-names and official documents must be written in both English and Welsh, and today some 20 per cent of the native population of 2.8 million speak Welsh.

Kick the Bar

For some reason, it is traditional when taking a bracing stroll along the Promenade to 'kick the bar', or railings, at the bottom of Constitution Hill at the north end of Marine Terrace. There are several explanations for this bizarre custom which is noted as far back as 1900. The most plausible theory is that male students, hanging around outside Alexandra Hall, the girls' hostel, would kick the bar in frustration and impatience while waiting for the girls to emerge. Alexandra Hall, opened by Princess Alexandra in 1896, was deliberately built as far away from the Old College as possible, to prevent unseemly behaviour. The Hall became run down when the university moved, but is now restored.

Constitution Hill

CONSTITUTION HILL overlooks Aberystwyth from the north and rises to a height of 430 ft (130 m), providing panoramic views of Cardigan Bay. At the summit is THE BIGGEST CAMERA OBSCURA IN THE WORLD, moved here from the castle in 1896 and restored in 1985. You can reach it either by climbing the steep cliff path or, as less active folk have been doing since 1896, via THE LONGEST ELECTRIC CLIFF RAILWAY IN BRITAIN. Sitting in one of the stepped compartments watching mid Wales unfold before you, while the sloping carriage trundles sedately up the 1 in 4 slope, is one of Wales's most rewarding experiences.

National Library

One of the institutions that can be seen from Constitution Hill, halfway up a neighbouring height, is the NATIONAL LIBRARY OF WALES, which opened in 1937. It is one of five copyright libraries in Britain that have the right to receive a free copy of every printed work published in Britain or Ireland. (The others are in London, Edinburgh, Oxford and Cambridge.) Amongst the library's five million or so books are the earliest surviving manuscripts of the *Mabinogion* (*see* Pembrokeshire), and THE FIRST BOOK WRITTEN IN Welsh, the *Black Book of Carmarthen*, dating from the 12th century. Thanks to the library and the university's own collection of over one million books, Aberystwyth is said to have THE HIGHEST RATIO OF BOOKS TO PEOPLE IN THE WORLD – six million books to 20,000 students and inhabitants.

Vale of Rheidol

(Afon Rheidol)

Last Steam Railway

THE LAST STEAM RAILWAY OPERATED BY BRITISH RAIL, until privatised in 1989, THE VALE OF RHEIDOL RAILWAY runs from the centre of Aberystwyth, along the south side of the Rheidol Valley to Devil's Bridge, 12 miles (19 km) inland. The journey takes one hour, climbs nearly 600 ft (180 m) and passes through some of the most rugged and dramatic scenery in Wales. The railway was built in 1902 to carry timber and ore from the lead mines down to the harbour at Aberystwyth. It had to be narrow gauge to negotiate the twists and gradients of the terrain, although the carriages are of normal width.

At DEVIL'S BRIDGE the waters of the River Mynach cascade down 400 ft (120 m) through a deep gorge to join the River Rheidol, creating a series of lively waterfalls. At one point the gorge is spanned by no fewer than three bridges, one on top of another. The highest is an iron bridge of 1901, below that a stone

bridge from 1753 and, at the bottom, the original Pont-y-gwr-Drwg or Devil's Bridge, also of stone, which legend says was put there by the Devil himself to lure souls across the water. In fact it was probably built by the monks of the abbey at Strata Florida, possibly as early as the 11th century.

The wild beauty of Devil's Bridge is somewhat diluted by the fact that this is now one of Wales's most popular tourist spots, and the narrow pathway past the bridges and the waterfalls can resemble a mob scene at busy times. You also have to pay. But none of this detracts from the essential magic of the dancing water and the beautiful woodland setting.

The main beneficiary of all this tourist attention is the Hafod Arms Hotel, built in the 1830s by the 4th Duke of Newcastle when he bought the Hafod estate.

Hafod House

Earthly Paradise

HAFOD HOUSE, which once stood at the centre of the Hafod estate, a few miles to the south near Pontrhydygroes, was the first house to be built in Wales solely for the purposes of beauty and pleasure. THOMAS JOHNES (1748–1816) inherited the estate on the death of his father in 1780. He was a passionate follower of the new 'Picturesque' movement sweeping the country whose adherents, rather than seeing nature as threatening and barbaric, believed that man could tame the wilderness by planting trees and flowers, creating gardens and vistas to enhance and frame the natural setting.

In 1786 Johnes commissioned Thomas Baldwin of Bath to build a neo-Gothic country house in this remote valley of the Ystwyth, around which he designed a magnificent park, planting thousands of trees and creating lakes, monuments, hidden gardens and grottoes. A line of illustrious visitors came to see this paradise. Turner painted the house against the mountain backdrop in 1811, and Samuel Taylor Coleridge was so taken with the place that apparently it was the 'stately pleasure dome' of Hafod that featured in the opium-induced dream which inspired him to write 'Kubla Khan'.

Thomas Johnes and his family were hit by a series of misfortunes in the early 19th century. In 1807 the house burned down and had to be rebuilt, possibly with the help of the leading architect of the Picturesque, John Nash. In 1811, Thomas's beloved daughter Mariamne, spirited and intelligent despite having a deformity of the spine, died at the age of 27, leaving her parents bereft. Eventually, the sheer cost of Hafod broke Thomas and he died in 1816.

Sir Francis Chantrey's moving sculpture of Mariamne in Hafod church was badly damaged when the church suffered a major fire in 1932. Hafod House passed through a number of owners before becoming vacant in 1946 and finally being declared unsafe and demolished in 1958.

It seems a tragic way for such a lovely place to end, but the glorious setting can never pale and the gardens and woods remain, slowly being restored to their former glory.

Strata Florida

Doorway to Wales

Fourteen miles (23 km) east of Aberystwyth, in the wild and lonely hills, are the ruins of the greatest abbey in Wales, Strata Florida, Ystrad Fflur, the Valley of Flowers.

Flowers still abound here, everywhere you look, sprouting from the remaining stones and monuments and mosaic tiled floors. There is very little left of the magnificent church, once bigger than St David's Cathedral, except the peaceful atmosphere and the wondrous arch of the west door, which seems to frame the whole of Wales with its shapely bands of rich and delicate stonework.

The arch has become an iconic image of Wales, and is a remarkable survivor from the Cistercian abbey founded here in 1184. Under the patronage of Lord Rhys ap Gryffudd, Strata Florida became not just a religious centre but the cultural and political heart of medieval Wales. Welsh princes were buried here and Welsh rulers assembled here on important 'state' occasions, such as in 1238 when they were summoned by Llywelyn the Great to swear allegiance to his son Dafydd. In 1294, the 'Westminster Abbey of Wales' was burned on the orders of Edward I, and suffered several further blows before Henry VIII finally had it destroyed in 1539.

In the abbey graveyard, buried beneath an ancient yew tree, is one of the greatest medieval Welsh poets, DAFYDD AP GWILYM. Considered on a par with Chaucer, Dafydd wrote with great humour of love and of his failed pursuit of women, in language that was both beautiful and bawdy.

Nearby is a modest headstone inscribed: 'The left leg and part of the thigh of Henry Hughes, cooper, cut off and interr'd here June 18th 1756'. Hughes lost his leg in a farming accident and then, despite having one foot in the grave, emigrated to America, where the rest of him is buried.

Perhaps most poignant of all is the grave of an unknown soldier from the Afghan wars, whose frozen body was found beside the mysterious Teifi pools, near the source of the River Teifi, in the hills north of the abbey in 1929. All he had in his pocket was a photograph of a young girl and a copy of *Old Moore's*

Almanack. The local people buried him here and wrote on his gravestone,

He died upon the hillside drear
Alone, where snow was deep.
By strangers he was carried here
Where princes also sleep.

Dafydd ap Gwilym would have been proud.

Nanteos

End of a Quest

The quest for the Holy Grail is over! It was in Wales all the time. At Nanteos, deep in the hills south-east of Aberystwyth.

The Holy Grail was the cup from which Jesus drank at the Last Supper, and was thought to have miraculous healing qualities. According to Sir Thomas Malory in his *Le Morte d'Arthur*, written in the 15th century, Joseph of Arimathea brought the cup to Glastonbury, where he built a church in which to house it. Guardianship of the Grail passed on to the monks of the subsequent abbey founded at Glastonbury in the 6th century by St David.

When Glastonbury was threatened with Dissolution at the time of Henry VIII, a group of the monks left with the Grail for the comparative safety of the Cistercian abbey at Strata Florida, hidden away in the wild folds of Wales. However, the King's commissioners soon caught up with them, and the monks had to flee again, this time west across the hills to the secluded valley of the nightingales, Nanteos, where the Lord of the Manor gave them sanctuary. The monks remained at Nanteos for the remaining years of their lives, and as the last monk lay dying, he placed the Grail into the hands of his host, bidding him to keep it safe at Nanteos, until such time as the church came to reclaim it. And there it remained. Pilgrims came from afar to sample its healing properties and miracles apparently occurred that enhanced the legend of the Grail.

The Nanteos of today, one of Wales's most handsome Georgian houses, was built in 1739 for Thomas Powell. His descendant, George Paul Powell, put the cup on show and opened up the house for people to come and look at it. Quite small, just 3 inches (7.5 cm) deep and 5 inches (13 cm)

round, there was not much left to see because, across the years, over-enthusiastic pilgrims had bitten chunks out of it. George Powell befriended the composer Richard Wagner in London and invited him to stay at Nanteos. Inspired by the Nanteos Cup, as it was called, Wagner is said to have begun composing *Parsifal*, his opera based on the story of the Holy Grail, in the music room at Nanteos.

The last of the Powells sold Nanteos in the 1980s, and when she left she took the cup with her. It is now said to be sitting in a bank vault somewhere in Herefordshire, but no one quite knows, so maybe the Quest for the Holy Grail is not quite over.

Whether any of this is true or not, Nanteos, tucked away in the hills at the end of its long drive, is a wonderfully romantic house, not spoiled at all by becoming a hotel. It certainly feels as though there could be monks buried beneath the house, or tunnels from the basement leading to Aberystwyth Castle . . .

Well, I never knew this ABOUT CARDIGANSHIRE

Close together on the high lonely moorlands of PLYNLIMMON, which have traditionally separated North and South Wales, are the sources of two of Britain's mightiest rivers, the Severn and the Wye. The River Severn is BRITAIN'S LONGEST RIVER. On its 217-mile (349 km) journey to the sea from Plynlimmon, it is crossed by 100 bridges, 40 of them in Wales. The River Wye is 152 miles (245 km) long and is regarded as Britain's most scenic river.

The coastline of Cardiganshire is never less than ravishing, but there are some places along the way that can even be inspirational. One such spot is the windswept headland of LOCHTYN, above the quaint fishing village of Llangranog, north-west of Cardigan. The composer SIR EDWARD ELGAR stayed near here in 1902 and loved to wander along the cliffs and enjoy the stunning views over Cardigan Bay. On one such occasion he heard some Welsh folk singing on the beach below, and their songs inspired him to write one of his most popular compositions, *Introduction and Allegro for Strings*.

The churchyard in the little village of ABERATH, a little way north of Aberaeron, is the proud possessor of the ashes of SIR GERAINT EVANS (1922–92), one of the world's greatest opera singers, who made the roles of Figaro and Verdi's Falstaff his own. Having performed at all the leading opera houses in the world, he began semi-retirement at his holiday home in Aberaeron in 1982, where he acted as a lifeguard. He died of a heart attack, and his ashes were laid to rest at Aberath, close to those of his brother-in-law, the talented Welsh rugby outside half-back Glyn Davies, winner of ten caps. Sir Geraint Evans was a co-founder of Harlech Television Wales in 1967.

For fans of the architect John Nash, a visit to LLANERCHAERON, just south of Aberaeron, is a must. This exquisite house, built in 1796 and bequeathed to the National Trust in 1989, is the finest and most complete of Nash's early works in Wales. It forms the centrepiece of a rare, unspoilt example of an 18th-century Welsh gentleman's estate.

Standing proudly on a rise at RHYDOWEN, south of New Quay, is a splendid Palladian chapel opened in 1733 as THE FIRST ARMINIAN CHAPEL IN WALES. In 1876, the chapel's minister, Dylan Thomas's great-uncle, William Thomas, was evicted by the landlord, who objected to his liberal sermons. A member of the congregation evicted with him was Anna Lloyd Jones, mother of the American architect FRANK LLOYD WRIGHT. Before they emigrated to America from New Quay in 1844, the Joneses had farmed at nearby Blaenalltddu, where there is a plaque on the farmhouse wall announcing the birthplace of Frank Lloyd Wright's uncle, Jenkin Lloyd Jones, who became a Unitarian preacher in Chicago. One of Frank Lloyd Wright's best early works was the Unity Temple in Chicago, built in 1905.

South of Rhydowen is the ROCK MILL WOOLLEN MILL, THE LAST WORKING WATER-POWERED WOOLLEN MILL IN WALES. It was built in 1890 by John Morgan, and his descendants still weave there today, in the traditional way. The Teifi valley was the centre of the Welsh woollen industry, based on Tregaron, where sheep drovers would assemble their flocks before driving them to markets in England.

Standing on the banks of the River Camddwr beside the lonely road from Tregaron to Llyn Brianne is SOAR-Y-MYNYDD chapel, THE MOST REMOTE CHAPEL IN WALES. It was built in 1820 by Ebeneezer Richards, the minister from Tregaron.

The eerily beautiful CORS CARON bog, north of Tregaron, is THE LARGEST AREA OF PEAT BOG IN ENGLAND AND

Soar-y-Mynydd

WALES. Working the peat ended in 1960, and much of the bog is now a National Nature Reserve. It is home to otters, polecats and water voles and has been at the forefront of the restoration of the red kite, once extremely rare but now often seen in the skies above Cors Caron. It is THE ONLY HABITAT OF THE BRITISH BLACK ADDER.

Buried in the churchyard at LLANDYFRIOG, 2 miles (3.2 km) east of Newcastle Emlyn, is THOMAS HESLOP (1780–1814), victim of THE LAST FATAL DUEL TO BE FOUGHT IN WALES. Heslop gallantly challenged a rascal called John Benyon to a duel, after Benyon had made ungentlemanly remarks about the barmaid at the Salutation Inn in Newcastle Emlyn. The duel took place in what are now the Old Cilgwyn Gardens a little to the north, and Heslop was shot dead. 'Alas, poor Heslop,' it says on the slate covering his grave. Benyon was run out of town and emigrated to America.

Buried in the churchyard at SILIAN near Lampeter, is JULIAN CAYO-EVANS (1937–95), leader of the Free Wales Army in the 1960s. He was one of several members rounded up and imprisoned for public order offences before the investiture of Prince Charles as Prince of Wales at Caernarfon Castle in 1969.

THE FIRST GAME OF RUGBY PLAYED IN WALES took place at ST DAVID'S COLLEGE, Lampeter, in 1850. St David's College was a founder member of the Welsh Rugby Union, established in the Castle Hotel, Neath, in 1881. The college is THE OLDEST INSTITUTION IN WALES and THE OLDEST IN ENGLAND AND WALES TO AWARD DEGREES, after Oxford and Cambridge.

THE FIRST PERMANENT PRINTING PRESS IN WALES was established in 1718 by Isaac Carter in the village of ADPAR, across the River Teifi from Newcastle Emlyn.

The sturdy 13th-century church of St David's at LLANDDEWI BREFI stands on a high mound of special significance. Sometime in the middle of the 6th century, a Synod was held here, attended by St David. The crowds were so huge that when St David stood up to preach no one except those at the front could see or hear him. As he began speaking, however, the ground rose beneath him until he stood in full view of everyone and his voice was carried on the wind so that he could be heard by all. Today, Llanddewi Brefi has found new fame as the home of Dafydd, 'the only gay in the village' from the television comedy series *Little Britain*.

CARMARTHENSHIRE

(SIR CAERFYRDDIN)

COUNTY TOWN: CARMARTHEN

Newton House at the heart of Dynevor Park

Carmarthen

(Caerfyrddin)

'When Merlin's Oak shall tumble down, then shall fall Carmarthen Town'

ANCIENT PROPHECY

In 1978, after much hand wringing, the petrified stump of the aforementioned MERLIN'S OAK was removed, very carefully, to the Civic Hall, because it was obstructing the traffic. The good people of Carmarthen have been holding their breath ever since. The Welsh name for Carmarthen, Caerfyrddin, means Merlin's Camp, and according to Geoffrey of Monmouth, the wizard was born here. He is said to be here still, imprisoned by a nymph called Vivien, in a cave on Merlin's Hill, just outside the town.

Carmarthen occupies the site of Moridunum, THE MOST WESTERLY ROMAN FORT IN BRITAIN, and shares with Caerleon in Monmouthshire the accolade of being THE OLDEST TOWN IN WALES. Remains of the Roman amphitheatre, one of only seven of its kind in Britain, can be seen off Priory Street, near where Merlin's Oak used to stand. Priory Street recalls the Augustinian Priory of St John, founded here in the 11th century, and where the BLACK BOOK OF CARMARTHEN was written in 1105. This is THE OLDEST BOOK IN THE WELSH LANGUAGE and is held in the National Library of Wales in Aberystwyth.

Carmarthen is THE MOST LONG-STANDING COUNTY TOWN IN WALES, having been given this status by Edward I in 1284, when he created the shire. Until the Industrial Revolution it was THE BIGGEST TOWN IN WALES.

Buried beneath a grand tomb in the 14th-century church of St Peter is SIR

RHYS AP THOMAS (1449–1525), who led the Welsh support for Henry Tudor at the Battle of Bosworth Field in 1485.

Also buried here is the essayist and dramatist SIR RICHARD STEELE (1671–1729) who, along with his Charterhouse classmate Joseph Addison, founded and published a number of influential 18th-century periodicals, including *The Tatler* (1709–11), the *Spectator* (1711–12) and the *Guardian* (1713), as well as THE FIRST THEATRICAL PAPER, the *Theatre* (1720). After the death of his second wife, Mary Scurlock, in 1718, heavy debts forced Steele to move to Wales, where he lived in Mary's house Ty Gwyn, at Llangunnor, just outside Carmarthen, now a farmhouse. He later moved into Carmarthen to what became the Ivy Bush Hotel, later the scene of a famous Eisteddfod in 1819 (*see* Cardiganshire). He was buried in the Scurlock vault in St Peter's, wearing a wig with black bow.

Someone else who moved to Carmarthen because of debts was the architect JOHN NASH, who lived here for 12 years. Sadly, little of the work he did in the town remains.

The landlord of the Ivy Bush Hotel in the 19th century was the father of Major-General Sir William Nott, victor of the first Afghan War in 1840, after whom Carmarthen's Nott Square is named.

Friend of Chopin and composer of 'God Bless the Prince of Wales', BRINLEY RICHARDS, was born in Hall Street in 1817.

In 1966, GWYNFOR EVANS gave his acceptance speech at Carmarthen Guildhall on winning the Carmarthen by-election and becoming THE FIRST PLAID CYMRU MEMBER OF PARLIAMENT.

Dolaucothi

Welsh Gold

Hidden away in the hills north of Llandeilo is one of the main reasons that the Romans came to Wales – there is, in fact, GOLD in them thar hills. DOLAUCOTHI, near the village of Pumpsaint (Five Saints), is THE ONLY KNOWN ROMAN GOLD-MINE IN BRITAIN. The gold from here, intended for the Imperial Mint in Rome, was retrieved partly by open-cast mining and also by driving shafts known as 'adits' horizontally into the hillside – the openings to these works, concealed by trees and rock falls, pockmark the slopes. The Romans cut ingenious stone aqueducts into the terrain, one of them over 7 miles (11 km) long, to bring water to the mines for washing the ore, and some sections of these aqueducts can still be traced. They abandoned Dolaucothi in about AD 140, and the mines lay undisturbed for centuries until they were reopened on a small scale in 1844. In 1867, while using explosives to open up new adits, workers came across wooden artefacts over 2,000 years old, at depths of 160 feet (50 m) or more. Dolaucothi finally closed for good in 1938, and the whole site is now run by the National Trust, who organise guided tours into the mines.

Pendine Sands

(Traeth Pentywyn)

Sun, Sand and Speed

For a brief but glorious time in the 1920s, Wales was at the centre of world land speed records, and a Welshman was the fastest man on earth. The six-mile stretch of Pendine Sands on Carmarthen Bay were the Bonneville salt flats of their day, and the setting for a gripping contest between speed hero SIR MALCOLM CAMPBELL and a motor engineer from Wrexham, JOHN PARRY THOMAS. In 1924, Campbell broke the world land speed record on Pendine Sands, reaching 146.16 mph (235.17 kph) in his V12 Sunbeam, the first of his famous *Bluebirds*. In July 1925, Campbell

became the first man to exceed 150 mph (241.35 kph), again on Pendine Sands. The following year Parry Thomas took to the sands in a huge, 27,000-litre, aero-engined monster he had acquired from his friend Count Zborowski, tragically killed at the Monza Grand Prix the year before. Zborowski had built his own cars, which became known as Chitty Chitty Bang Bangs after the noise emitted from their exhaust pipes – one such car inspired Ian Fleming's book of the same name. Parry Thomas re-designed his Chitty Chitty Bang Bang, named it

'Babs' and, in 1926, set a new world record of 171.02 mph (275.17 kph) on Pendine Sands.

In February 1927, Malcolm Campbell just managed to snatch the record back at Pendine with an average speed of 174.8 mph (281.25 kph). Parry Thomas was not going to stand for that. On 3 March he took a slightly modified Babs for another run across the sand, just missing the record. On his second attempt, the car overturned at 180 mph (289.62 kph) and Parry Thomas was killed instantly, decapitated by the broken drive chain.

This was the last world land speed record attempt made at Pendine. For more than 40 years Babs lay buried in the sand where she had crashed, until, in 1969, she was uncovered and slowly restored to her original condition. Babs now sits proudly in the Museum of Speed in Pendine village.

In 1933, flying ace AMY JOHNSON and her husband JIM MOLLISON took off from Pendine Sands and achieved THE FIRST EVER NON-STOP FLIGHT FROM BRITAIN TO THE USA. Their aircraft ran out of fuel and crash landed at an aerodrome in Connecticut, just short of their ultimate destination of New York, slightly injuring both pilots.

During the Second World War Pendine Sands were taken over by the Ministry of Defence for use as a firing range. In 1943, Winston Churchill, General Eisenhower and Field-Marshal Montgomery stood on the beach at Wiseman's Bridge to watch as 100,000 men stormed ashore during rehearsals for the D-Day Normandy landings.

In June 2002 Sir Malcolm Campbell's grandson, Don Wales, evoked some nostalgia by bringing a *Bluebird* back to Pendine Sands and setting a speed record – the UK electric land speed record of 137 mph (220 kph), in *Bluebird Electric 2*.

Pendine Sands are still owned by the MoD, and on some days access is restricted, but the vast beach is now more of a holiday destination – there are some who wish that the MoD would train their guns on the swarming caravan parks that have sprung up as far as the eye can see.

Laugharne

'timeless, beautiful, barmy town'

DYLAN THOMAS

In the sloping hillside churchyard of 13th-century St Martin's, set back from the road, there is a simple white wooden cross that brings people from all over the world to this most lovely and remote of Welsh towns, set on the 'mussel pooled and heron priested shore' of the Taf estuary. Here, above LAUGHARNE, the 'strangest town in Wales', where he 'got off the bus and forgot to get on again', lies the best-known Welsh poet of them all, DYLAN THOMAS (1914–53). From the church it is a gentle walk into the town, along a road lined with sweet Georgian houses. It takes you past Thomas's favourite Brown's Hotel, where he would sup his midday bitter and listen to the gossip, past his parents' home opposite, past the Rose and Crown, now 'Dylan's Diner', on past the castle and over the cliffs, along Dylan's Walk, to finally look down upon the BOAT HOUSE, squeezed between the cliff and the water's edge. Thomas spent the last four years of his life in this 'seashaken house on a break-neck of rocks'.

The local people seem indifferent to the excitement of those who come here to worship Dylan Thomas, perhaps because they, like the poet himself, came here to get away from it all, or perhaps because they slightly resent being looked at as characters out of *Under Milk Wood* – however much Thomas tried to deny it, the rest of the world, if not all the critics, see Laugharne and its inhabitants as the model for Llareggub. After all, if you reverse the letters you will discover what Dylan Thomas thought happened in Laugharne – which is the main reason why he wanted to live here.

Thomas came to live in Laugharne in 1938, but it was not until 1949 that he moved into the Boat House with his wife Caitlin and their two children – a third child, Colm, was born there. The Boat House was bought for them, for £3,000, by Mrs Taylor, the wife of the historian A.J.P. Taylor. Above the Boat House, springing out from the cliff and supported at one end by steel legs anchored in the garden below, is a blue-painted wooden shed, with a board over the door on which is written: 'In this building Dylan Thomas wrote many of his famous works seeking inspiration from the panoramic view of the estuary'. A glass window inserted in the door allows the pilgrim to gaze in at the small, plain, sparsely furnished room where Thomas worked every afternoon, and where he composed *Under Milk Wood*. The shed had originally been built as a garage, to house a previous owner's German DKW car which had no reverse gear, and therefore needed to be garaged on the flat, where it could be easily manhandled in and out.

Like so many of the best writers, Dylan Thomas drank too much, was

exciting to know, impossible to live with, and always in debt. It was the drink that finished him, in a New York bar in 1953, at the age of 39, while he was on a speaking tour of America to try to raise some money. Many years later, as a tribute to his idol, the American singer Robert Allen Zimmerman changed his own name – to Bob Dylan.

The Boat House is now open to the public.

Laugharne's picturesque castle, subject of a dramatic painting by J.M.W. Turner, dates from the 13th century and was transformed into a comfortable dwelling by Sir John Perrot, an illegitimate son of Henry VIII. Between the wars, RICHARD HUGHES, author of *A High Wind in Jamaica*, lived in Castle House next door.

Llanelli

Saucepans

LLANELLI is the largest town in Carmarthenshire and is famous for its rugby team, the SCARLETS, who celebrated their centenary in 1972 by beating the New Zealand All Blacks at Stradey Park. Many of the great Welsh rugby players have turned out for the Scarlets, including Ray Gravell, Derek Quinnell and Ieuan Evans. The rugby posts at Stradey Park are topped with saucepans, and the club's anthem 'Sospan Fach' (Little Saucepan) is a tribute to Llanelli's industrial heritage – the town was once THE LARGEST MANUFACTURER OF TINPLATE IN THE WORLD. The TROSTRE plant on the edge of the town is now THE ONLY TINPLATE WORKS LEFT IN BRITAIN.

At the start of the 20th century, Stepney Street in Llanelli became famous for the production of a hugely successful invention by Walter Davies, the STEPNEY SPARE MOTOR WHEEL, an inflated tyre on a solid spokeless rim that could be temporarily attached to a car wheel in the event of a puncture. Stepney Wheels were sent all over the world, and in India the term is still applied to any spare tyre.

LLANELLY HOUSE in Bridge Street is widely praised as 'THE FINEST GEORGIAN TOWN HOUSE IN WALES'. It was restored to pristine condition as a result of being voted the Welsh finalist in the BBC *Restoration* programme of 2005.

The Rebecca Riots

Road Charging

Beside the road at EFAILWEN there is a commemorative stone that marks the site of the first of the 'REBECCA RIOTS', which took place on the night of 13 May 1839, when the 'Daughters of Rebecca' attacked a tollgate operated here by the Whitland Turnpike Trust. It was a time of severe economic depression after the Napoleonic Wars, and the local farmers disguised themselves as women to protest against having to pay tolls to use poorly maintained roads, something they saw as a symbol of oppression. The riots continued sporadically until 1843, with miners and metalworkers joining in, and although they became increasingly violent and many of the ringleaders were transported to Australia, the 1844 Turnpike Trust Act conceded many of their demands. The Daughters of Rebecca took their name from The Book of Genesis, Chapter 24, Verse 60: 'And they blessed Rebekah and said unto her, "and let thy seed possess the gates of those which hate them".'

BORN IN CARMARTHENSHIRE

Stage actress RACHEL ROBERTS was born in Llanelli in 1927. She was married to Rex Harrison for nine years.

Actress SIAN PHILLIPS was born in Betws, near Ammanford, in 1934. Perhaps best known for her role as the devious Livia in the BBC TV series *I Claudius*, Sian was married for 20 years to hell-raising actor Peter O'Toole.

Actor HYWEL BENNETT, best known for playing the title role in the long running television sitcom *Shelley,* was born in Garnant, near Ammanford, in 1944.

Rugby star BARRY JOHN was born in Cefneithin, Llanelli, in 1945.

Television presenter ALEX JONES, known for her work on S4C, and as co-presenter on BBC'S THE ONE SHOW, was born in Ammanford in 1977.

Rugby star JONATHAN DAVIES was born in Trimsaran in 1962.

BURIED IN CARMARTHENSHIRE

Alone in the Tabernacle cemetery at GLANAMAN, beneath the Black Mountains, lies JAMES COLTON (1858–1936), a miner who was married to one of the most controversial figures of the early 20th century, feminist and anarchist Emma Goldman (1869–1940), described by J. Edgar Hoover as 'the most dangerous woman in America'. Colton sympathised with Goldman's views and admired her courage in standing up for them, and he offered to marry her so that she could gain a British passport, after she was thrown out of the USA. In Warren Beatty's epic film *Reds*, Emma Goldman was played by Maureen Stapleton, who won an Oscar for the role.

An obelisk in LLANFAIR-AR-Y-BRYN CHURCHYARD outside Llandovery marks the resting-place of WILLIAM WILLIAMS, PANTYCELYN (1717–91), one of Wales's great hymn writers, composer of, amongst other hymns, 'Guide Me, O Thou Great Jehovah'.

Buried in a modest family vault in the lonely churchyard at CAEO, near Llandovery, is a victim of one of the most infamous Victorian melodramas of the 19th century. JUDGE JOHN JOHNES was murdered in the study of his ancestral home, Dolaucothi, by his butler, HARRY TREMBLE, whom he had just dismissed. The butler did it, and then killed the Judge's dogs before turning the gun on himself. Tremble's body was left lying by the side of the road for some time before eventually being buried in the churchyard in an unmarked grave. Also buried with the Johnes family is SIR JAMES HILL-JOHNES (1833–1919) who, as James Hill, won a Victoria Cross at the siege of Delhi in 1857, and married Judge Johnes's daughter in 1882.

Well, I never knew this

ABOUT

CARMARTHENSHIRE

Carmarthenshire is THE LARGEST COUNTY IN WALES.

The NATIONAL BOTANICAL GARDEN OF WALES opened in the grounds of Middleton Hall in Llanarthne, east of Carmarthen, in 2000 – THE FIRST NEW NATIONAL BOTANICAL GARDEN OF THE NEW MILLENNIUM ANYWHERE IN THE WORLD.

The GREAT GLASSHOUSE in the Botanic Garden was designed by Sir Norman Foster and IS THE LARGEST SINGLE-SPAN GLASSHOUSE IN THE WORLD, 312 ft (95 m) long and 180 ft (55 m) wide. The glasshouse is home to over 1,000 species of plant and is able to recreate a number of climates, including those of Chile and South Australia. In a 2006 nation-wide poll to decide the Seven Wonders of Wales, it was voted No. 1 by readers of the *Western Mail*, just ahead of Mt Snowdon.

PAXTON'S TOWER, a Gothic folly and banqueting hall 1 mile (1.6 km) to the north, has spectacular views over the gardens as well as the Twyi valley. It was built around 1810 for a former owner of Middleton Hall, William Paxton, a banker who had made his money in India. The tower is dedicated to Lord Nelson.

Paxton's Tower

The garden at ABERGLASNEY, near Llandeilo, is one of the oldest in Britain. It was first mentioned in 1477 by the bard Lewis Glyn Cothi, who described it as 'a white painted court, built of dressed stone, surrounded by nine gardens of orchards, vineyards and large oak trees'. In the 17th century the estate was bought by Bishop Anthony Rudd of St David's, who laid out the gardens in the style we see them today. They have been restored by the Aberglasney Restoration Trust as a unique example of a Jacobean garden and include a parapet walk that is THE ONLY SURVIVING EXAMPLE OF ITS KIND IN BRITAIN.

The hill fort of CARN COCH, 700 ft (213 m) up in the foothills of the Black Mountains between Llandovery and Llandeilo, is THE LARGEST HILL FORT IN WALES and covers and area of some 15 acres (6 ha).

Below Carn Coch is BETHLEHEM, a small community that takes its name from a nonconformist chapel on the hillside. At Christmas time the village post office is inundated with sacks of Christmas cards from across Britain, all sent here to be appropriately franked.

TALLEY ABBEY, established in 1180 and now a peaceful ruin set in wooded country north of Llandeilo, is THE ONLY HOUSE OF THE ORDER OF THE WHITE CANONS TO BE FOUNDED IN WALES.

Just north of Llandovery is the graceful DOLAUHIRION BRIDGE across the River Twyi, built by William Edwards. When it was constructed in 1773 it was one of the longest single-span bridges in the world – outdone only by another bridge designed by Edwards, the famous bridge across the River Taff at Pontypridd.

CAPEL YSTRAD FFIN, a tiny, single-chambered church on the Cardigan border near Llyn Brianne, was founded in 1117, and used to belong to the monks of Strata Florida. It was rebuilt by the Cawdor family in 1821 and is thought to have been used as THE FIRST MEETING-PLACE FOR METHODISTS IN WALES.

Built in 1972, the LLYN BRIANNE DAM, north of Llandovery, is 299 ft (91 m) high, THE HIGHEST DAM IN BRITAIN.

The main road into the picturesque hill-top market town of LLANDEILO crosses the River Twyi over THE LONGEST STONE ARCH IN WALES. THE TWYI BRIDGE was built in 1848 and is 365 ft (111 m) long with a central span of 145 ft (44 m).

CARREG CENNEN CASTLE, 4 miles (6.4 km) south-east of Llandeilo, has the most commanding and impressive situation of any castle in Wales. It stands on top of a limestone crag with a sheer drop of 300 ft (91 m) to the River Cennan below, and dominates the countryside beneath the Black Mountain. The crag has been fortified since before Roman times, but the present ruins date from the 13th century and create an unmistakable landmark that has lured generations of visitors and artists, notably Turner, to this remote spot. A steep, walled passageway, lit by a succession of arched windows, tunnels its way down the cliff face and leads to a cavern where prehistoric remains have been found. The views are sensational.

On 17 June 1928, history was made at BURRY PORT, near Llanelli, when a seaplane called *Friendship* landed in the harbour after a flight of 20 hours and 49 minutes from Newfoundland. On board as a passenger was AMELIA EARHART, and she had just become THE FIRST WOMAN TO FLY ACROSS THE ATLANTIC. The buoy that *Friendship* was tethered to has been restored and sits proudly on the harbour front, along with a commemorative plaque and signposts showing the distances to Newfoundland and New York. Burry Port sits at the eastern end of CEFN SIDAN SANDS which, at 7 miles (11 km) long, is WALES'S LONGEST BEACH.

DENBIGHSHIRE

(SIR DINBYCH)

COUNTY TOWN: DENBIGH

The Georgian Pin Mill at Bodnant Gardens, brought here from Gloucestershire in 1939

Denbigh
(Dinbych)

A Town to Explore

Edward I glowers out over the charming old hill town of DENBIGH, from his niche above the huge triangular gatehouse of Denbigh Castle. This was one of the biggest and most powerful of Edward's castles, begun in 1282 on the site of a previous Welsh fortification. Like Caernarfon and Conwy, the town of Denbigh was turned into a fortified English borough, surrounded by high walls. One of the original gates, Burgess Gate, is still there, as well as long stretches of the wall, which provide an exhilarating walk offering commanding views of the town, with the moors and vales beyond.

Much of the original medieval street pattern survives within the walls, but most of the buildings date from the 16th century, when the town was rebuilt after being burned to the ground during the Wars of the Roses. In the time of Elizabeth I, the Castle and Lordship of

Denbigh was held by the Queen's favourite Robert Dudley, Earl of Leicester, who started to build Leicester's church by the castle in the hope of attracting the bishopric from St Asaph. This never happened and the church was not finished.

Denbigh possesses a fine collection of chapels, of which CAPEL LON SWAN in Chapel Street, founded in 1742, is the oldest. Also in Chapel Street, CAPEL PENDREF is THE FIRST PURPOSE-BUILT WESLEYAN CHAPEL IN WALES, opened in 1804.

ST MARCELLA S, Denbigh's parish church, sits 1 mile (1.6 km) outside the town to the east at Llanfarchell, above a holy well where Marchell the Virgin had her hermitage. It's a grand church from the 15th century, with a double nave and large perpendicular Gothic windows.

There are a number of fine monuments inside. On the north side, HUMPHREY LLWYD (1527– 68), who was born in Denbigh, kneels beside an angel holding a globe. A scholar, musician and MP for Denbigh, he has been called 'the Father of Modern Geography' and produced THE FIRST PRINTED MAP OF WALES, which was published in Antwerp in 1573 and proved so popular that it was reprinted regularly until 1741.

Nearby is a monumental brass of Richard Myddelton and his wife and 16 children. One son, Sir Thomas Myddelton, became head of the Chirk Castle Myddeltons, and another, Sir Hugh Myddelton, developed the ingenious 'New River' system that brought water to London from Hertfordshire early in the 17th century.

Remembered in the north aisle, but buried in the churchyard, is Thomas Edwards, or TWM O'R NANT (1739–1810). Known as 'the Cambrian Shakespeare', he was the first Welsh playwright of note and was born near Llannefydd, 3 miles (5 km) north-west of Denbigh.

Henry Morton Stanley

A Bit Presumptious

John Rowlands was born in 1841 in a cottage by the castle gates, the illegitimate son of John Rowlands and Elizabeth Parry (later Jones). He was sent away to the workhouse in St Asaph, from where he ran away to sea at the age of 16. In 1859, he sailed to New Orleans as a cabin boy and was adopted by a merchant called Henry Stanley, whose name he took. As HENRY MORTON STANLEY, he fought for both sides in the American Civil War and then made use of his experiences to become a journalist.

In 1869 Stanley was sent by the *New York Herald* to look for the Scottish missionary and explorer David Livingstone, who had gone to search for the source of the Nile and hadn't been heard from since 1866. It took Stanley two years to track his man down, but he eventually found Livingstone in a remote part of what is now Tanzania, near Lake Tanganyika and greeted him, supposedly, with the immortal sound bite 'Dr Livingstone, I presume?' It was one of the world's first great journalistic 'scoops' and made Stanley more famous than his subject.

In later years Henry Morton Stanley returned frequently to Africa to explore further. With the support of King Leopold II of Belgium, he opened up the Belgian Congo and prepared the ground for the creation of the Congo Free State.

On returning to Britain he toured the country, lecturing and writing about his experiences, and became MP for Lambeth, in London. He died in 1904 and is buried at Pirbright, in Surrey, under a stone with the simple epitaph 'Africa'.

Ruthin

(Rhuthun)

Square Eyes

Ruthin is one of the nicest little towns in Wales, an eclectic mix of attractive buildings gathered around a hilltop square, with breezy views of the Vale of Clwyd and the Clwydian Hills.

The handsome wrought-iron gates leading to St Peter's Church are by Robert Davies of Bersham. Nantclwyd House in Castle Street is a 15th-century timbered cruck house, one of the oldest in Wales, and was once the home of Dr Gabriel Goodman, who became Dean of Westminster for 40 years and founded Ruthin School in 1595.

The Myddelton Arms is an

The Eyes of Ruthin

unusual Dutch-style building, with a huge sloping roof pierced by seven dormer windows known as the 'eyes of Ruthin'. Prominent in the square is the Maen Huail, a large stone which local legend says marks where King Arthur beheaded Huail, his rival in love.

Ruthin Castle, once home to the Cornwallis-West family and now an hotel, is a huge castellated mansion of the early 19th century, built on the site of a 13th-century castle of Edward I. Only the battlemented gatehouse remains from the original castle.

Top Formula One racing driver TOM PRYCE (1949–77) was born in Ruthin. On entering Formula One in 1974, Pryce was tipped as a future world champion, before being tragically killed in a freak accident at Kyalami in South Africa, when a 19-year-old marshal ran out on to the track in front of him.

Pop star Elton John's half-brother GEOFF DWIGHT lives in a small terraced house in Ruthin.

Beatle John Lennon's first wife CYNTHIA lived in Ruthin during the 1970s and 80s, and ran a bistro called Oliver's in Well Street. Julian, her son by John, went to Ruthin School. Paul McCartney is thought to have had Julian in mind when he wrote his sad song 'Hey, Jude', around the time of Cynthia and John's break-up.

Nantclwyd Hall

Oh, I say!

Wimbledon Centre Court, Dan Maskell's 'Oh, I say!', Henman Hill, Maria Sharapova, tennis elbow – we owe them all to the gardens at NANTCLWYD HALL, a 17th-century country house, 3 miles (5 km) south of Ruthin. It was on the lawns here, in 1873, that MAJOR WALTER WINGFIELD sowed the seeds of lawn tennis, after playing a game with a new kind of India rubber ball designed to bounce on grass. It was such fun that he was inspired to write down some rules.

Later that year he published THE FIRST SET OF LAWN TENNIS RULES, and in 1874 he registered a patent for the game, which he called sphairistike. He put together a kit of net, posts, rackets and balls, which he sold along with the book of rules, and the game quickly became hugely popular.

The first Wimbledon tournament took place in 1877, and the Lawn Tennis Association was founded in 1888.

Nantclwyd Hall is a private home, but the exotic 3-acre (1.2 ha) gardens, designed by Sir Clough Williams-Ellis for the Naylor-Leyland family, are sometimes open under the National Gardens Open Day scheme. Amongst the follies, temples and gazebos, dovecote, ceremonial arch and clock tower, as well as formal gardens, it might just be possible to find and walk on THE VERY FIRST LAWN WHERE TENNIS WAS PLAYED.

Wrexham

(Wrecsam)

Lager Town

WREXHAM, red brick and gritty, is the largest town in North Wales and its industrial and commercial capital. A market centre since the 14th century, Wrexham has grown prosperous on leather, iron and coal.

Just a step or two away from the busy, noisy, pedestrianised town centre, a quite beautiful set of wrought-iron gates opens on to another world, the calm, peaceful world of St Giles Church. Wrexham may not be the prettiest town, but it does possess one of the most glorious Gothic towers in the world, the tower of ST GILES, 136 ft (41 m) high, richly carved and pinnacled, one of the Seven Wonders of Wales.

Lying at the foot of the tower, near the west door, in a big stone chest tomb, is ELIHU YALE (1649–1721), benefactor of Yale University in Connecticut, USA. His epitaph begins:

Born in America, in Europe bred
In Africa travell'd, and in Asia wed

Yale was born in Boston, Massachusetts, but was brought to England when he was four. His family's ancestral home, about 10 miles (16 km) west of Wrexham, was called Plas yn Ial, which was how they got the name Yale, an anglicised version of Ial. Elihu Yale made his fortune with the East India Company and as Governor of Fort George, Madras. In 1718, he helped to raise money for a new building at the Collegiate School of Connecticut, which had been founded in 1701, by donating valuable books and paintings. The building was named after him, and then the university which grew from it.

Yale University in New Haven, Connecticut, is the third oldest institution of higher education in America, and a member of the Ivy League, a group of eight prestigious private universities in the north-east of America that play each other at sports. Wrexham Tower, overlooking Yale University, is a replica of St Giles tower.

As an adult, Elihu Yale lived at Plas Grono, a house near Erddig, just outside Wrexham, that was demolished in 1876. There is a tertiary college named Yale College, after Elihu Yale, in the centre of Wrexham, and in 1999 they were the subject of a lawsuit by Yale University over the use of the name.

In 1881, THE FIRST LAGER BREWERY IN BRITAIN was opened in Wrexham by German immigrants. WREXHAM LAGER was, for a long time, THE ONLY DRAUGHT BEER SERVED ON BRITISH SHIPS, as it was unaffected by the motion of the sea, unlike traditional beer. Because it travelled well, Wrexham Lager was exported all over the world and was even found at General Gordon's palace in Khartoum, according to a letter posted to the brewery from the Sudan in 1898. Eventually, Wrexham Lager was swallowed up by what became Carlsberg Tetley. In 2000, it was closed down and the factory demolished, except for the historic red-brick, original brewery building which is listed. Wrexham Lager is now brewed in Leeds.

JUDGE GEORGE JEFFREYS (1645–89), the infamous 'Hanging Judge' who presided over the 'Bloody Assizes' after the Monmouth Rebellion in 1685, was born at Acton Hall on the northern outskirts of Wrexham.

JOHN GODFREY PARRY-THOMAS (1884–1927), who broke the world land speed record at Pendine Sands (*see* Carmarthenshire), was born in Wrexham.

ANN WILKINSON, wife of John 'Iron Mad' Wilkinson, is commemorated inside St Giles church with a classical urn.

Bersham

Iron

In the latter half of the 18th century, BERSHAM, to the west of Wrexham, was THE FOREMOST IRON-MAKING CENTRE IN THE WORLD. At Croes Foel Farm, just outside the village, a plaque marks the site of the Davies brothers' smithy, where they produced THE FINEST WROUGHT-IRON GATES IN BRITAIN. Examples of their work in Wales are the churchyard gates of St Giles in Wrexham, forged in 1720 (*see* above), the White Gates of 1726 at Leeswood Hall near Mold, over 100 ft (30 m) long, and the Great Gates at Chirk Castle, their greatest masterpiece, completed in 1721.

The nearby Bersham Ironworks had been in use since 1640, producing cannons for the Civil War. In 1762, JOHN 'IRON MAD' WILKINSON took over the Bersham ironworks from his father, and from 1774 began producing superior cannons of incredible accuracy, using a revolutionary new technique he had patented for boring cannon cylinders from solid cast iron. Bersham cannon were used in the American War of Independence and during the Napoleonic and Peninsular Wars to great effect.

Wilkinson's cylinders were the only cylinders precise enough to make James Watt's new steam engines work, and the Boulton and Watt steam engines that powered the Industrial Revolution were built at Bersham.

In 1792, Wilkinson bought the coal-rich Brymbo Hall estate, 3 miles (5 km) to the north, and set up a new ironworks out of which grew the Brymbo Steel Company, which finally closed its doors in 1990.

Bersham Ironworks has been restored and can be visited in the summer months.

Bersham Colliery was first sunk in 1864, and coal was dug here for over 100 years until the mine closed in 1986. The pit-head gear, the last in North Wales, has been preserved and can be seen from the A483 Wrexham bypass.

Llangollen

Blessed is a world that sings,
Gentle are its songs

(Motto for the International Music Eisteddfod) T. GWYNN JONES

For most of the year LLANGOLLEN is a quiet, respectable Victorian village, clustered around its famous four-arch bridge, one of the Seven Wonders of Wales. But every July the town fills with singers, dancers, musicians and choirs from all over the world, who descend on the Royal International Pavilion for the INTERNATIONAL MUSICAL EISTEDDFOD. The first International Musical Eisteddfod took place in 1947 and was aimed at promoting peace, through music, between the nations after the Second World War. The occasion now attracts participants from over 50 countries.

There has been a bridge at Llangollen since 1284, but the first stone bridge was built in 1345 by the Bishop of Asaph, John Trevor, after whom the present bridge is named. The first bridge was replaced in 1656, and the downstream side of the bridge dates from this time. The upstream side has been altered twice since, in order to widen the bridge, once in 1873 and again in 1968.

The road north from Llangollen, before it starts to snake its way up the dizzying, self-explanatory Horseshoe Pass, goes by the picturesque ruins of VALLE CRUCIS ABBEY, founded in 1201, THE LAST CISTERCIAN ABBEY BUILT IN WALES. The cross referred to in the name is ELISEG'S PILLAR, erected in the 9th century in memory of Eliseg by his great-grandson, Cyngen, Prince of Powys. It stands 8 ft (2.4 m) high, and is beside the road about half a mile (0.8 km) from the abbey.

Dear Ladies

Buried beneath a three-sided Gothic tombstone in the churchyard of St Collen are the celebrated LADIES OF LLANGOLLEN, *Eleanor Butler (1739–1829) and Sarah Ponsonby (1755–1831), along with their maid Mary Caryll. The two ladies eloped from their homes in Ireland, after many adventures, and set up home at* PLAS NEWYDD, *a modest cottage on a hill overlooking the village. They were on their way to England, along the A5 from Holyhead, but fell in love with Wales, which they thought the most beautiful country in the world, and decided to stay.*

They were an odd couple, and would walk around Llangollen dressed in dark riding gear so that they looked more like men, and they spent their time gardening, painting and reading. They grew their own fruit and vegetables, kept cows as well as dogs and cats, and loved collecting things, especially anything carved in oak. The house is still bulging with all their treasures.

The Ladies of Llangollen became one of the sights of the village, and before long it was de rigueur *for any prominent figure travelling between London and Holyhead to stop off and see them. A small gift of a wooden carving was always welcome. Sarah Siddons, Edmund Burke, Sir Walter Scott, the Duke of Wellington and William Wordsworth – all dropped by and were entertained, for the Ladies could talk to anyone on any subject.*

After the Ladies had died, Plas Newydd passed through several hands before being taken on by a retired general who converted the house and collection into a museum, formalised the garden and had the Elizabethan timbering we see today added to the cottage. The house and gardens are now owned by Denbighshire County Council, and are open to the public during the summer months.

Valle Crucis Abbey

Pontcysyllte

Stream in the Sky

Take a boat east along the Llangollen Canal from Llangollen, and you will soon find yourself floating 126 ft (38 m) above the River Dee, on THE WORLD'S HIGHEST BOAT RIDE ABOVE LAND, courtesy of Thomas Telford's supreme PONTCYSYLLTE AQUEDUCT, at 1,007 ft (307 m), THE LONGEST AQUEDUCT IN BRITAIN. Completed in 1805, it was THE FIRST AQUEDUCT IN THE WORLD TO USE A CAST-IRON TROUGH, SET ON HIGH PILLARS, of which there are 18. Even by Telford's standards Pontcysyllte was an astoundingly bold and brilliant piece of engineering. Sir Walter Scott called it the finest work of art he had ever seen.

It is a toe-tingling experience to walk along the towpath over the aqueduct, beside THE LONGEST IRON TROUGH IN BRITAIN, as gaily painted narrow boats glide by, separated from the awful drop by no more than a few inches of fragile cast-iron lip. If you can bring yourself to look, the prospect of the Dee valley from the centre of the aqueduct is tremendous, and includes a distant view of Telford's earlier Chirk Aqueduct, running alongside Henry Robertson's huge railway viaduct of 1848.

Rhos-on-Sea

The Smallest Chapel and the First Americans

Right on the border with Caernarfonshire, Rhos-on-Sea sits on a promontory between the sands of Colwyn Bay and Penrhyn Bay. At the western end of the Promenade, almost on the beach, is the tiny, stone, buttressed ST TRILLO'S CHAPEL, THE SMALLEST CHAPEL IN BRITAIN, measuring only 11 ft (3.4 m) by 8 ft (2.4 m). The original structure, built next to a drinking well, was 6th-century, and was related to a nearby monastery founded by St Trillo, a monk from Brittany. The chapel seats six people and is used each Wednesday for an Anglican Communion service. Out on the sands, low tide reveals the remains of a small, stone-walled enclosure built by the monks to trap fish, which would be stranded within when the water receded.

A brass plaque in a garden near the chapel commemorates the historic voyage of PRINCE MADOC, who is said to have sailed from here in 1170 to discover America, 300 years before Christopher Columbus. Prince Madoc, born at Dolwyddelan Castle, was an illegitimate son of King Owain Gwynedd. In 1170, to escape the fighting after his father's death, he sailed west from Rhos-on-Sea with two ships, to try and find the promised land beyond the western horizon. Madoc returned with tales of a wonderful new country across the sea and persuaded others of his countrymen to accompany him back there and start a new life. In 1171 Madoc and his companions sailed towards the setting sun and were never heard of again.

Many people believe that Prince Madoc did survive, landing at Mobile Bay in Alabama, and travelling inland up the Alabama River. Explorers who followed after Columbus discovered a series of forts along the Alabama River, apparently dating from well before Columbus's arrival, and closely resembling the hill forts of Wales. One of the forts, on Lookout Mountain, near DeSoto Falls, Alabama, showed striking similarities, both in its setting and in its design, to Madoc's birthplace, Dolwyddelan Castle.

Later explorers came across a tribe of blue-eyed Red Indians with fair skin and brown hair, living on the banks of the Missouri River, who called themselves Mandans. They spoke, in a language very like Welsh, of their tribe coming originally from the Gulf of Mexico, and they fished in round boats like Welsh coracles. And their settlements were built on rocky outcrops, as in Wales. Were they the descendants of Madoc and his companions, and did the Welsh discover America?

Buried in the church at Llandrillo-yn-

Rhos is HOWARD LOWE (1882–1944), Fifth Officer on the *Titanic*, and one of the few men to row back to the sinking ship to look for survivors. He was played in the Oscar-winning film *Titanic* by Welsh actor Ioan Gruffydd.

Well, I never knew this ABOUT DENBIGHSHIRE

Pistyll Rhaeadr and Wrexham steeple,
Snowdon's mountain without its people,
Overton yew trees, St Winefride's Well,
Llangollen Bridge and Gresford bells

Denbighshire possesses four of the 'Seven Wonders of Wales'. These 'wonders' feature in the above poem, written anonymously in the late 18th century, and have sparked lively debate ever since – especially as they are all in North Wales!

The bells in the lovely 15th-century pinnacled bell tower of ALL SAINTS CHURCH in GRESFORD, one of the finest churches in Wales, are amongst the Seven Wonders of Wales. A new set of lighter bells was added in 2006.

GRESFORD, once a mining town, is known for its disasters as well as its wonders. In 1934, a series of explosions inside the Gresford coal-mine killed 262 miners, three rescuers and a surface worker, in one of the worst mining disasters in British history.

Denbigh was one of the few places in Wales that the old curmudgeon DR JOHNSON approved of. For a short while he was a guest of the Myddeltons of GWAENYNOG HALL, just outside the town, and in the grounds you can still see the riverside cottage where he stayed, as well as Johnson's Monument, erected by Colonel Myddelton to commemorate the good doctor's visit.

The gardens of GWAENYNOG HALL are the setting for Beatrix Potter's *Tale of the Flopsy Bunnies*. The hall belonged to her mother's family, and while staying here, Beatrix drew inspiration for her illustrations from the wonderful Victorian gardens. Mr McGregor's potting-shed is still there, as are plenty of flopsy bunnies, and the present owner, Janie Smith, Beatrix Potter's great-great-niece, has restored the gardens to how they would have looked when Beatrix was here in the 1890s.

In the grounds of TY'N DWR HALL, near Llangollen, which is now a Youth Hostel, is THE LARGEST YEW TREE IN WALES.

The entrance to the spreading grounds of CHIRK CASTLE (NT), in the Marcher lands south of Wrexham, is through the most breathtakingly beautiful set of wrought-iron gates in Britain, the finest

masterpiece of the Davies brothers of Bersham. The castle, on top of a small hill, is low and brooding with huge round drum towers at each corner. It was begun by Edward I's mightiest Marcher lord, Roger de Mortimer, in the 13th century, and oozes power and intimidation. You approach, with some trepidation, the soaring entrance arch, emblazoned with a coat of arms in stone and barred by vast, iron-studded wooden doors. The awe is palpable. The hand trembles. And there, beside the door, is a tiny bronze doorbell saying 'Myddelton'. Just so the postman knows.

The underground workings of Bersham Colliery reached beneath the wonderful, late 17th-century ERDDIG HALL, and although a large pillar of solid coal was left in place directly under the house, Erddig was nevertheless seriously damaged by subsidence. The last owner, Philip Yorke, handed Erddig over to the National Trust in 1973, complete with contents. Erddig is the only stately home where the world of the servants takes pride of place. The Yorkes, who lived there from the early 18th century, commissioned portraits of all their servants and kept notes of their daily lives together, creating a unique record of servant life in a country house over two and a half centuries.

LLANFAIR TALHAEARN, a pretty village beside the River Elwy, west of Denbigh, was the birthplace of the poet and architect JOHN JONES (1810–89). Jones worked under Sir Joseph Paxton and oversaw the construction of the Crystal Palace for the Great Exhibition of 1851.

Regarded as one of the best builders and architects of his day, he had to retire far too young owing to crippling arthritis, and spent the rest of his life trying, unsuccessfully, to win the Chair at the National Eisteddfod. He is buried under a yew tree in the steeply rising churchyard.

The small town of LLANRWST, north of Betws-y-Coed, is the market centre for the Conwy Valley and is known for its steep and narrow bridge, thought to be the work of Inigo Jones – certainly there is a Stuart coat of arms dated 1636 on the parapet. In the Gwydir Chapel of the church of St Grwst is a tomb, said to be that of LLYWELYN THE GREAT, first moved from his abbey at Aberconwy to Maenan Abbey in 1283, and then to Llanrwst at the Dissolution.

PISTYLL RHAEADR, one of the Seven Wonders of Wales, is THE TALLEST WATERFALL IN ENGLAND AND WALES. Tumbling down off the moorland of Berwyn, the Afon Disgynfa falls 240 ft (73 m), after which it becomes the Afon Rhaeadr. As George Borrow, the 19th-century author of *Wild Wales* put it, 'I never saw water falling so gracefully . . .' Pistyll Rhaeadr is located at the head of the valley some 3 miles (5 km) north-west of the village of Llanrhaeadr-ym-Mochnant, where William Morgan was Rector and worked on his translation of the Bible into Welsh.

Buried in the church at LLANNEFYDD, high up on the moors north-west of Denbigh, is CATRIN O FERAIN (1534–91), known as 'Mam Cymru' or 'Mother of Wales'. She was a direct descendant of Henry IV and one-time owner of Penymyndd, the ancestral home of the Tudors on Anglesey. Four times she married, each time to a rich and influential man. Her second husband was Elizabeth I's factor in Antwerp, merchant banker and architect Richard Clough, who founded the London Stock Exchange and was an ancestor of Portmeirion architect Sir Clough Williams-Ellis. Amongst her descendants were the Williams Wynns of Wynnstay, near Ruabon, at one time the richest and most powerful landowning family in North Wales. It is said that she disposed of her many lovers by pouring molten lead in their ears, and burying them in the garden.

Monty Python star TERRY JONES was born in COLWYN BAY in 1942.

James Bond actor TIMOTHY DALTON was born in COLWYN BAY in 1946.

TV personality PAULA YATES (1960–2000) was born in COLWYN BAY. Presenter of *The Tube* and *Big Breakfast*, she married Live Aid star Bob Geldof, with whom she had three children, Fifi Trixibell, Peaches and Pixie. She later had a daughter by INXS singer Michael Hutchence, Heavenly Hiraani Tiger Lily. Late in life she discovered that her real father was not the *Stars on Sunday* TV presenter Jess Yates, as she had been told, but another TV presenter, Hughie Greene of *Opportunity Knocks*.

ST MICHAEL'S CHURCH, ABERGELE, is THE LARGEST CHURCH WITH A DOUBLE NAVE IN WALES.

In the churchyard of St Michael's Church, Abergele, there is a memorial to the 33 people who died in a terrible train crash at Llanddulas, a little west of Abergele. The Irish Mail express from Chester ran into some runaway wagons, loaded with paraffin, that had rolled down the hill from quarry sidings. The passengers were locked into their compartments for safety, and when the gas lighting in the train ignited, 33 of them were burned alive. In 1969, two Welsh separatists, Arwel Jones and George Taylor, were killed while trying to place a bomb on the railway line at Abergele, to sabotage the train bringing Prince Charles to Caernarfon Castle for his Investiture.

CAPTAIN MATTHEW WEBB trained in the sea off PENSARN before becoming THE FIRST MAN TO SWIM THE ENGLISH CHANNEL in 1875.

FLINTSHIRE

(SIR FFLINT)

COUNTY TOWN: MOLD

St Asaph Cathedral, the smallest medieval cathedral in Britain

St Asaph

(Llanelwy)

Smallest Cathedral

ST ASAPH CATHEDRAL is THE SMALLEST MEDIEVAL CATHEDRAL IN BRITAIN. A church was built here by St Kentigern, Bishop of Strathclyde, also known as St Mungo, in AD 560. When St Kentigern returned to Scotland in AD 573, he left his student, Asaph, in his place as Bishop.

The present cathedral building dates mainly from the 13th and 14th centuries. Buried inside, close to the Bishop's throne, is WILLIAM MORGAN, BISHOP OF ASAPH (1545–1604), whose translation of the Bible into Welsh (*see* Caernarfonshire) is considered to be the most important single contribution to the preservation of the Welsh language. The cathedral possesses to this day a 1588 first edition of Morgan's Welsh Bible, which was used at Prince Charles's investiture as Prince of Wales at Caernarfon Castle in 1969.

There is a memorial in the cathedral

to the poetess FELICIA HEMANS (1793–1835), who lived most of her life in and around St Asaph. Her best-known poem was called 'Casablanca' and starts with the line 'The boy stood on the burning deck . . .'

As the seat of an ancient cathedral, St Asaph was historically considered a city, but is not recognised as such today. The widespread belief that having a cathedral or a university automatically confers city status is mistaken. Brecon and St Asaph are the only two Welsh cathedral towns denied city status, despite St Asaph having applied twice in recent years. (The other four Welsh cathedral cities are Bangor, St David's, Cardiff (Llandaff) and Newport, Monmouthshire.)

Former Liverpool and Wales footballer IAN RUSH was born in St Asaph in 1961. He is WALES'S RECORD GOAL-SCORER with 28 goals in 73 appearances.

LISA SCOTT-LEE, former member of the band Steps, was born in St Asaph in 1975.

Holywell
(Treffynnon)

Well, Well

Some 1300 years ago, in the 7th century, a gentle young girl of noble birth called Winefride was studying alone at home, when the evil Prince Caradog forced his way in and attempted to ravish her. She managed to escape and fled towards her uncle St

Beuno's church on the hill, but Caradog caught up with her and, maddened with rage and lust, sliced her head off with his sword. St Beuno and Winefride's brother Owain returned at that moment, and Owain slew Caradog where he stood. St Beuno picked up Winefride's head and replaced it on her shoulders, praying as he did so. She was miraculously restored to life, and she and St Beuno sat down on the stone that today bears his name.

At the spot where her head had fallen, a spring gushed forth, and St Beuno told Winefride that anyone who drank from the spring and prayed for her help would find succour. Winefride went on to become an Abbess at Gwytherin Convent near Llanrwst, and her well at Holywell has been a place of pilgrimage ever since. She is buried in Shrewsbury Abbey.

Although the holy well of ST WINEFRIDE has been recorded as a place of pilgrimage since the 11th century, and Henry V came here in 1416 after the Battle of Agincourt, it is one of the unknown places of Wales. It is about a quarter of a mile (0.4 km) outside the little industrial market town of Holywell, with its wide main street, just far enough removed from the bustle and the A55 to remain a real sanctuary of peace and tranquillity. Possibly because it is so easy to overlook, St Winefride's Well is THE ONLY SHRINE IN WALES TO HAVE SURVIVED IN CONTINUOUS USE FROM ITS FOUNDATION TO THE PRESENT DAY.

A beautifully vaulted crypt has been built around the well, with access from the north through a graceful triple arcade. A rather worn pendant boss, carved with the tale of St Winefride, hangs over the spring, while built directly above the crypt is a divine little pilgrim's chapel. All of this is the work of Margaret Beaufort, mother of Henry VII, and was constructed in 1490. This is one of the most special places in all of Wales, and for most of the time is blissfully uncrowded.

St Winefride's Well is one of the traditional Seven Wonders of Wales mentioned in the famous 19th-century rhyme.

The poet GERALD MANLEY HOPKINS (1844–89) loved St Winefride's Well, and was inspired by the beauty of the area to write what is regarded as his finest poetry. He first came here in 1874 while studying at the Jesuit college of St Beuno, nearby at Tremeirchion.

Actor JONATHAN PRYCE was born in Holywell in 1947.

Flint
(Y Fflint)

Old and Thick

FLINT was once the port for Chester and has THE OLDEST TOWN CHARTER IN WALES, dating from 1284.

The ruins of Flint Castle, the first of Edward I's iron ring of fortresses, stand on a rocky platform above the marshes of the Dee estuary. Flint is THE ONLY CASTLE IN BRITAIN TO HAVE A SEPARATE DONJON, or Great Tower, detached from the rest of the castle, and used to be surrounded by a moat, filled from the Dee. The walls of the donjon, which was built in 1277–80, are 23 ft (7 m) thick, THE THICKEST CASTLE WALLS IN THE WORLD. In 1399, Richard II was made captive here and forced to surrender to Henry Bolingbroke, later Henry IV. The scene was re-enacted in Act III, Scene iii of William Shakespeare's *Richard II*.

Edward's Iron Ring

King Edward I's iron ring of fortresses were the most ambitious building project of medieval Europe, and were designed to contain and subdue once and for all the heartlands of the Welsh Princes of Gwynedd, Anglesey and Snowdonia. The major castles of the iron ring are Flint, Rhuddlan, Conwy, Harlech, Caernarfon and Beaumaris. They were all the work of the foremost architect of the day, James of St George, and are considered to be the most advanced and sophisticated strongholds of their time anywhere in the world.

Film star TOM CRUISE'S great-great-grandfather emigrated to America from Flint in 1850.

Hawarden Castle

Home of a Grand Old Man

In St Deiniol's church in HAWARDEN there is a gorgeous stained-glass window by Sir Edward Burne-Jones, honouring the only man to be Prime Minister four times, WILLIAM GLADSTONE (1809–98). The window was unveiled in 1898, the year that Gladstone died, and was BURNE-JONES'S LAST WORK, for he passed away later that same year.

Nearly 60 years earlier William Gladstone came to Hawarden to marry Catherine Glynne, heiress to Hawarden Castle. Hawarden became his 'Temple of Peace', away from the hurly-burly of Westminster politics. His greatest relaxation was felling the trees on the estate, and that is precisely what he was doing when summoned for the first time by Queen Victoria to form a government. He later opened the grounds to the public, and they flocked to see him at work with his axe.

Felling trees was not without its hazards. On one occasion, he was almost blinded in one eye by a splinter that flew up from the tree he was chopping at. Many years later, in 1892, his other eye was equally badly damaged when he was hit in the face by a ginger biscuit, thrown by a woman at his open carriage as he was driving to make a speech in Chester. On another occasion, he was walking through the park with Catherine when they were charged at by a wild heifer. Gladstone threw himself in front of his wife to protect her and was sent sprawling in the dirt. The heifer was later caught and shot, and its head displayed in the village pub.

The park also contains the ruins of the original 13th-century Hawarden Castle, an impressive stone motte and bailey fort, sitting amongst trees not far from the present, romantically castellated Hawarden Castle, which dates from 1752.

Next to St Deiniol's church stands the St Deiniol Library, based on Gladstone's personal library of over 30,000 books. It is probably the greatest collection of books about the Victorian era that exists outside the British Library.

The huge bronze statue of Gladstone in the village was intended for Dublin, but was rejected by the city following Irish independence – ironically, Irish Home Rule being the one great aspiration of Gladstone's that he never managed to achieve in his lifetime.

Mold
(Yr Wyddgrug)

Cape Town

Mold is a busy, bustling market town gathered around the foot of the Mont Haut or 'high mound' that gives the town its name. Its Welsh name Yr Wyddgrug also means high mound, and refers to the motte that survives on Bailey Hill at the top of the High Street.

At the foot of Bailey Hill, casting its benevolent gaze over the town, is Mold's pride and joy, the beautiful church of St Mary's, founded by Margaret Beaufort to commemorate her son Henry VII's victory at Bosworth Field in 1485. The impressive tower was added in 1773.

Antiquities

Mold has a rich artistic heritage that goes back a long way. In 1833, workmen quarrying for stone at Bryn yr Ellyllon, or Goblin's Hill, to the north of the town, uncovered a Bronze Age burial mound. Inside was a skeleton, some amber beads and THE LARGEST GOLD OBJECT EVER FOUND IN WALES, a unique cape, weighing 1¼ lbs (560 g) and produced from a single gold ingot. The MOLD GOLD CAPE, as it became known, is around 4,000 years old, of high-quality gold, gloriously decorated, and thought to be a ceremonial or religious garment. Discovery of the cape went some way towards explaining the well-documented stories of hauntings in the area, with a number of people over the years reporting sightings of a gigantic man standing on Goblin's Hill, 'glittering and shining in gold'.

The cape was sold to the British Museum and is regarded as one of the Museum's top 10 exhibits. Many local people feel it should be returned to the town where it was found.

Art

Outside in the churchyard of St Mary's, close to the north wall of the church, is the simple stone tomb of RICHARD WILSON (1714–82), Wales's greatest artist and THE FATHER OF BRITISH LANDSCAPE PAINTING. He was born at Penegoes, near Machynlleth, where his father was the Vicar, but spent most of his childhood in Mold, having moved there after his father died.

He showed prodigious talent as an artist from an early age and went to London in 1729 to become a portrait painter. His subjects included Bonnie Prince Charlie's Flora Macdonald and the young royal princes. His real passion, though, was for landscapes, and he spent six years in Italy studying and developing his own natural style. On his return, under the auspices of his two patrons Sir Watkin Williams-Wynn and the 1st Lord Lyttelton, Wilson began to paint the wild mountains and dramatic landscapes of his Welsh homeland and so build his reputation. Particularly admired are his paintings of Mt Snowdon, Cader Idris, and Caernarfon and Cilgerran castles. He was one of the founders of the Royal Academy in 1768, becoming the Academy Librarian in 1776.

Richard Wilson was the first British artist to concentrate on landscapes. At the time, however, these were considered inferior to portraits and so commissions were scarce. In 1781, sick and impoverished, he retired to his cousin's house, Colomendy Hall, near Mold, where he died a year later.

Richard Wilson was not much honoured in his lifetime, but his powerful and romantic pictures inspired people to come and see Wales for themselves. As a result, a land that had previously been seen as barbaric and fearsome suddenly won appreciation for its beauty, and it was explored by artists such as J.M.W. Turner and John Constable, who willingly acknowledged his influence on them. Today his pictures are highly prized and grace some of the world's greatest art collections.

Literature

Outside the town library there is a bronze statue of DANIEL OWEN (1836–95), generally acknowledged as WALES'S

A Sign and a Saying

About three miles outside Mold, beside the road to Ruthin, at the entrance to the Loggerheads Country Park, stands the ancient Three Loggerheads Inn. Richard Wilson, who lived nearby at Colomendy Hall, was a regular visitor and, in return for a couple of pints, he painted the inn sign, a replica of which swings in the wind outside the pub today. The original hangs on a wall inside, a unique and precious memento of the first great British landscape artist. The sign shows two men's heads above the words 'We Three Loggerheads', the third person being the one looking on. The story behind the picture is of a local vicar and landowner who were in dispute, and were persuaded by the landlord of the Loggerheads to meet at the inn to try and resolve their long-running differences. Hence, the expression to be 'at Loggerheads' came to mean to be in disagreement with someone.

GREATEST NOVELIST. The statue is adorned with his own words which, translated from the Welsh, read, 'I wrote, not for the wise and learned, but for the common man.' Owen was born in Mold and spent most of his life there. He wrote only in Welsh and is sometimes referred to as 'the Welsh Dickens' for his vivid stories of real, everyday life. He is buried in Mold Municipal Cemetery.

Music

The area of craggy limestone hills to the west of Mold is said to have inspired FELIX MENDELSSOHN when writing his opus *Rivulet*.

A plaque on the former Assembly Hall, now a bank, commemorates a visit from THE BEATLES, who played there on 24 January 1963.

JONNY BUCKLAND, the lead guitarist of the band COLDPLAY, came with his family to live in Pantymwyn, 2 miles (3 km) from Mold, when he was four. Between the ages of 11 and 18 he attended Mold Alun school.

Architecture

Wales, while famous for its castles, is not particularly noted for its 'stately homes' or domestic architecture. In fact, there are countless houses of great quality and interest hidden away behind walls and trees throughout the country, but they are rarely advertised. The area around Mold positively abounds in lovely houses. Below are two of the most fascinating examples in Flintshire.

THE TOWER, built around 1445 for Rheinallt ap Gruffydd ap Bleddyn, is an exquisite example of a Welsh tower-house. It is also a rarity – thereafter it was generally thought less necessary to fortify homes. In the early 18th century, the Tower was extended and remodelled to make it more comfortable to live in. The original defensive turret with its superb, pyramid-shaped stone roof was cleverly incorporated into the new house, and the whole effect is very satisfying. The Tower, which is near Nercwys, about 2 miles (3 km) south of Mold, stands in delightful gardens with a pond and can be visited by appointment.

PLAS TEG looms above the Flint countryside some 3 miles (5 km) south-east of Mold. It was built for Sir John Trevor, Surveyor of the Queen's Ships, in 1610, THE EARLIEST JACOBEAN HOUSE IN WALES. It was an extraordinarily advanced house for its day, the grandest private home in Wales, an unmistakable expression of the prestige and power of the Trevor family. Plas Teg remained in the Trevor and, latterly, Trevor-Roper family until after the Second World War, when it started to fall into decline. After several rescue attempts the house was bought by a private owner Cornelia

The Tower, Nerewys

Bayley, in 1986 and is now restored to its full glory. It can be visited on Sundays or by appointment. Plas Teg has one other claim to fame. It is considered to be THE MOST HAUNTED HOUSE IN WALES.

Bangor-is-y-coed

Britain's First Monastery

BANGOR-IS-Y-COED, sometimes known as Bangor-on-Dee, a small village in the detached portion of Flintshire beyond Wrexham to the south-east, is the site of THE EARLIEST MONASTERY IN BRITAIN, founded in AD 180. One of the Abbots here, PELAGIUS, preached a doctrine that became known as the 'Pelagian Heresy', which maintained that every individual had the free will to accept or reject Salvation as they wished.

In AD 613, after the Battle of Chester, the 1200 monks of Bangor-is-y-coed were massacred by the Saxons from Northumbria, for refusing to give up their Celtic Christianity in favour of the doctrines of the Roman Catholic Church, as espoused by St Augustine. The few monks that survived fled to Bardsey Island, where they established a new monastery.

There is nothing left at all of the abbey, which was razed to the ground. The village is known today for its bridge, thought to be by Inigo Jones, and for the Bangor-on-Dee racecourse, one of only two racecourses in Wales, the other being at Chepstow.

Plas Teg – the most haunted house in Wales?

Rhyl

(Y Rhyl)

Brash and Breezy

Although a Victorian seaside resort in North Wales like its neighbour Llandudno, RHYL is everything that Llandudno is not: brash, lively and unrestrained. The sandy beach stretches for miles, and every conceivable type of attraction is offered. There is BRITAIN'S OLDEST MINIATURE RAILWAY, opened in 1911, one of Britain's first all-weather leisure attractions, the Sun Centre, with THE FIRST POOL IN EUROPE TO FEATURE INDOOR SURFING, and a 240 ft (73 m) high Sky Tower.

RUTH ELLIS, THE LAST WOMAN TO BE HANGED IN BRITAIN, in 1955, was born in Rhyl in 1927.

'Liver Bird' NERYS HUGHES was born in Rhyl in 1941.

The A6 murderer JAMES HANRATTY claimed to be staying in Rhyl, at a guest-house in Kinmel Street, at the time of the murder in 1961. His alibi didn't stand up, and he was found guilty and executed. There are some who still think him innocent.

Countdown presenter CAROL VORDERMAN learned her passion for numbers from her maths teacher Mr Parry, while attending the Blessed Edward Jones school in Rhyl.

The 1973 film of *On the Buses*, starring Reg Varney, was shot in Rhyl.

Rhyl was the scene of the celebrated incident, during the 2001 General Election, when the Deputy Prime Minister, JOHN PRESCOTT, threw a punch at a member of the public who had hit him with an egg.

Rhuddlan

The Cradle of Wales

Rhuddlan Castle was the first of the concentric castles James of St George built in Wales, a design which reached its apogee at Beaumaris (*see* Anglesey). It stands on a mound known as Twthill, 60 ft (18 m) above the River Clwyd, and in another extraordinary feat of engineering, the castle was made accessible from the sea, 3 miles (5 km) away, by canalising the final stretch of the river.

Edward I made Rhuddlan his headquarters during his Welsh campaigns, and in March 1284 he issued the Statute of Rhuddlan, uniting the Principality of Wales with England. The Statute, which lasted until the Act of Union in 1536, replaced the Welsh legal system with the English and created the new Welsh counties of Flintshire, Caernarfonshire, Merioneth, Cardiganshire and Carmarthenshire. There is a plaque commemorating the event on the wall of Parliament House, which stands where Edward proclaimed the Statute, and from where he promised to make his son 'Prince of Wales'.

Well, I never knew this ABOUT FLINTSHIRE

Flintshire is THE SMALLEST COUNTY IN WALES.

Flintshire boasts two of the 'Seven Wonders of Wales': St Winefride's Well (*see* above) and the 21 yew trees that surround St Mary's Church at OVERTON, a village in the detached portion of Flintshire south-east of Wrexham. In 1992 a new yew tree was planted by Queen Elizabeth II.

Standing beside the road in a field near the village of Whitford, north-west of Holywell, is MAEN ACHWYFAEN, the 'Stone of Lamentation', a sculptured Celtic wheel cross, dating from the early 10th century. It is THE TALLEST CROSS OF ITS KIND IN BRITAIN.

The village church of TREMEIRCHION, near St Asaph, is THE ONLY MEDIEVAL CHURCH IN BRITAIN DEDICATED TO CORPUS CHRISTI.

Nestling on the slopes of the northern Clwydian hills, between the two holy sites of St Asaph and Holywell, is Flintshire's most dauntingly named village, SODOM.

BODELWYDDAN HALL, a mid-19th-century battlemented house set in 260 acres (105 ha) of parkland west of St Asaph, is now an outstation of the National Portrait Gallery, exhibiting a permanent collection of Victorian portraits and furniture. Nearby is the ebullient, unrestrained Marble Church of gleaming local white limestone, with a 200 ft (60 m) spire, commissioned by Lady Willoughby de Broke in 1860, in memory of her husband. Lying in the north-east corner of the churchyard is Elizabeth Jones, mother of Sir Henry Morton Stanley (*see* Denbighshire).

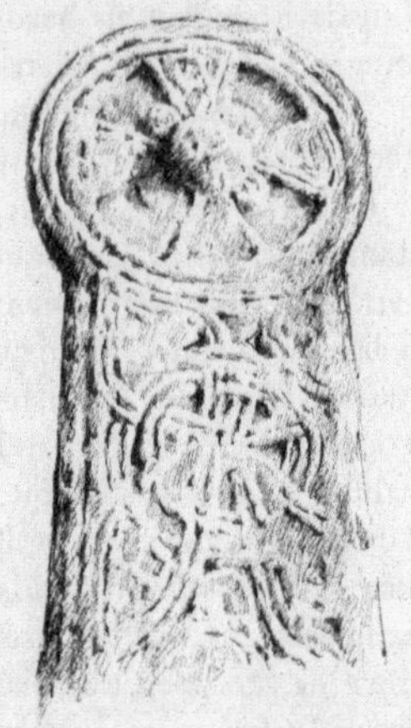

MOEL FAMAU, 'the Mother of Mountains', stands 1,820 ft (555 m) high, the highest point on the Clwydian range of hills. At the summit are the gaunt remains of the Jubilee Tower, built in

1810 to commemorate the Golden Jubilee of George III in 1809. It consisted of a tall pillar standing on a vast square base and was celebrated as THE FIRST MONUMENT IN BRITAIN TO BE BUILT IN THE EGYPTIAN STYLE. The pillar was blown down by a storm in 1852, and nowadays just the dilapidated base remains.

BODRHYDDAN HALL, just west of Dyserth, is a picturesque 17th-century house belonging to the Conwy family. The Charter of Rhuddlan is held here, and in the Drawing Room there are wooden panels from the chapel of a Spanish Armada ship, wrecked off the coast of Anglesey.

PRESTATYN stands at the northern end of Offa's Dyke.

MIKE PETERS, front man of the biggest Welsh band of the 1980s, THE ALARM, was born in Prestatyn in 1959. The Alarm played their first gig at the Victoria Hotel in Prestatyn on 10 June 1981.

Britain's first major offshore wind farm, the NORTH HOYLE OFFSHORE WIND FARM, was opened 4 miles (7 km) off the coast of Prestatyn in 2003. Thirty turbines with a combined maximum capacity of 60 megawatts generate enough energy to power 40,000 homes.

Bodrhyddan Hall

GLAMORGAN

(MORGANNWG)

COUNTY TOWN: CARDIFF

Castle Coch, or Red Castle, built by William Burges for the 3rd Marquess of Bute between 1875 and 1891

Cardiff

(Caerdydd)

Capital of Coal

CARDIFF, county town of Glamorgan and successor to Machynlleth as CAPITAL OF WALES since 1955, is THE LARGEST CITY IN WALES and was once THE LARGEST COAL-AND IRON-EXPORTING PORT IN THE WORLD.

Although most of what we see today is the product of the Industrial Revolution and modern regeneration, Cardiff was first settled by the Romans in the 1st century. and the name is thought to derive from 'Caer Didius', or 'Fort of Didius', Audius Didius Gallus being the Roman governor of a nearby province.

Castle

One thousand years later, the Normans built a castle on the site of the Roman fort, and it was around this castle that the town of Cardiff began to grow. The stone keep of the Norman castle, built in 1121, still stands as the centrepiece of the whole

Cardiff Castle complex. Roman bricks can be seen incorporated in its walls.

By the end of the 18th century, most of the land around Cardiff had passed by marriage into the hands of the 1st Marquess of Bute, and it was he who took the huge gamble to build the docks at Cardiff, to exploit the burgeoning coal and iron industries of the Welsh valleys. It paid off spectacularly, and in 1868 the 3rd Marquess put much of his wealth back into refurbishing the castle as a vast, flamboyant neo-Gothic palace, designed by the eccentric architect William Burges, and boasting opulent state rooms full of marble fireplaces and stained glass.

Across the road from the castle is what is often called THE FINEST CIVIC CENTRE IN BRITAIN, built in the first years of the 20th century, after Cardiff was granted city status by Edward VII in 1905. Included in a range of distinguished, white Portland stone buildings are the domed City Hall with its elaborate clock tower and marble statues of Welsh heroes, and the Welsh National Museum containing the fabulous collection of impressionist paintings donated by the Davies sisters of Gregynog (*see* Montgomeryshire).

Docks

What kick-started the development of Cardiff, from a quiet market town on the Taff river into one of the world's

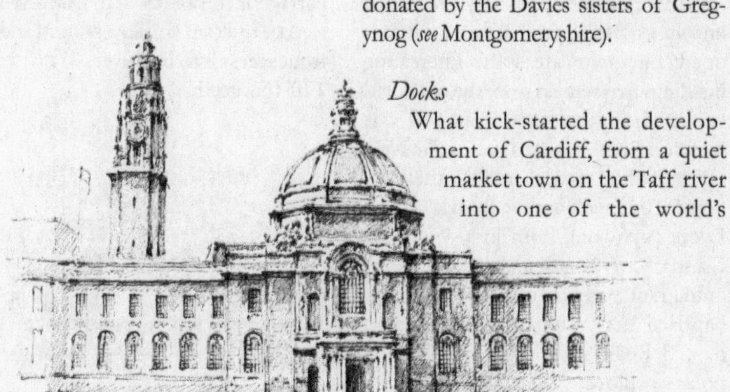

busiest ports, was the opening in 1794 of the Glamorgan Canal, constructed to transport iron from Merthyr Tydfil, the largest town in Wales at that time, and home to the two largest ironworks in the world. Various reminders of this canal can still be seen, running from near the castle, south under the shopping centre and alongside Bute Street towards the sea. An old canal tunnel is now used as a pedestrian underpass beneath North Street near the castle.

In 1839, the 2nd Marquess of Bute opened the WEST BUTE DOCK, then THE BIGGEST MASONRY DOCK IN THE WORLD, ¾ mile (1.2 km) long and 200 ft (60 m) wide, carved out of 18 acres (7.3 ha) of swamp. The Taff Railway arrived the next year, bringing coal from the Valleys, more docks were built, and for the next 100 years Cardiff flourished.

Tiger Bay

During this time the area around the docks became known as TIGER BAY, a tough, uncompromising place that gained notoeriety in the 1959 film *Tiger Bay*, starring Hayley Mills.

Almost all the Tiger Bay area, now known as Butetown, has been redeveloped, but there are some interesting buildings that remain from the old docklands. The NORWEGIAN CHURCH was built in 1869 for the many Scandinavian sailors who made Cardiff their home. Children's author ROALD DAHL (1916–90), born in Llandaff of Norwegian immigrant parents, was baptised here. He was named Roald after the polar explorer Roald Amundsen. In 1987, the church was dismantled and removed from its site near the West Bute Dock to its present location adjoining Roath Basin.

Back a bit from the docks, in Mount Stuart Square, is the COAL EXCHANGE, completed in 1886 when the price of the world's coal was determined in Cardiff. In 1907 THE WORLD'S FIRST ONE MILLION POUND DEAL was struck here. The Coal Exchange is now a music venue.

There is a wonderful clash of visions on the waterfront, where the gorgeous and distinctive terracotta PIERHEAD BUILDING of 1897 squats in the shadow of the looming new WALES MILLENNIUM CENTRE, opened in 2004 as an arts and cultural venue, and home of the Welsh National Opera. Nearby is the SENEDD, new home of the National Assembly for Wales, which opened on St David's Day 2006.

Key to the regeneration of the docks has been the CARDIFF BAY BARRAGE, stretching across the mouth of the bay for half a mile (0.8 km), which has created a huge 500-acre (200 ha) freshwater lake for sailing and water sports. The barrage incorporates THE LARGEST FISH PASS IN EUROPE, to allow salmon and sea trout access into the River Taff for breeding.

Cathedral

A 2-mile (3.2 km) walk north-west along the River Taff from the city centre, but a world away from the bustle and the tumult, is LLANDAFF CATHEDRAL, nestling in a hollow on a site made holy in the 6th century. The present building was begun in 1107 and has been substantially altered over the centuries. The Victorian restoration was badly bombed in 1941, but the cathedral was rebuilt and reopened in 1957. This is a lovely quiet spot with a cloistered village atmosphere, although the cathedral looks a bit lopsided with just one of the western towers carrying a spire. The interior is unexpected and breathtaking, with the nave spanned by a huge parabolic arch, crowned with a cylinder housing the organ pipes, and carrying an aluminium statue of *Christ in Majesty* by Jacob Epstein.

BORN IN CARDIFF

IVOR NOVELLO (1893–1951), silent movie star, musical theatre actor and songwriter, born David Ivor Davies in Cowbridge Road East. His song 'Keep the Home Fires Burning' was hugely popular with British troops during the First World War, and he had another wartime success in the Second World War with 'We'll Gather Lilacs'. His name lives on in the IVOR NOVELLO AWARDS, established by the British Academy of Composers and Songwriters to honour the talents of songwriters and composers.

TERRY NATION, television scriptwriter and inventor of Doctor Who's greatest foe, the Daleks, born in Llandaff in 1930. Fittingly, the new generation *Doctor Who* series is filmed in Cardiff, as is the adult spin-off, *Torchwood*, which is also set in and around Cardiff.

Dame SHIRLEY BASSEY, singer, born in Tiger Bay, in 1937, the the youngest of seven children, to Eliza and Nigerian sailor Henry. Famed for her 'big' voice, she has had many hits including 'Kiss Me Honey Honey Kiss Me' and 'Hey, Big Spender'. She also sang the theme tunes to three James Bond films, *Goldfinger*, *Diamonds are Forever* and *Moonraker*.

JOHN HUMPHRYS, journalist and broadcaster, best known as anchor for the *Today* programme on Radio 4, born in 1943.

KEN FOLLETT, thriller writer, born in 1949.

GRIFF RHYS JONES, TV comedian, born 1953. Came to prominence in *Not the Nine O'Clock News* and *Alas Smith and Jones*, and recently presented the BBC's *Restoration* programme.

JEREMY BOWEN, TV journalist and broadcaster, born in 1960.

COLIN JACKSON, world record-breaking athlete, born in 1967.

CERYS MATTHEWS, singer, born in 1969. Now a solo artist, she found fame as lead singer of the band Catatonia.

CHARLOTTE CHURCH, singer, born in Llandaff in 1986. In 1998 she became THE YOUNGEST ARTIST EVER TO TOP THE CLASSICAL CHART with her debut album *Voice of an Angel.*

Well, I never knew this ABOUT CARDIFF

The Arthurian knight SIR LANCELOT is said to have sailed from Cardiff after his banishment from King Arthur's court.

In 1910, ROBERT FALCON SCOTT sailed from Cardiff in the *Terra Nova* to begin his fateful trip to the South Pole. There is a monument to him in Roath Park in the form of a lighthouse, with a replica of the *Terra Nova*, and in 2003 a Captain Scott Memorial was unveiled on the waterfront, near the spot from where the ship sailed.

Cardiff's MILLENNIUM STADIUM hosted the final of THE LAST WORLD SPORTING EVENT OF THE 20TH CENTURY, the RUGBY WORLD CUP in 1999.

Cardiff is home to THE ONLY FIRST-CLASS COUNTY CRICKET TEAM IN WALES, GLAMORGAN COUNTY CRICKET CLUB.

CARDIFF CITY are THE ONLY NON-ENGLISH FOOTBALL CLUB EVER TO WIN THE FA CUP. They beat Arsenal 1–0 in the final at Wembley in 1927.

Cardiff has MORE PARKS AND OPEN SPACES PER HEAD OF POPULATION THAN ANY OTHER CITY IN BRITAIN.

SPILLERS RECORDS, in Cardiff's The Hayes, opened in 1894 and is THE OLDEST RECORD SHOP IN THE WORLD and THE OLDEST RECORDED MUSIC BUSINESS IN THE WORLD.

Port Talbot and Margam

From Longest Orangery to Longest Steelworks

At PORT TALBOT is one of the last remaining steelworks in Britain. Film director Ridley Scott said that Port Talbot at night, with its endless miles of fiery smoke stacks and belching chimneys, was the inspiration for his vision of the future in the 1982 science fiction film *Blade Runner.* Port Talbot was once one of the biggest steelworks in Europe. The Abbey Works is over 1 mile (1.6 km) long.

Abbey

The abbey referred to is MARGAM ABBEY, just across the motorway to the south-east. It was founded as a Cistercian house in 1147 by Robert of Gloucester, and grew into one of the largest and wealthiest in Wales. Most of it has disappeared, but the magnificent Norman nave of the abbey church is now used as the parish church. Two campanile bell towers were added in the 19th century, giving the church an Italian look, all of which makes the superb Norman doorway and pillars come as an unexpected delight.

The medieval buildings beside the church, which once housed one of Britain's oldest schools, are now the home of the Margam Stones Museum, an extraordinary collection of early Christian sculpture, dating from Roman times to the 11th century. The star of the collection is, without doubt, the intricate 10th-century CROSS OF CYNFELYN.

At the Dissolution of the Monasteries Margam passed to the Mansel family, whose impressive alabaster tombs can be seen in the church. By the 18th century, through various marriages, Margam had passed to an English branch of the family, the Talbots of Lacock in Wiltshire, and it is this family that gave its name to Port Talbot.

Orangery

Alongside the church is the highlight of Margam, the astounding Georgian ORANGERY. It was designed in 1787 by Anthony Keck for Thomas Mansel Talbot and is 275 ft (84 m) in length – THE LONGEST ORANGERY IN BRITAIN.

Castle

In 1830, Christopher Talbot, the long-time Liberal MP for Glamorgan, asked Thomas Hopper, architect of Penrhyn Castle in Caernarfonshire, to build him a huge Gothick country castle to replace that of his ancestors. Today, MARGAM CASTLE forms the centrepiece of Margam Country Park.

It is an almost surreal experience to

wander around the peaceful bowers of Margam, enjoying the old church, the elegant Orangery, the red deer grazing in the woods, the children playing on the lawns in front of the great Victorian castle, while in the background great apocolyptic clouds of smoke and chemicals billow into the air from the steelworks.

Neath

From Rome to Riches

In one small area of NEATH, by the river, it is possible to see monuments from every stage of the town's development over the last 2,000 years.

Neath was founded in AD 120 as an important Roman base called Nidum, at the crossing place of the River Neath. Traces of Nidum can still be seen near the ruins of Neath Abbey, founded in 1129 and once the largest abbey in Wales. John Leland, the 16th-century antiquary, described Neath Abbey as 'the fairest abbey of all Wales'. The remains of the abbey are quite well preserved, as is the Tudor mansion built within the precincts after the Dissolution of the Monasteries. Best of all is a gorgeous 13th-century undercroft.

In the 18th century industry arrived, and dotted along the river there are the remnants of some substantial smelting furnaces and chimneys. One of the first to realise the potential of Neath's location, near the coast, with fast-flowing rivers and plenty of raw materials, was SIR HUMPHREY MACKWORTH (1657–1727), founder of the SPCK, or Society for the Promotion of Christian Knowledge.

The first NEATH FAIR was held on 1280. It is still held every September and is THE OLDEST FAIR IN WALES.

The WELSH RUGBY UNIOn was founded at the Castle Hotel in Neath in 1881. Neath RFC is THE OLDEST RUGBY CLUB IN WALES.

BORN IN PORT TALBOT/NEATH

RAY MILLAND (1907–86), film star, born Reginald Alfred John Truscott-Jones. He chose the name Milland from an area of his home town, Neath. He was a trooper with the Royal Household Cavalry for three years. Won the Best Actor Oscar in 1945 for his portrayal of an alcoholic writer in *The Lost Weekend.*

RICHARD BURTON (1925–84), actor, born Richard Walter Jenkins, in a modest end-of-terrace house below the viaduct at Pontrhydyfen, between Neath and Port Talbot. The 12th of 13 children, he took his stage name from his English teacher Philip Burton. He was twice married to and twice divorced from Elizabeth Taylor, and his most memorable film roles were playing opposite her in *Cleopatra, Who's Afraid of Virginia Woolf?*, *The Taming of the Shrew* and *Under Milk Wood.* He was buried in Celigny, on Lake Geneva, to the strains of the Welsh rugby anthem 'Sospan Fach', and with a copy of *The Complete Works of Dylan Thomas.* A few feet away lies Alastair Maclean, author of the novel *Where Eagles Dare*, adapted for one of Richard Burton's most memorable screen roles.

LORD HOWE OF ABERAVON, longest surviving minister from Margaret Thatcher's original 1979 Cabinet, born in Port Talbot in 1926. Being attacked by Geoffrey Howe was, according to Denis Healey, 'like being savaged by a dead sheep'. He managed to bring down Margaret Thatcher, however, with a little help from Swansea-born Michael Heseltine.

SIR ANTHONY HOPKINS, actor, born in Port Talbot in 1937. Best known for playing the flesh-eating serial killer Hannibal Lecter in the film *Silence of the Lambs*, for which he won the Best Actor Oscar in 1991. On becoming President of the National Trust's Snowdonia Appeal, he said, 'Supporting the National Trust's purchase of this part of lovely Snowdonia gave me the opportunity to do something positive for Wales, my birthplace.'

BONNIE TYLER, singer, born in the village of SKEWEN, near Neath Abbey, in 1953. Best known for her 1980s hit singles 'Holding Out for a Hero' and 'Total Eclipse of the Heart'.

KATHERINE JENKINS, 'the world's most glamorous soprano', was born in Neath in 1980. At the age of 23 she signed THE BIGGEST CLASSICAL RECORDING DEAL OF ALL TIME for six albums with Universal Music. She is THE ONLY PERSON EVER TO HAVE HELD THE NO. 1 AND NO. 2 SPOTS IN THE CLASSICAL ALBUM CHART AT THE SAME TIME, and THE ONLY FEMALE ARTIST EVER TO WIN TWO CONSECUTIVE CLASSICAL BRIT AWARDS. She is also the official mascot for the Welsh rugby team. Despite all this international acclaim she says, 'I love coming back to Neath – this is home and always will be.'

Swansea

'Ugly, lovely town'

DYLAN THOMAS

SWANSEA IS THE SECOND LARGEST CITY IN WALES after Cardiff. Destructive heavy industries, one of Britain's worst-ever earthquakes, measuring 5.2 on the Richter scale, in June 1906, and severe bombing during the Second World War destroyed much of the architectural heritage, but one of the world's largest regeneration projects has transformed the Lower Swansea Valley, and the town has maintained its long-held reputation as a dynamic cultural centre.

The name Swansea comes from 'Sweyne's Ey', or island, and it was the Danish King Sweyne who first settled a small fishing village at the mouth of the River Tawe. A Norman castle followed in the 12th century, and shipbuilding flourished. But it was at the start of the Industrial Revolution that Swansea boomed, with its cheap coal and plentiful supply of water power. Copper from Cornwall was brought to Swansea for smelting, and by the early 19th century the Lower Swansea Valley was THE BIGGEST COPPER PROCESSING AREA IN THE WORLD, and the Hafod works, THE LARGEST COPPER WORKS IN THE WORLD. At this time Swansea was known as 'Copperopolis'.

In 1850, Isambard Kingdom Brunel's LONGEST-EVER WOODEN VIADUCT, 1,760 ft (536 m), across the River Tawe at Landore opened up the area for more industry. In 1868, at Landore, William Siemens built THE FIRST STEELWORKS TO SUCCESSFULLY MANUFACTURE STEEL USING THE NEW OPEN-HEARTH FURNACE METHOD, and this factory became, for a time, THE BIGGEST STEELWORKS IN THE WORLD.

Copper processing is a particularly messy business, and when the copper factories finally shut up shop in the 1960s (the Vivian works was the last to close in 1982), they left a dead wasteland of slag-heaps and foul water, where no trees would grow and yellow clouds of sulphur hung over the landscape. It was THE LARGEST AREA OF INDUSTRIAL DERELICTION IN EUROPE. Since then, thanks to a huge regeneration project, the Lower Swansea Valley has been transformed into shopping and sports complexes, a yachting marina and Maritime Quarter, parks and cycling trails.

In the Maritime Quarter is WALES'S NEWEST MUSEUM, THE NATIONAL WATERFRONT MUSEUM, which tells the story of Wales's industrial and maritime history. Wales was, in fact, THE WORLD'S FIRST INDUSTRIAL NATION – it was THE FIRST NATION IN THE WORLD TO EMPLOY MORE PEOPLE IN INDUSTRY THAN IN AGRICULTURE.

Nearby is THE OLDEST MUSEUM IN WALES, THE SWANSEA MUSEUM, which records the history of Swansea.

At the top of the extraordinary, Phoenician-looking TOWER OF THE ECLIPTIC OBSERVATORY, on the beach, is THE LARGEST TELESCOPE IN WALES.

Swansea's GRAND THEATRE, in the city centre, was opened in 1897 by the diva Adelina Patti. Today it is home to the Ballet Russe, THE ONLY CLASSICAL BALLET COMPANY RESIDENT IN WALES.

South-west of the city centre at Victoria Park is the Patti Pavilion, donated to

Swansea by Adelina Patti in 1918. The building was originally the 'winter garden' at her home Craig-y-Nos in Breconshire. It is now used as a theatre.

The BRANGWYN HALL, part of the Guildhall complex, houses the five colourful British Empire Panels by war artist Frank Brangwyn, depicting the Empire in all its majesty. They were completed in 1932 for the House of Lords, but rejected for being too vivid and unrestrained. Westminster's loss was Swansea's gain.

Swansea produced both THE FIRST WELSH NEWSPAPER, *The Cambrian* (1804), and THE FIRST WELSH-LANGUAGE WEEKLY, *Seren Gomer* (1814)

Swansea is home to the WELSH NATIONAL POOL, THE LARGEST COVERED MARKET IN WALES, and the DVLA, the Driver and Vehicle Licensing Agency.

BORN IN SWANSEA

RICHARD 'BEAU' NASH (1674–1762), the 'King of Bath'.

DYLAN THOMAS (1914–53), poet, born at 5 Cwmdonkin Drive. Thomas's birthplace is used for occasional literary events, and there is a memorial to him in Cwmdonkin Park, where 'the ball I threw while playing in the park has not yet reached the ground' (*see* Carmarthenshire). The Dylan Thomas Centre in Swansea was opened in 1995 by one of his greatest fans, former US President Jimmy Carter.

SIR HARRY SECOMBE (1921–2001), singer, entertainer and Goon. He shared a birthday, 8 September, with fellow Goon Peter Sellers.

MICHAEL HESELTINE, politician, in 1933. He was Margaret Thatcher's nemesis, along with Geoffrey Howe of Port Talbot.

DR ROWAN WILLIAMS, Archbishop of Canterbury, in 1950.

RUSSELL T. DAVIES, television scriptwriter and producer of the new *Doctor Who* series, in 1963.

JACK, Swansea's famous black labrador retriever. Over seven years he rescued 27 people from drowning in Swansea docks. There is a monument to him on the foreshore near St Helen's stadium.

The Mumbles

World Class

THE MUMBLES, a Victorian resort town on the southern tip of Swansea Bay, was the western terminus for THE WORLD'S FIRST PASSENGER RAILWAY. On 25 March 1807, a converted railroad car, full of paying passengers, was hitched up to a horse and drawn on rails around the perimeter of Swansea Bay, and into history. For the next 150 years the Swansea to Mumbles Railway continued to convey passengers along the 5-mile (8 km) long route, utilising at various times horses, sail, steam, diesel and THE LARGEST TRAMS IN BRITAIN. It closed, sadly, in 1960, but there is a Mumbles Railway Preservation Society that hopes one day to resurrect this important part of Wales's, and the world's, heritage.

The Mumbles LOVESPOON GALLERY gives a fascinating insight into a uniquely Welsh custom that dates back many centuries, to when young men would carve out intricately patterned spoons from a single piece of wood, and present them to the object of their desire as a sign of devotion. If the girl kept the spoon it showed that she returned the affection.

CATHERINE ZETA-JONES, the actress and British Tap Dancing Champion, was born in The Mumbles in 1969. Catherine's middle name Zeta is a tribute to her grandmother, who was named after a boat in Swansea harbour. Catherine first came to prominence in Britain as Mariette in the television adaptation of H.E. Bates's *The Darling Buds of May*. In 2000, she married Hollywood superstar Michael Douglas, and in 2003, she won the Best Supporting Actress Oscar for her role in *Chicago*. Catherine and Michael Douglas now maintain a home in The Mumbles.

The Mumbles gets its name from the French word 'mamelles', meaning 'breasts', and refers to two little islands just offshore. This sauciness cannot have pleased the most famous resident of the churchyard of All Saints in Oystermouth, the little fishing village around which The Mumbles originally developed. THOMAS BOWDLER (1754–1825) was a literary censor whose most famous work was an expurgated 'Family Shakespeare', cleansed of any smutty words or phrases unfit to be read out in front of the whole family. So strict were his criteria, particularly as applied to sex, that the term 'bowdlerise', meaning to censor prudishly, has entered the English language.

Merthyr Tydfil

Iron and Steam

Like some sleeping volcano, Merthyr Tydfil slumbered in peace for many hundreds of years, overlooked, undiscovered and insignificant. Then, one day, it stretched, spasmed, erupted,

Cyfarthfa Castle

spewed forth iron, basked in the glow of a million furnaces, made the world take notice, and then went quiet again.

It's quiet today. Just a few tendrils of steam and not much left to show of its turbulent past. Walking around it now you would never guess that Merthyr Tydfil built the world. From here came the cannons that beat Napoleon, the railways that encircled the globe, the girders that raised towers into the sky. The name Merthyr Tydfil is somehow quaint, unthreatening, the sort of place you might have heard of but you don't really know where it is. However, in the space of 200 years, this little town lived through more history than most places on earth ever will. In 1700, it was a little village of 700 souls, its back to the Brecon Beacons, gazing down a long valley to the sea. A mere 100 years later it was THE BIGGEST TOWN IN WALES, home to 50,000 workers, IRON CAPITAL OF THE WORLD and the workshop of the Industrial Revolution.

Dowlais

Ore in the hills, limestone in the Beacons, water running down from both. Merthyr was the perfect place to make iron. When wars and industries and new inventions demanded iron, they came to Merthyr Tydfil. The first large ironworks in Merthyr was the DOWLAIS IRONWORKS, established in 1759. Dowlais manufactured the rails for the world's first passenger steam railway from Stockton to Darlington in 1821, for the Trans-Siberian railway and for the railways that opened up the West in America. It was THE FIRST MAJOR IRONWORKS IN THE WORLD TO PRODUCE IRON USING THE BESSEMER PROCESS.

In 1835, a boiler exploded at Dowlais, killing a number of men, and one of the ironworks' engineers, ADRIAN STEPHENS, realised that some sort of warning device was needed to indicate when too much pressure was building up inside the boiler. He devised a copper tube, inserted into the boiler, which whistled when the pressure reached a dangerous level. This STEAM WHISTLE was later adapted for trains and steamships.

In 1833, the owner of Dowlais, JOSIAH JOHN GUEST, married Lady Charlotte Bertie, the Earl of Lindsey's only daughter who, as LADY CHARLOTTE GUEST, translated and wrote down the Mabinogion, from Welsh myths and Dark Age tales (*see* Pembrokeshire).

By 1865 Dowlais was THE BIGGEST IRONWORKS IN THE WORLD, taking over from Cyfarthfa (*see* below). It was the last of the great ironworks to close, in 1936, and all that is left of it today is the grand Georgian stable house, saved from demolition and converted into accommodation.

Cyfarthfa

CYFARTHFA IRONWORKS opened in 1765 and, by the start of the 19th century, had, in its turn, become THE LARGEST IRONWORKS IN THE WORLD. In 1802, Nelson came to Cyfarthfa to see the cannons being made for his ships, and was shown around by the owner RICHARD CRAWSHAY. In 1825, Crawshay's grandson WILLIAM built himself a castle at the top of the hill, from where he could look down upon his empire. CYFARTHFA CASTLE is now a school and museum, while the surrounding gardens afford the most fascinating views over Merthyr. The Cyfarthfa Ironworks reached their greatest heights under Robert Thompson Crawshay (1817–89), who is buried outside the church he had built at Vaynor, on the edge of the Brecon Beacons north of the town. His tombstone is inscribed 'God Forgive Me'.

Close to the site of the Cyfarthfa Ironworks, which closed in 1919 and were dismantled in 1928, you can still see THE WORLD'S FIRST IRON RAILWAY BRIDGE, the PONTYCAFNAU, constructed in 1793.

First steam

21 February 1804 was a momentous day that saw THE FIRST STEAM LOCOMOTIVE EVER TO RUN ALONG RAILS, complete THE WORLD'S FIRST RAILWAY JOURNEY BY STEAM, 9 miles (14.5 km) from Penydarren, Merthyr Tydfil, to Navigation, Abercynon. Ironmaster SAMUEL HOMFRAY of the Penydarren Works had bet Richard Crawshay of Cyfarthfa, 500 guineas that RICHARD TREVITHICK'S self-propelling steam locomotive could haul 10 tons of iron along the route, and Homfray won his bet. Trevithick covered the distance in just over four hours at a speed of 5 mph (8 kph), carrying not only five wagon-loads of iron but also 70 passengers who clung on to the wagons to enjoy the experience. It is possible to follow the route of this historic journey most of the way on foot. There are various memorials along the way and, best of all, you can actually walk through THE WORLD'S FIRST RAILWAY TUNNEL, underneath the site of the old Plymouth Ironworks.

The footpath takes you close to CHAPEL ROW, a fascinating example of workers' houses that has survived from the early 19th century, and where, at No. 4, the composer JOSEPH PARRY (1841–1903) was born.

Merthyr Riots

In 1831 there was an outbreak of sustained rioting that became known as the MERTHYR RIOTS. Iron workers complaining about their appalling wages and conditions marched on the Castle Hotel in the town centre, where troops opened fire on the crowd, killing 26. This was a worse loss of life than at the infamous Peterloo Massacre of 1819 in Manchester, but it got no headlines. Much followed from the Merthyr Riots, however. It was the first time workers had marched under the RED FLAG, in this case a shirt soaked in calf's blood, and when KIER HARDIE was elected by Merthyr Tydfil as THE FIRST-EVER LABOUR MP in 1900, he campaigned under the banner of the Red Flag, which has remained a symbol of the genuine Labour movement ever since. The man who carried the Red Flag, Richard Lewis, known as DIC PENDERYN, was sentenced to death for stabbing and wounding a soldier, and is buried at the gate of St Mary's Church in Aberavon, one of the first working-class martyrs.

Pontypridd

Beautiful Bridge

PONTYPRIDD sits at the confluence of the Rhondda and Taff rivers at the entrance to the Rhondda Valleys. The name is Welsh for 'bridge at the earthen house', where the Taff was shallow enough to ford.

In 1756, WILLIAM EDWARDS, a Methodist preacher and farmer who had taught himself stonemasonry, decided there should be a new way to cross the Taff, without having to get your feet wet, and so he built a bridge. And what a bridge! A single, perfect, rainbow arch, 140 ft (43 m) across, THE LONGEST SINGLE STONE ARCH IN THE WORLD, for many years to come. And a sign that the Industrial Revolution was on its way to the Valleys.

It took three attempts to build the bridge. The first structure, made of wood, was washed away by floods, and the second, built of stone, collapsed under its own weight. Success was finally achieved by inserting three holes in the stonework at each end of the bridge, to make the structure lighter and less wind resistant. It has now stood for 250 years, an elegant symbol of this 'Gateway to the Valleys'. Some people think that the glory of the arch has been spoilt by the flat road bridge built alongside it in 1857, but for others it just goes to accentuate the sublime grace of the original.

In Pontypridd's Ynysangharad Park there is a monument consisting of two statues representing Poetry and Music, designed in 1930 by Sir Goscombe John, as a memorial to local weaver EVAN JAMES (1809–78) and his son JAMES JAMES (1832–1902), who together composed the WELSH NATIONAL ANTHEM, 'Hen Wlad Fy Nhadau', or 'Land of My Fathers'.

Near here was the chain works of Brown Lenox, which produced chains using a revolutionary new kind of link, devised by SIR SAMUEL BROWN, that enabled chains to be used for bigger and heavier structures. Brown Lenox's chains were used in the construction of the world's first suspension road bridge, the Union Chain Bridge in Northumberland, and the world's first seaside pleasure pier, the Chain Pier in Brighton, Sussex, as well as on many ships such as the *Queen Mary* and HMS *Hood*.

On Pontypridd Common is the Rocking Stone, at the centre of a Druid's Circle of smaller stones constructed by Victorian Druid revivalists, and used for rituals by, amongst others, Dr William Price (*see* Llantrisant). It is called the Rocking Stone because, if you push on the top part of the stone, it gently rocks.

Born in Pontypridd

Opera stars SIR GERAINT EVANS (1922–92) and STEWART BURROWS (born 1933) both come from Cilfnydd, near Pontypridd, and were born in the same street.

Legendary singer and entertainer SIR TOM JONES was born Thomas Jones Woodward in Treforest, Pontypridd, in 1940. Renowned for his unmistakable delivery of hit songs such as 'It's Not Unusual' (1965), 'The Green Green Grass of Home' (1966) and 'Delilah' (1968). In 2000 he was invited by US President Bill Clinton to sing at the foot of the Lincoln Memorial as part of the Washington Millennium Celebrations. In May 2005 he gave his first performance in Pontypridd since 1964 for a special concert in Ynysangharad Park in front of 25,000 people, including Katherine Jenkins, to mark his 65th birthday.

Porth

Just north of Pontypridd is PORTH, where one of Wales's worst mining disasters occurred in 1856, when 114 men and boys were killed in an explosion at the Cymmer mine. In 1887, a new mine next to the Cymmer pit flooded, and for ten days the world held its breath while dramatic attempts were made to rescue the trapped miners using divers. Five miners were eventually brought safely to the surface, while nine were lost. The incident inspired Joseph Parry to compose the 'Miner's Anthem'.

In 1895, in Porth, William Evans began to manufacture his home-made ginger beers and lemonades that became CORONA 'POP', exported around the world. Closed in 1987, the Corona Pop factory was reborn in the new millennium as the Pop Factory, a music studio and TV complex.

Llantrisant

The Hole with the Mint

LOCAL WIT

LLANTRISANT is the home of the ROYAL MINT, which moved here in 1968 from Tower Hill in London.

In the centre of the town is a statue commemorating the amazing DR WILLIAM PRICE (1800–93). He believed he was a descendant of Druids and held Druidical ceremonies at the Rocking Stone in Pontypridd. He was going to build himself a Druid palace at Glyntaf, but only got around to putting up two round towers as a gatehouse (they are still there). His idea of natty dressing was a scarlet waistcoat, green trousers, a white cloak and a whole fox fur on his head, complete with dangling legs and brush. As a doctor he was an advocate of free love, nudism and a vegetarian diet, and he was also an early 'Green', issuing dire warnings about the perils of encroaching industrialisation.

In 1884, his eccentricity suddenly took on a national significance, when he went to Caerlan, a hill outside Llantrisant, and set fire to an oil drum, inside which was the body of his five-month-old son, who had died in infancy a couple of months earlier. He was arrested and tried in Cardiff, but argued so effectively for the right of people to have their remains cremated rather than buried, that he was acquitted, and the case led directly to THE LEGALISATION OF CREMATION IN BRITAIN. He lived happily ever after, even becoming a father again, by his young housekeeper, at the age of 90. When he died in 1893, he was legally cremated on the hill at Caerlan in front of a large crowd, in THE FIRST PUBLIC CREMATION IN BRITAIN.

St Donat's

Hollywood in Wales

Winston Churchill, JFK, Charlie Chaplin, Bob Hope and Bing Crosby, Arthur Conan Doyle – what brought them all to a rugged 14th-century castle on a windswept cliff top in South Wales?

In 1925, the world's most powerful newspaper tycoon, WILLIAM RANDOLPH HEARST, bought ST DONAT'S CASTLE for his mistress, the talented actress and comedienne Marion Davies, and spent huge sums of money restoring it. He scoured Europe for treasures to fill the castle, installing not just pictures and furniture but ceilings, screens, fireplaces and sometimes whole rooms from other medieval castles, abbeys and churches. St Donat's was transformed into the Hollywood ideal of a castle, and Hearst invited a Hollywood-style guest list to complete the image. Eventually, as tycoons do, Hearst got bored with the project and started to dismantle St Donat's in order to provide for his new toy, Hearst Castle, at San Simeon in California.

In 1960, KURT HAHN, the founder of Gordonstoun school in Scotland, turned St Donat's into the UNITED WORLD COLLEGE OF THE ATLANTIC, THE WORLD'S FIRST INTERNATIONAL SIXTH-FORM COLLEGE – its current President is Nelson Mandela.

Well, I never knew this
ABOUT
GLAMORGAN

CAERPHILLY CASTLE is THE LARGEST CASTLE IN WALES and there are only two bigger, Dover and Windsor, in the whole of Britain. Caerphilly was begun in 1268 by Gilbert de Clare, and was THE VERY FIRST PURPOSE-BUILT CONCENTRIC CASTLE IN BRITAIN. The curtain wall is 960 ft (293 m) in circumference, and is itself surrounded by a huge, water-filled moat, creating a fortified area of 30 acres (12 ha). When Oliver Cromwell's troops slighted the castle during the Civil War, to make it no longer 'fit for purpose', they failed to bring down the south-east tower, which now tilts at an alarming angle. Indeed, at 82 ft (25 m) high and 10 ft (3 m) out of true, the 'Leaning Tower of Caerphilly' leans further than Pisa's celebrated monument.

Creamy, crumbly CAERPHILLY CHEESE, after some years' absence, is once more made in Caerphilly.

The peerless comedian TOMMY COOPER (1922–84) remembered for his fez and his conjuring tricks was born in Caerphilly.

THE WORST MINING DISASTER IN BRITISH HISTORY occurred at the UNIVERSAL COLLIERY AT SENGHENYDD, near Caerphilly, when an explosion wrecked the pit-head gear and sent flames shooting through the miles of tunnels below. At the time the day shift was working at full capacity, and 439 men and boys perished.

There is no more poignant place in all the Valleys than the hillside cemetery at ABERFAN, where two long rows of graves stand testament to that awful morning on 21 October 1966, when an avalanche of slurry, from a coal-pit on Merthyr Hill, engulfed Pantglas Primary School, killing 144 people, 116 of them children.

Actor STANLEY BAKER (1937–76), best remembered for his role as Lt John Chard in the film *Zulu*, was born in FERNDALE.

The TOWER COLLIERY in HIRWAUN, run as a co-operative by the miners themselves, is THE LAST WORKING DEEP MINE IN WALES. In 1757, an ironworks was opened here by John Maybery, THE FIRST PLACE IN WALES THAT USED COKE TO SMELT IRON ORE IN PLACE OF CHARCOAL.

Entertainer MAX BOYCE was born in GLYNNEATH in 1945.

The coal-mine at GLYNNEATH is THE LARGEST OPEN-CAST COAL-MINE IN EUROPE.

In 1979, the Rhondda village of MAERDY elected MRS ANNIE POWELL as BRITAIN'S FIRST COMMUNIST MAYOR.

The tiny mining village of GILFACH GOCH, to the west of Pontypridd, was the setting for Richard Llewellyn's 1939 novel *How Green Was My Valley*, turned into a classic film by John Ford in 1941.

When completed in 1930, the CEFN COLLIERY at Creunant, near Neath, was THE DEEPEST ANTHRACITE MINE IN THE WORLD, 2,250 ft (686 m) deep. It is now home to the Cefn Coed Colliery Museum.

THE WORLD'S FIRST MESSAGE EVER SENT BY RADIO was transmitted by Guglielmo Marconi on 11 May 1897, from LAVERNOCK POINT, south of Penarth, to a mast on Flat Holm in the Bristol Channel, a distance of 3 miles (4.8 km). The message read: 'Are you ready?' There is a plaque on the wall of St Lawrence's churchyard marking the exact spot.

In 1956, the GOWER PENINSULA was designated THE FIRST 'AREA OF OUTSTANDING NATURAL BEAUTY' IN BRITAIN.

In the little Norman church at RHOSSILI there is a plaque to the memory of EDGAR EVANS (1876–1912), the first of Captain Robert Scott's men to perish on the return journey from the South Pole, in 1912. Evans was born in the next-door village of Middleton on Gower, and the plaque was placed in the church by his widow, Lois. He was the first Petty Officer to have a naval building named for him, the Edgar Evans Building on Whale Island, Portsmouth.

RHOOSE POINT, just west of Barry is THE SOUTHERNMOST POINT OF MAINLAND WALES. A sign there proclaims the fact.

MERTHYR MAWR, 3 miles (5 km) outside Bridgend, is an idyllic collection of ridiculously pretty, thatched, grey stone cottages, grouped around a wide green. A short walk away is the haunting, ivy-covered ruin of CANDLESTON CASTLE, a 14th-century fortified manor house that once stood at the centre of the lost village of Treganlaw, now smothered by the shifting sands of Merthyr Mawr, THE LARGEST DUNE SYSTEM IN EUROPE. Some of the dunes are over 200 ft (60 m) high, and one dune, known as the 'Big Dipper', is thought to be THE HIGHEST SAND DUNE IN EUROPE. Scenes from the 1962 David Lean film *Lawrence of Arabia*, starring Peter O'Toole, were filmed on the dunes at Merthyr Mawr.

R.D. BLACKMORE (1825–1900), author of *Lorna Doone*, grew up at NOTTAGE

Nottage Court

COURT, a beautiful Jacobean house belonging to his Aunt Mary, where he was sent to live after his mother died when he was a baby. Nearby is the mysterious SKER HOUSE, one of Wales's haunted places – Blackmore was inspired to write *The Maid of Sker* after hearing the true tale of a young woman imprisoned in the house, in a room with blocked-up windows. The Elizabethan house has recently been restored.

Sker House

WHITEFORD LIGHTHOUSE stands at the southern entrance of the channel to Llanelli, off the northern tip of the Gower Peninsula at Whiteford Burrows. Built in 1865, it is THE ONLY OFF-SHORE CAST-IRON LIGHTHOUSE IN BRITAIN.

The massive capstone covering the neolithic chambered tomb at TINKINSWOOD weighs 40 tons and is THE LARGEST CAPSTONE IN BRITAIN. Some 50 bodies were found inside the tomb when it was excavated in 1914.

Beautiful ABERDULAIS FALLS, near Neath, is one of the birthplaces of Welsh industry, a power source for over 400 years. In 1584, a copper-smelting business was set up here, followed by a tin-plate works. Aberdulais is one of the most picturesque industrial sites anywhere and has long been a favourite for painters. Today the falls are run by the National Trust, and have been harnessed to run a unique self-sufficient hydro-electric scheme. The water-wheel at Aberdulais is THE BIGGEST WATER-WHEEL IN EUROPE BEING USED TO GENERATE ELECTRICITY.

During its short life, the THREE-WHEELED ELECTRIC C5 CAR designed by SIR CLIVE SINCLAIR was manufactured at the Hoover factory in MERTHYR TYDFIL.

There are only 16 examples of LEY'S WHITEBEAM, THE WORLD'S RAREST TREE, growing anywhere in the world – and they are all in the Taff valley near MERTHYR TYDFIL.

LLANTWIT MAJOR is a quite lovely old town centred on the great church of St Illtyd, described by John Wesley in 1777 as 'the most beautiful parish church in Wales'. St Illtyd was a 5th-century monk who had been a soldier of fortune, and is thought by some to have been Sir Galahad from the Knights of the Round Table. He established a college here, on the site of an earlier school, founded in the 3rd century by Eurgain, a daughter of Caratacus, which was THE EARLIEST KNOWN SEAT OF LEARNING IN BRITAIN.

One of Wales's greatest rock bands, THE STEREOPHONICS, started out in CWMAMAN, near Aberdare.

The derelict 13th-century parish church of LLANDEILO TALYBONT, near Pontardulais, famed for its wall paintings, is THE FIRST MEDIEVAL CHURCH IN BRITAIN TO BE DISMANTLED AND RE-ERECTED IN A MUSEUM, in this case the Museum of Welsh Life at St Fagan's, near Cardiff.

Merioneth

(MEIRIONNYDD)

County Town: Dolgellau

Portmeirion – Italy comes to Wales

Dolgellau

Lost Gold

The old county town of Dolgellau lies in the shadow of Cader Idris at the head of the Mawddach estuary. Its streets are dark and narrow, lined mainly with Georgian houses, and there is a lovely bridge of seven arches dating from 1638. The 18th-century church of St Mary has rare oak pillars. Dolgellau has long been at the centre of the Welsh gold trade. The Romans came here for gold and so did the Victorians, and the Clogau Gold Mine in Bontddu, near Barmouth, was at one time producing three-quarters of all the gold in Britain.

Welsh gold has been mined since prehistoric times. It is known for its unique 'rose' hue and has always been highly sought after. Celtic craftsmen fashioned exquisite gold items, and Welsh princes would display gold jewellery to show off their wealth and power. For over a hundred years royal wedding rings have been made from Welsh gold, a tradition begun by the future George V and Queen Mary when they married in 1893, and continued by the Queen Mother, Elizabeth II, Princess Diana and the Duchess of Cornwall. Hollywood actor Michael Douglas bought himself one to celebrate his marriage to Catherine Zeta-Jones in 2000.

There never was a great quantity of Welsh gold, and in 2007 the last two gold mines of any substance, Gwynfynydd Gold Mine in Dolgellau and the Clogau Gold Mine, finally closed. Such scarcity serves to make Welsh gold THE MOST VALUABLE GOLD IN THE WORLD.

Blaenau Ffestiniog

Oldest in the World

The FFESTINIOG RAILWAY, running between Blaenau Ffestiniog in Merioneth and Porthmadog in Caenarfonshire, is THE OLDEST INDEPENDENT RAILWAY COMPANY IN THE WORLD. It was founded in 1832 to transport slate from the mines around Blaenau to the sea at Porthmadog, from where it was shipped around the globe. The line is 14 miles (22.5 km) long, with a track gauge of just 23 inches (58 cm), and drops 700 ft (213 m) from Blaenau to sea level at Porthmadog. The gradient was designed to be gentle and consistent, allowing full wagons to descend westwards by gravity alone, while the empty wagons could be hauled back up by horse.

The construction of a railway through such inhospitable terrain necessitated a raft of innovative engineering techniques. The rapid success of the Ffestiniog line brought engineers to Wales from all over the world, and Ffestiniog has had an influence on the design and construction of railways everywhere. The first steam engines were introduced in 1863, and in the same year Ffestiniog became THE FIRST NARROW-GAUGE RAILWAY IN THE WORLD TO CARRY PASSENGERS.

Painted bright red and still working the line is PRINCE, one of the original steam-engines built for the Ffestiniog railway in 1863. Prince is now THE OLDEST STEAM LOCOMOTIVE WORKING IN REGULAR SERVICE IN THE WORLD.

Another innovation pioneered on the

Ffestiniog line was a double bogie engine, back-to back-locomotives articulated in the middle, designed by Robert Fairlie to provide more power for climbing the gradient and taking sharp curves. The Fairlie 'Little Wonder' was first demonstrated in 1870, and a number of Double Fairlies are still in service on the line today.

Just north of the station at Tan-y-Bwlch the line runs past a little cottage built in 1873 for a railway inspector. There is a tiny platform here where the train will stop on request for walkers to alight. Between the wars the cottage was rented out as holiday accommodation, and amongst those who stayed there were St John Philby, father of Stalinist spy Kim Philby, and William Joyce, the treacherous Lord Haw-Haw, who mentioned the cottage in several of his infamous wartime propaganda broadcasts for the Nazis.

The name of the cottage is COED-Y-BLEIDDIAU, or 'The Wood of the Wolves', and is reputed to be near the place where THE LAST WOLF IN WALES WAS KILLED.

The trip from Porthmadog to Blaenau runs through some of the most ravishing scenery in the world, but entering BLAENAU FFESTINIOG is like going back to black-and-white television after colour. Everything is a shade of grey. Grey slates, grey mountains, grey houses, grey sky – Blaenau is pretty much the greyest and the wettest town in Wales. It is all terribly bleak, and yet that very bleakness seems to attract artists and writers from everywhere, keen to 'get away from it all'.

The controversial Hungarian writer and political commentator ARTHUR KOESTLER lived in a farmhouse called Bwlch Iccyn, near Blaenau Ffestiniog, for a number of years, after the end of the Second World War.

The overlooked but talented writer JOHN COWPER POWYS spent the last eight years of his life in Blaenau, having fled here after finding his home town of Corwen had become 'too crowded'.

Internationally renowned sculptor DAVID NASH has lived and worked in Blaenau Ffestiniog for 40 years, and the multi-talented artist FALCON D. HILDRED has converted an old water-mill in Blaenau into a studio and exhibition space.

During the Second World War pictures from the royal art galleries and the Tate and National Galleries were transported to Blaenau Ffestiniog in disguised delivery vans, for storage in the tunnels and caves of the Manod Quarry, 1,000 ft (300 m) below the summit of the mountain. The storage caves were specially heated and ventilated to protect the priceless paintings from damp and cold.

Today, you can visit two of the slate-mines, LLECHWEDD SLATE CAVERNS and GLODDFA GANOL, once THE LARGEST SLATE-MINE IN THE WORLD.

Bala

(Y Bala)

Bibles to Patagonia

The BALA LAKE RAILWAY runs alongside BALA LAKE, OR LLYN TEGID, THE LARGEST NATURAL LAKE IN WALES. Four miles (6.4 km) long, nearly

1 mile (1.6 km) wide and up to 150 ft (46 m) deep, the lake is of great ecological importance, rich in unusual plants, fish and bird life. Bala Lake is the only lake in Britain where you can find the reclusive GWYNIAD, a kind of freshwater herring that lives in deep water and feeds on plankton. Rarely seen, the gwyniad cannot be caught with a rod, as it is not attracted by any normal bait, and has to be netted.

The town of BALA, or Y Bala, sits at the head of the lake to the north-east and consists largely of one long, tree-filled street, lined with shops, municipal buildings and chapels.

Outside the Methodist Capel Tegid is a statue of THOMAS CHARLES (1755–1814), the Methodist preacher who was inspired to help create THE BRITISH AND FOREIGN BIBLE SOCIETY, in 1804, by the courage and determination of a schoolgirl called MARY JONES.

Mary Jones was a weaver's daughter who lived with her parents in the remote mountain hamlet of Llanfihangel-y-Pennant, on the southern slopes of Cader Idris, and attended the school at Abergynolwyn which Thomas Charles had founded. At the age of ten she started to save up for her own Welsh bible, something very scarce in the rural community where her home was. It took her six years to save the money, selling eggs and honey and doing chores on the nearby hill farms.

One morning in 1800, when she had saved enough, she set off across the mountains, alone and barefoot, to call on Thomas Charles in Bala, 25 miles (40 km) away, and to buy a bible from him. When she got there, exhausted and hungry, Thomas Charles had to tell her that he had no bibles left, that they were all sold and the printers were refusing to print any more. Mary was devastated, and Charles was so moved by her devotion and commitment that he gave her his own bible, and determined that from that time on anyone who wanted a bible in their own language should have one, no matter what.

A monument to Mary stands in the ruins of her family's cottage in Llanfihangel-y-Pennant.

Another celebrated resident of Bala was MICHAEL D. JONES, a Nationalist and Nonconformist preacher who was the inspiration behind the Welsh community in Patagonia, in what is now Argentina. His idea was to create an

independent Welsh community away from the interference of the English, where they could run their own affairs, speak their own language and practise their own religion. Australia, New Zealand and even Palestine were considered, but an offer by the Argentinian government of 100 square miles (259 sq km) of virgin territory along the

Chubut River in Patagonia seemed too good an opportunity to pass up.

Having received good reports of the area from prospectors Lewis Jones and Sir Love Jones-Parry of Madryn (*see* Caernarfonshire), Michael Jones raised the finance and found the volunteers, and, in May 1865, the good ship *Mimosa* sailed away from Liverpool with 153 brave souls aboard, to found a free Welsh paradise on the other side of the world. After much hardship and struggle the community established itself and still exists today. Although fully integrated with the Spanish now, there are still Welsh speakers amongst the descendants of the original settlers, and Welsh culture is kept alive with Welsh chapel services and a yearly eisteddfod. On the seafront in Puerto Madryn there is a monument at the spot where the *Mimosa* landed, showing the first immigrants with their bibles.

Rhiwlas

Horses, Dogs and Whisky

Buried in his pyramid-crowned family mausoleum at the top of the churchyard in Llanfor, half a mile (0.8 km) outside Bala, is RICHARD JOHN LLOYD PRICE (1843–1923). He was saved from financial ruin when his race horse Bendigo won the Cambridgeshire, and his epitaph reads:

'As to my latter end I go,
To win my Jubilee,
I bless the good horse Bendigo,
Who built this tomb for me.'

Lloyd Price was the squire of RHIWLAS, a fine house in the hills above Bala, since rebuilt by Clough Williams-Ellis in 1951. As a sportsman Price didn't just love horses but dogs too, and in 1873 he inaugurated THE FIRST MODERN SHEEP-DOG TRIALS on his land at Rhiwlas.

He also pioneered the distilling of Welsh Whisky, and in 1887 he opened a huge distillery on the River Tryweryn at Fron Goch, just up the road, which produced 'the most wonderful whisky that ever drove the skeleton from the feast or painted landscapes on the brain of man', according to his publicity. Unfortunately the enterprise went bust in 1910, and at the start of the First World War the distillery buildings were requisitioned by the government as a prisoner-of-war camp. After the 1916 Easter Rebellion hundreds of Irish republicans were interned at Fron Goch, including key figures such as Terence MacSweeney, J.J. O'Connell and Michael Collins. There is a monument to those times by the roadside, written in English, Welsh and Gaelic.

Barmouth

(Abermaw)

A Bridge to Remember

Overlooking the funfair and amusement parks of sunny Barmouth is DINAS OLEU, the 'Fortress of Light', THE FIRST POSSESSION EVER GIVEN TO THE NATIONAL TRUST. This 4½ acres (1.8 ha) of gorse-covered hillside was donated in 1895 by a wealthy resident who lived nearby, Mrs Fanny Talbot, and marks the start of the heavenly Panorama Walk across the hills of the Mawddach Valley. It can be easily reached from the main street in Barmouth via a footpath.

Down by the beach is Barmouth's oldest building, TY GWYN, an ancient house dating from 1460 and used as a meeting-place for supporters of Harry Tudor and the House of Lancaster.

The centre of Barmouth is dominated by the church of St John the Evangelist, built in 1898, and paid for by Mrs Perrins of Lea & Perrins sauce fame. In the 1880s the Perrins family built themselves a substantial holiday home at Barmouth called Plas Mynach, set in its own grounds, with wide views over the sea and the Mawddach estuary. Barmouth has left such genteel Victorian days behind, and now goes in for more robust pleasures.

Since 1977 Barmouth has been the starting line, on midsummer's day, for the annual THREE PEAKS RACE, in which competitors attempt to sail to, and climb, the three highest peaks in Wales, Scotland and England – Mt Snowdon, Ben Nevis and Scafell Pike.

Spanning the Mawddach estuary is the magnificent BARMOUTH RAILWAY BRIDGE, built in 1867, over half a mile (0.8 km) long and made almost entirely of wood, except for a swing bridge section towards the Barmouth end, which hasn't swung open since the 1960s. It was put there to allow boats in and out of the Mawddach estuary and used to be opened regularly to keep it in working order. Now nobody dares to open it again in case they can't close it – which would be a shame for not only would it curtail the scenic train ride, but it would also close one of the most unique footpaths in Britain. The views, from the middle of the bridge, of the thickly wooded estuary and bare mountains are

incomparable, and to stand above the gurgling water while the tide races out and the oyster-catchers bob and duck on the sandbanks is truly one of the wonders of Wales.

Harlech

Men of Harlech

Even in a country of such superlative panoramas as Wales, the view from the ramparts of HARLECH CASTLE is special. The awestruck visitor stands on a high wall, itself perched on a tall crag of rock – Harlech means 'bold rock' – and gazes across the shimmering sea to the gnarled, receding coastline of Lleyn. Laid out below, like a green and gold tapestry, the flat, sunlit marshes and sands of Morfa Harlech lead the eye across Tremadog Bay to the brooding, thunderous mass of Snowdon, one moment stark, proud and clear, the next veiled in dark and swirling clouds. Professor Tolkien must have been standing right here when he thought of Mordor. It is a view that holds you mesmerised, intimidated and elated.

Harlech is the best of castles to explore, with its dungeons, hidden passageways and spectacular walks around the battlements. A testing way to get to it is to climb the old harbour stairway clinging to the western rock face. Before the land where the golf course now is was reclaimed, waves used to lap against the foot of the rock, and when besieged, the castle could be supplied from the sea.

During the Wars of the Roses, Harlech Castle was a Lancastrian stronghold and held out under siege for seven years, until finally it fell to the Yorkists in 1468, a feat remembered in the song 'Men of Harlech'. In the Civil War, Harlech was

THE LAST ROYALIST CASTLE IN WALES TO SURRENDER TO OLIVER CROMWELL'S TROOPS.

Salem Chapel

A few miles south of Harlech, in the tiny village of Cefncymerau, near Llanbedr, is the 'SALEM' CHAPEL, THE MOST FAMOUS CHAPEL IN WALES. The interior is immortalised in an iconic painting by Sydney Curnow Vosper, showing a woman in traditional Welsh dress arriving late for morning service. Hidden deep in the folds of the woman's cloak is an image of the Devil, designed to represent vanity, for it is thought that the woman arrived late, during the period of silence before the service, in order to make an entrance. The original was purchased by the 1st Viscount Leverhulme, the owner of Sunlight Soap, and he offered a free reproduction to anyone buying £7 of soap. The picture captures an appealing 'Welshness' and piety, and hangs on the wall of many a Welsh Nonconformist home. The model for the woman in the picture was SIAN OWEN (1837–1927), buried in the churchyard of St Mary's in Llanfair, just up the road.

Portmeirion

Mediterranean Wales

It shouldn't work, but it does. There is no more romantic place in Wales than PORTMEIRION, and it is hard not to fall under its spell. This is the culmination of the life's work of SIR CLOUGH WILLIAMS-ELLIS (1883–1978). The beauties of the landscape enhanced rather than spoilt, man and nature clasped together in perfect harmony. The setting could not be more spectacular: a sheltered hillside on Tremadog Bay, with sea and woods and cliffs, and a purple backdrop of mountains.

Touring Italy in the 1920s, Williams-Ellis had fallen in love with the Mediterranean fishing village of Portofino, and he returned home determined to recreate that special atmosphere in his own homeland. After a lengthy search he settled on an untamed, derelict scrap of land between Porthmadog and Harlech, and transformed it into an Italianate extravaganza. Grouped around a central piazza are domes and campaniles, statues and fountains, boxed windows and weather boarding, clocks and colonnades, all bedecked with shrubs and flowers and trees. Portmeirion took Clough Williams-Ellis 50 years to complete, and it looks as if it has been there 500 years.

The distinctive Portmeirion pottery was established in 1960, by Clough Williams-Ellis's daughter Susan, who fashioned and created the original designs, inspired by the beauties of Portmeirion village. She and her husband Euan took over a pottery business in Stoke on Trent to manufacture the pottery, which is now exported all over the world.

NOËL COWARD wrote *Blithe Spirit* during a two-week stay at Portmeirion in 1941, after his London office had been destroyed in the Blitz.

In 1966–67 Portmeirion became 'The Village' in the cult television series THE PRISONER, starring Patrick McGoohan.

Among other television series that have featured Portmeirion are *Doctor Who*, *Citizen Smith*, *Brideshead Revisited* and *Cold Feet.*

On the cliffs above the village there are trails through a subtropical woodland known as Y Gwyllt, literally 'the wild place', with rhododendrons, camellias, Californian redwoods, New Zealand broadleaf trees and THE TALLEST CHILEAN MAITEN TREE IN BRITAIN.

Walk across the wide, open sands of Traeth Bach in the twilight, while the distant waves of Tremadog Bay pound on the wind at your back, the estuary gleams in the pale light of the rising moon, and the twinkling domes of Portmeirion beckon out of the dusk, and just for a moment, you really could be in Paradise.

Well, I never knew this ABOUT MERIONETH

Wales is known for its 'great little railways' and Merioneth has four of the best, the Bala Lake, the Ffestiniog, the Talyllyn and the Fairbourne.

A ferry ride across the estuary from Barmouth is WALES'S SMALLEST NARROW-GAUGE RAILWAY, with a gauge of just 12¼ inches (31 cm). The FAIRBOURNE STEAM RAILWAY runs for 2½ miles (4 km) from the dunes of Penryhn Point to Fairbourne Village. The track was laid in 1895 by Sir Arthur McDougall of McDougall's flour, to transport building materials for the new beach resort at Fairbourne. The station by the golf club boasts THE LONGEST PLACE NAME IN BRITAIN, Gorsafawddachaidraigddanheddogleddollonpenrhynareurdraethceredigion, meaning 'The Mawddach station and its dragon teeth at the Northern Penrhyn Road on the golden beach of Cardigan Bay'. This beats the station name at Llanfair PG on Anglesey by nine letters. The folk at Llanfair PG complain that the Fairbourne name was just manufactured to get into the *Guinness Book of Records*, and this is true, but then Llanfair PG was also concocted to attract the tourists. So, you take your pick. They are both in the *Guinness Book of Records.*

THE TALYLLYN RAILWAY was opened in 1866 to carry slate from the Bryn Eglwys quarry to the Cambrian railway line at Tywyn, and runs for 7 miles (11 km) along the beautiful Afon Fathew valley from Tywyn to Abergynolwyn. After the quarry closed in 1947, and the railway was no longer viable, a group of enthusiasts got together to run the line as a tourist attraction, and in 1951 they formed THE WORLD'S FIRST RAILWAY PRESERVATION SOCIETY.

Reaching a height of 1,790 ft (546 m), the BWLCH-Y-GROES PASS linking Bala with Dinas Mawddwy is the HIGHEST ROAD IN WALES.

ST CADFAN'S CHURCH in TYWYN, remarkable for its enormous, solid Norman nave, also possesses a gravestone with THE EARLIEST KNOWN INSCRIPTION IN THE WELSH LANGUAGE. The tall stone pillar dates from the 8th century and is thought to read, 'The body of Cingen lies here'. It was discovered in a nearby field, being used as a gatepost.

Buried under a yew tree in the lonely churchyard at LLANFIHANGEL-Y-TRAETHAU, north of Harlech, is RICHARD HUGHES (1900–76), author of *A High Wind in Jamaica.* His 1924 play *Danger* was THE FIRST PLAY TO BE BROADCAST ON RADIO. Also lying in the same churchyard is WILLIAM DAVID ORMSBY-GORE, 5TH LORD HARLECH, British Ambassador in Washington during the Kennedy years.

St Cadfan's Church

Writer and philosopher BERTRAND RUSSELL (1872–1970), lived in a house called Plas Penrhyn, in Penrhyndeudraeth, for the final years of his life. He won the Nobel Prize for Literature in 1950 and was the inaugural recipient of the Jerusalem Prize, an award for writers interested in the freedom of the individual in society.

One of the most restful places in Wales lies just along the River Dee from Corwen, where two simple churches

The whole problem with the world is that fools and fanatics are always so certain of themselves, but wiser people so full of doubts.

Few people can be happy unless they hate some other person, nation or creed.

The desire to understand the world and the desire to reform it are the two great engines of progress.

Quotes from Bertrand Russell

stand peacefully almost side by side in fields. LLANGAR CHURCH, or Llangaewgwyn, meaning Church of the White Stag, was built on the spot where a white stag appeared to some villagers who were praying in the open air. It has a single nave, a fine medieval roof and some faded wall paintings. The other church, called Y RUG, once the private chapel of Colonel William Salusbury (1580–1660), sits in grounds laid out later by Humphry Repton. The plain exterior hides an interior rich with wood carvings, canopied pews, ornate bench ends and a wonderful gallery.

Five miles (8 km) from Portmeirion, in Llanfrothen, is PLAS BRONDANW, where Sir Clough Williams-Ellis lived until his death in 1978. The magnificent gardens he laid out around the house are now open to the public.

The distinctive shape of BIRD ROCK, CRAIG-YR-ADERYN, soars 760 ft (232 m) over the water-meadows of the Dysynni valley. Bird Rock is a sea cliff that was left stranded, 4 miles (6.4 km) inland, when the sea retired behind a new spit of sand. The local cormorants have yet to accept that the sea has gone and continue to nest on the rock – making it

THE ONLY INLAND CORMORANT NESTING SITE IN BRITAIN.

In the middle of the village of TRAWSFYNYDD there is a statue of ELLIS HUMPHREY EVANS, born here in 1887. He was a shepherd and a poet, and he won the chair at the Eisteddfod of 1917, held that year in Birkenhead. When the winner's name was announced, it was discovered that Evans had died in the trenches in Flanders. His chair was draped in black and became known as the Black Chair of Birkenhead. The vast and sinister concrete blocks of the now decommissioned Trawsfynydd Power Station loom incongruously over the trees – it is THE ONLY NUCLEAR POWER STATION EVER TO BE LOCATED IN THE MIDDLE OF A NATIONAL PARK (Snowdonia).

Eight miles (13 km) south of Dolgellau, in an abandoned slate quarry, is Europe's leading Eco village, the CENTRE FOR ALTERNATIVE TECHNOLOGY. The site is almost self-sufficient: they grow their own organic foods, and energy is drawn from windmills, water-powered generators and solar panels. A unique water-balanced railway, similar to those used in the old slate quarries, carries passengers 180 ft (55 m) up the hillside.

Monmouthshire

(SIR FYNWY)

County Town: Monmouth

Tintern Abbey, on the banks of the River Wye, once the richest abbey in Wales

Monmouth

(Trefynwy)

Famous Sons and a Unique Bridge

There are few more attractive towns in Britain than MONMOUTH, sited on a hilly peninsula between the Monnow and Wye rivers. Still faithful to its 15th-century layout, the town is full of Georgian shop-fronts, colourful markets and medieval coaching inns.

The best way to enter the town is from the west, across the mighty 13th-century MONNOW BRIDGE, with its great towering gatehouse, the only surviving fortified bridge in Britain. Next to the bridge is a small church dedicated to St Thomas Becket, built in 1180 and possessing a wide, Norman chancel arch.

Monmouth's main street, Monnow Street, starts broad here, where the cattle markets were held, and then funnels up the hill to the site of the original Norman castle of 1068. St Mary's Church marks the site of the

Priory where, around 1135, the Prior, Geoffrey of Monmouth (1090–1155), wrote his epic *History of the Kings of Britain*, which traces back the line of British kings and introduced the world to King Lear, King Arthur and the wizard Merlin.

Monmouth Castle was rebuilt in 1375 by John of Gaunt, and in 1387 his grandson, the future HENRY V, was born there. There is not much left of the castle now, but a little way down the hill is Agincourt Square, named after Henry V's great triumph over the French in 1415. Victory at Agincourt, against a much greater French force, was secured by the brilliance of Henry's Welsh archers and their longbows. Shakespeare tells us they wore leeks in their 'Monmouth caps'. These round hats, knitted from brown wool and with a button on top, were produced only in Monmouth and were very popular in Tudor times. There is only one example left in existence, and that can be seen in the Nelson Museum in Monmouth.

Henry V stands on a pedestal high up on the impressive facade of the 18th-century Shire Hall, overlooking Agincourt Square and a statue of another of Monmouth's famous sons, CHARLES STEWART ROLLS, younger son of Lord and Lady Llangattock and co-founder of Rolls-Royce, whose family home, The Hendre, lies just outside the town.

Lady Llangattock was fascinated with Lord Nelson and collected everything

With its tales of gallantry, courage and magic, Monmouth's History of the Kings of Britain *is considered to be the most influential and important contribution to European literature and culture of its time. Although later added to and embellished by others, the vision that Monmouth drew of Arthur and his struggles has survived almost untouched to the present day, through Thomas Malory's* Le Morte d'Arthur *of 1470, to Lord Tennyson's* Idylls of the King *and even Tolkien's* Lord of the Rings. *Geoffrey of Monmouth's own source is thought to have been a 9th-century Welsh monk from Bangor called Nennius, who mentions a great warrior leader named 'Artorius' in his* Historia Britonum. *It places Arthur and his court firmly in Wales, with Arthur's fortress, which later became known as Camelot, located at Caerleon. William Shakespeare drew his King Lear from Monmouth's* History of the Kings of Britain, *in which he appears as Leir.*

connected with him that she could find. The telescope he raised to his blind eye at Copenhagen, his chair from HMS *Victory*, Emma Hamilton's harp and the Romney miniature of her that Nelson kept in his cabin, his sword, books, a Bible: hers is the most comprehensive collection of Nelson memorabilia outside the National Maritime Museum in Greenwich. She gave it all to Monmouth, where it is housed in the Nelson Museum in Glendower Street.

Nelson did once visit Monmouth in 1802, on his way back from visiting Sir William Hamilton's docks at Milford Haven. He stayed the night at the Beaufort Arms, and next morning went up Kymin Hill to look at the view over the Wye valley and see the Naval Temple, erected two years earlier in tribute to him and other famous British admirals. It is a captivating spot.

Blaenavon

Industrial History

Blaenavon is an astonishing place. Here on the edge of mountain and moorland, at the head of the River Llwyd, sits possibly THE MOST COMPLETE AND IMPORTANT INDUSTRIAL HERITAGE SITE IN THE WORLD.

It all began in 1782, with three industrialists, Thomas Hopkins, Benjamin Pratt and Thomas Hill, who leased some land near Blaenavon from the 1st Earl of Abergavenny, and dug a coal-pit. A few years later, they were ready to create THE FIRST PURPOSE-BUILT MULTI-FURNACE IRONWORKS IN WALES, hard up against a cliff face, with three furnaces powered by a steam engine, and utilising all the latest cutting-edge technology. It quickly grew into one of the largest ironworks in the world, rivalled only by the huge ironworks at nearby Merthyr Tydfil (*see* Glamorgan). The structures of the ironworks at Blaenavon survive almost intact, forming THE BEST-PRESERVED 18TH-CENTURY IRONWORKS IN THE WORLD.

Big Pit

The BIG PIT MINE at Blaenavon was worked for over 100 years, longer than almost any other colliery in Wales. It was first dug in 1880, on the site of an earlier mine sunk in 1860, and it closed in 1980. It has reopened as a museum and is THE ONLY COAL-MINE IN WALES WHERE THE PUBLIC CAN GO UNDERGROUND IN THE ORIGINAL PIT CAGE.

Hill's Tramroad

As the ironworks got busier, new transport links were needed, and in 1812, Thomas Hill began to construct a primitive railway across the hills to connect with the Brecon and Abergavenny Canal. There is a footpath the runs along the route of Hill's Tramroad, as it became known, and it makes for an exhilarating walk, along the level terraces that Hill had cut into the mountainside, and on down past the counter-balanced inclines to Llanfoist, outside Abergavenny. A branch line leading to the quarry at Pwll-Du tunnels under the mountain for 1½ miles (2.4 km), through THE LONGEST TUNNEL EVER BUILT IN BRITAIN FOR A HORSE-DRAWN RAILWAY.

Gilchrist Thomas

In 1878, two young men working as chemists at Blaenavon, metallurgy student SIDNEY GILCHRIST THOMAS and his cousin PERCY CARLYLE GILCHRIST, made a breakthrough that would have far-reaching effects for the future of mankind around the world, and for Blaenavon.

Twenty years earlier Henry Bessemer had invented a converter for making steel in large quantities, but only from ores with a low phosphorus content, such as those found at Blaenavon, which were relatively rare. Sidney Gilchrist Thomas and his cousin devised a lining for the Bessemer converters which absorbed the excess phosphorus, allowing common, high-phosphorus ores to be used, and within four years the process had been sold to the Russians, to European countries, such as Austria, Hungary and Luxembourg, and to the USA. Andrew Carnegie, the Scottish-born Steel King of Pittsburgh, Pennsylvania, paid $250,000 for the rights to use the process in America and commented, 'These two young men, Thomas and Gilchrist of Blaenavon, did more for Britain's greatness than all the Kings and Queens put together.'

Six years after his momentous achievement, Sidney Thomas Gilchrist died at the young age of 35, his lungs destroyed by the dust and chemicals produced by his experiments. A granite memorial and bust of him can be seen near to the restored Blaenavon Ironworks.

Ironically, the discovery at Blaenavon had an adverse effect on the town itself. The fact that steel could now be made from high-phosphorus ore, which could be found anywhere, meant that other countries were able set up their own steelworks, and this caused a drop in demand for steel from Blaenavon, which gradually began to decline.

Blaenavon is now a World Heritage Site.

Pontypool
(pont-y-Pwl)

Japanware

PONTYPOOL is the site of WALES'S FIRST RECORDED IRON FORGE, known to have been operating in around 1425. At the end of the 16th century an early ironworks was established in Pontypool, and in 1652 emigrants from here by the name of Leonard are said to have set up THE FIRST IRON-MAKING FORGE IN AMERICA, on the Saugus River, north of Boston, Massachusetts.

At the end of the 17th century, PONTYPOOL became THE FIRST TOWN IN BRITAIN TO MANUFACTURE TIN PLATE on a large scale, when ironmaster JOHN HANBURY developed a heated rolling process that produced a high-quality tin plate smooth and thin enough to be made into kitchenware.

At the start of the 18th century one of his managers, THOMAS ALLGOOD, developed a material that, when baked on to the tin plate, created a protective layer of hard lacquer. This 'baked varnish' technique had been developed in China, for articles of furniture, and perfected in Japan. Hence, goods treated in this way became known as 'japanned', and Pontypool became the leading producer of JAPANWARE in the western world. Although competition grew, for the next 100 years Pontypool japanware was considered to be the very best. The only memorial to this unique industry left in Pontypool today is the name Japan Street, where the japanware premises were once located.

Gelligroes Mill

First Signs of a Disaster

In the early hours of 15 April 1912, amateur wireless enthusiast ARTHUR MOORE was dozing fitfully in front of his radio in the old water-mill at Gelligroes, near Pontllanfraith, when he was jerked awake by an insistent tap-tapping coming across the airwaves, in Morse code. It was hard to make out, but it sounded like a distress call and Arthur thought he could make out the call sign of the RMS *Titanic*, then on her maiden voyage. However, it was very faint and a most unlikely scenario, and the next morning when Arthur told others what he had heard they were convinced he must have been mistaken. After all, the *Titanic* was unsinkable, wasn't she? And then the news started to come in . . .

The mill, which is 400 years old, is fully restored and now houses a workshop for making candles as well as a small radio museum. Arthur Moore went on to work for Marconi – the firm that had made the radio with which he picked up the signals.

Caerleon

(Caerllion)

Camelot?

Slip off the M4 motorway at Junction 25 into CAERLEON and you go back in time 2,000 years, to THE ONLY ROMAN LEGIONARY FORT IN WALES, and one of only three in Britain (the others being Chester and York). Wales was Rome's furthest outpost, a wild and dangerous place, and Caerleon, or Isca Silurum, was not just a fortress but a staging post and supply base. It was constructed by the River Usk in AD 75, about the same time as the Colosseum in Rome, and was home to the 2nd Augustan Legion. Caerleon is now THE ONLY PLACE IN EUROPE WHERE YOU CAN SEE A SURVIVING EXAMPLE OF A ROMAN BARRACKS.

In his *History of the Kings of Britain*, Geoffrey of Monmouth places the court of King Arthur at 'The City of the Legions', and it seems likely that he was referring to Caerleon, which in Welsh means 'Fortress of the Legions'. This possibility brought Lord Tennyson to Caerleon in 1865, when he was researching his Arthurian *Idylls of the King*. He stayed at the Hanbury Arms by the river, and there you can still sit by the mullioned window where he sat looking out at the Usk and wrote, 'The Usk murmurs by the windows and I sit like King Arthur at Caerleon . . .'

Tennyson was particularly intrigued by the mystery of a low grassy mound on the edge of the town, known as King Arthur's Round Table. He never did get to find out what it was, since excavations of the mound didn't start until 1926. It was then discovered that the mound was in fact the remains of THE BIGGEST ROMAN AMPHITHEATRE IN WALES, large enough to seat the entire legion of 6,000 men.

Using the Venerable Bede as his source, Geoffrey of Monmouth also mentions the City of the Legions as being the burial place of two Romano-Welsh Christian martyrs, JULIUS and AARON. In the late 3rd and early 4th centuries, the Roman Emperor Diocletian launched a persecution of Christians throughout the Empire, and three Romano-British Christians are known to have died for their faith. One was St Alban, who had a city named after him, and, according to Geoffrey, the others were, 'two townsfolk in the City of the Legions, Julius and Aaron, who stood firm in the battle-line of Christ. They were torn limb from limb and mangled with unheard-of cruelty.'

CAERWENT, or Venta Silurum, lies some 5 miles (8 km) to the east of Caerleon, Isca Silurum, and the two centres grew up more or less alongside each other. Caerwent means 'fortress with a market' and is the derivation of the county name of Gwent. It was THE LARGEST CIVILIAN ROMAN SETTLEMENT IN WALES, and much of the modern village is still contained within the massive Roman walls and their bastions. You can still walk along much of the southern section of the walls, which in some places reach a height of 17 ft (5 m).

Newport
(Casnewydd)

What is this life if, full of care,
We have no time to stand and stare?

W. H. DAVIES

Of the three conurbations along the South Wales coast, NEWPORT, on the River Usk, is the least known and the least modernised. It is, however, the oldest of the three, first recorded 2,000 years ago as a harbour and gateway for the Roman fort at Caerleon, 3 miles (5 km) inland. There are the remains of a Norman castle and a real unexpected gem, a Norman cathedral gloriously situated on a hilltop and described by the historian E.A. Freeman as 'a Norman jewel in a Gothic casket'.

Cathedral

The mighty tower of the Cathedral Church of St Woolas has stood as a landmark for ships in the Bristol Channel since the 15th century, when it was erected by Jasper Tudor, uncle of Henry VII. The view from the top is superb.

Within the church is the Galilee Chapel built by the Normans on the site of the original Saxon church. The doorway through to the nave is possibly the finest Norman arch in Wales, and is thought to incorporate stone from the camp at Caerleon. It is worth taking a minute to look through this arch at the sturdy pillars marching down the nave – a fine sight.

Chartist March

In the churchyard is a plaque commemorating those who died in the Chartist March on Newport in 1839, ten of whom are buried here in unmarked graves. On 4 November, led by the former mayor of Newport JOHN FROST, some 3,000 workers, mostly miners, descended on Newport in support of the People's Charter drawn up the previous year, demanding voting and other democratic rights which are now commonplace. The size and mood of the gathering outside the Westgate Hotel alarmed the authorities, who ordered their soldiers to fire into the crowd, in an echo of the Merthyr Riots eight years earlier. More than 20 Chartists died, and the ringleaders were arrested and condemned to death for high treason. This sentence was commuted and they were transported to Tasmania. In 1854, they received a pardon and John Frost returned to live out the rest of his days in Bristol. He is now remembered in Newport by John Frost Square.

The highlight of the Newport Museum in John Frost Square is a 4th-century pewter bowl from Caerwent that is thought to be THE EARLIEST CHRISTIAN ANTIQUITY EVER FOUND IN WALES.

Transporter Bridge

By the beginning of the 19th century Newport was exporting as much coal and iron as Cardiff, and in order to remain competitive it became essential to have some method of linking the docks with the industries across the River Usk. The Usk has A GREATER TIDAL RANGE THAN ANY OTHER RIVER IN BRITAIN, and it also has low banks, so constructing a bridge high enough to clear the busy shipping lanes beneath was quite a challenge. The answer was provided by a French engineer Ferdinand Arnodin, and in 1906 the NEWPORT TRANSPORTER BRIDGE was opened by the 1st Viscount Tredegar.

There is only one other transporter bridge in Britain, in Middlesbrough, and only four left working in the whole world. Newport's is 645 ft (197 m) across, and can carry up to six cars and 120 people across the river at a height of 177 feet (54 m). It is slow, these days completely pointless, goes nowhere of interest and is the best ride in Wales, utterly spine-tingling as you dangle on slender wires above the swirling waters. It is also magnificent to gaze upon Newport's emblem and arguably the most magnificent of the many monuments to Wales's mighty industrial history. The bridge closed because of corrosion in 1985, but was refurbished, and reopened in 1995. You can walk across the top, or take the gondola at weekends.

Fourteen Locks

Another unsung industrial monument can be found in Newport's northern suburb of Rogerstone, now virtually cut off from the rest of Newport by the M4 motorway. Here, the Monmouthshire and Brecon Canal descends from the hills via THE STEEPEST LOCK SYSTEM IN BRITAIN, a flight of 14 interdependent locks that falls 164 ft (50 m) in just under half a mile (740 m). The canal and the locks were built in 1790 to transport coal and iron to Newport, an incredible engineering feat for the time and still very impressive. There are wonderful canal-side walks from the Fourteen Locks Visitor Centre at the top of the system, at High Cross.

W.H. Davies

Newport's most famous son was the original 'super-tramp', poet WILLIAM HENRY DAVIES. He was born, according to his *Autobiography of a Super-Tramp*, on 20 April 1871, in the Church House Inn, on the corner of Portland Street, and in 1938 he watched from the crowd as a plaque was unveiled on the inn wall, by John Masefield, recording Davies's birthplace. In fact, he was born on 3 July 1871, at No. 6 Portland Street, which is now gone.

Details were never very important to Davies, who did indeed like to stand and stare (*see* above). At the age of 22, he took himself off to America to look for adventure, but instead lost a leg trying to jump onto a goods train, and returned to wander around England and Wales as a pedlar, writing poems about the countryside and the simple life. In 1908, his own simple life changed when *Autobiography of a Super-Tramp* was published, and its success opened the doors of literary society and a more conventional lifestyle. But he will always be best remembered as the super-tramp, and it was in this guise that he was a hero to Dylan Thomas.

Tredegar House

A Special Nest Egg

TREDEGAR HOUSE is the finest classical house in Wales but, no doubt thanks to its unprepossessing position next to the M4, on the edge of Newport, it is grievously unknown. It has been sympathetically restored by Newport Council and sits there, glowing a lovely orange pink, in a reduced parkland of some 60 acres (24 ha), a little oasis amongst the tumult.

The house as we see it today dates largely from the Stuart period of Charles II, circa 1664–72, but by then Tredegar had been home to the Morgan family for at least 150 years. It was Sir Charles Gould Morgan of Tredegar, president of THE WORLD'S FIRST LIFE ASSURANCE COMPANY, EQUITABLE LIFE, who was largely responsible for the growth of Newport as an industrial centre in the 18th century. He began the exploitation of the coal and iron on the estate, and built up a network of canals and roads giving access to the docks, including a toll road through the park that proved so lucrative that it became known as the 'Golden Mile'.

His great-grandson, Captain Godfrey Morgan, took part in the Charge of the Light Brigade in 1854. Sir Briggs, the horse that bore Godfrey into the Valley of Death – and out again – was brought back to the stables at Tredegar for a well-earned retirement. The horse used to miss his master so much that he would frequently break out of his stall and wander through the house, whinnying, until he found Godfrey. Sir Briggs is buried beneath a cedar tree in the park, along with Godfrey's two Skye terriers Peeps and Friday. Godfrey, a bachelor, was eventually made the 1st Viscount Tredegar in recognition of his public works in Newport.

Whereas his successor was a good huntin', shootin', fishin' sort, the next Viscount Tredegar, Evan, was a little different. He saw himself as an artist and poet and filled Tredegar with exotic

animals such as gorillas, bears and, his particular favourites, kangaroos, with whom he used to box. To break the ice at stuffy parties he trained his parrot, Blue Boy, to climb up inside his trousers and peep out through the fly, causing strong men to pale and well-bred ladies to swoon.

His mother, the former Lady Katharine Carnegie, thought she was a bird, and would go about the house making nests where she could roost. Apparently, when hungry, she would emit a noise something like a jackdaw and a footman would appear with her favourite tiffin, a dish of corn seed, steeped in medium sherry.

Evan was the last of the Morgans to live at Tredegar. He died childless in 1949, and the house was sold to become a boarding school. After years of neglect it was acquired by the town in 1974 and now serves as a shining example of what can be achieved by an enlightened council. Drivers rushing by on the M4 little know what a delight they are missing.

Captain Morgan

Another member of the Morgan family who made a name for himself was CAPTAIN SIR HENRY MORGAN (1635–88). He was born either at Llanrumney, near Cardiff, or Abergavenny – no one seems sure – and is believed to have lived at what is now the Penllwyn Hotel in Pontllanfraith, west of Pontypool. At the age of 20, Morgan sailed to the West Indies with an expedition led by Admiral Penn, father of the William Penn who would found Pennsylvania. The expedition captured Jamaica, and for the next 15 years, with the blessing of the English government, Captain Morgan sailed the Spanish Main as a buccaneer, looting and sacking Spanish ports and vessels. He eventually settled down to become Governor of Jamaica and is best remembered today as a brand of rum.

Chepstow
(Cas-Gwent)

First Stone Castle

The border market town of CHEPSTOW stands at the southern end of Offa's Dyke. Chepstow Castle, perched on a rocky bluff 90 ft (27 m) above the River Wye, was THE FIRST STONE CASTLE IN BRITAIN. The central keep, 100 ft (30 m) by 40 ft (12 m), was begun in 1068 and is THE OLDEST OF ITS KIND IN BRITAIN. A third storey was added to the keep in the 13th century.

The best view of the castle is obtained from the elegant cast-iron bridge built across the Wye by John Rennie in 1816, one of the first of its kind in the world. A little further down river the railway used to cross the Wye on Isambard Kingdom Brunel's tubular bridge, the first large iron bridge he ever built, opened in 1852. This was replaced in 1962. The contractor who created the tubes for the bridge used his experience to manufacture the first iron masts for ships. Brunel's *Great Eastern*, launched in 1858, was the first vessel in the world to have masts made of iron, masts that were also manufactured at Chepstow.

There is a plaque down by the river commemorating the departure of John Frost, William Jones and Zephaniah Williams, the leaders of the Chartist March on Newport, who were deported from here to Van Diemen's Land (Tasmania) on 3 February 1840.

Monmouth Politics

Leading in Labour

Labour politician ANEURIN BEVAN (1897–1960) was born in TREDEGAR. Leader of the South Wales miners during the General Strike in 1926, he went on to become Labour MP for Ebbw Vale. As Minister for Health in the post-war Labour Government he was the chief promoter of the NATIONAL HEALTH SERVICE, which came into being on 5 July 1948. When Bevan died in 1960, the Ebbw Vale constituency was taken over by Michael Foot, who would go on to lead the Labour Party from 1980 to 1983.

Labour politician NEIL KINNOCK, Lord Kinnock of Bedwellty, was born in Tredegar in 1942. In 1983 he became THE ONLY WELSH LEADER OF THE LABOUR PARTY.

Politician ROY JENKINS, Lord Jenkins of Hillhead (1920–2003), was born in ABERSYCHAN, son of local MP Arthur Jenkins. As Home Secretary in the 1960s he is responsible for creating the 'Permissive Society'. In 1977 he became President of the European Commission and oversaw the introduction of the European Monetary System, forerunner of the Euro. In 1981 he left the Labour Party to co-found the Social Democratic Party, or SDP, along with Shirley Williams, David Owen and William Rodgers.

Well, I never knew this ABOUT MONMOUTHSHIRE

An oddity in the churchyard of St Mary's Church in Monmouth is the grave of JOHN RENIE, who died in 1832 at the age of 33. His epitaph, 'Here lies John Renie', is written in the form of an acrostic that can be read upwards, downwards and backwards in scores of different directions – someone apparently worked out that if you included doglegs and zigzags it could be read in more than 40,000 ways.

In the church at LLANGATTOCK-VIBON-AVEL, 4 miles (6.4 km) north-west of Monmouth, is a plain brass that marks the last resting-place of CHARLES STEWART ROLLS (1877–1910). His family home, THE HENDRE, a fine gabled house, is just down the road. Charles Rolls was a dashing adventurer with a passion for the new machinery of the age. He drove one of the four first cars seen in England, made over 200 balloon ascents, and went over to America to meet Wilbur Wright so that he could bring back one of the first aeroplanes, a Wright Flyer. In 1904, he met engineer Henry Royce at the Midland Hotel in Manchester and they agreed to form a company, Rolls-Royce, to manufacture 'the best car in the world'. In 1910, he became THE FIRST MAN TO FLY ACROSS THE ENGLISH CHANNEL AND BACK AGAIN, NON-STOP. One month later he was dead, THE FIRST BRITISH MAN TO DIE IN AN AEROPLANE ACCIDENT, when his Wright Flyer crashed during a flying exhibition over Bournemouth.

THE SKIRRID INN, north of Monmouth, dates from 1110 and is THE OLDEST INN IN WALES. Inside is a square spiral staircase which was used as a gallows, THE ONLY ONE OF ITS KIND IN BRITAIN. Condemned prisoners were hanged over the stairwell until dead.

It is almost impossible to miss the huge vault in the churchyard of St Bartholomew's in LLANOVER, on the road from Pontypool to Abergavenny. Here lies 'Big Ben', SIR BENJAMIN HALL, Lord Llanover (1802–67) who, as Chief Commissioner for Works, oversaw the installation of the clock in St Stephen's Tower at the Houses of Parliament, which ever since has borne his name. The battlemented gatehouse is all that remains of his home, Llanover Court, where he lived with his wife, AUGUSTA WADDINGTON, a great Welsh folklorist who assisted Lady Charlotte Guest with her translation of the *Mabinogion.*

On 16 August 1679, ST DAVID LEWIS, born in Abergavenny in 1616, was hung, drawn and quartered in the little town of USK, east of Pontypool. A victim of the hysteria surrounding Titus Oates's 'Popish Plot' allegations, he was THE LAST CATHOLIC PRIEST TO DIE FOR HIS FAITH IN BRITAIN. He was canonised by Pope Paul VI in 1970.

THE FIRST GOLF COURSE EVER DESIGNED AND BUILT SPECIFICALLY TO HOST THE RYDER CUP has been constructed at the CELTIC MANOR RESORT in the Usk valley, 2 miles (3.2 km) outside Newport. The event will take place there in 2010, THE FIRST TIME THE RYDER CUP HAS EVER BEEN HELD IN WALES.

THE WORLD'S BIGGEST LUMP OF COAL, weighing 15 tons, can be seen in the grounds of BEDWELLTY HOUSE, in Bedwellty.

One of Wales's most popular rock bands, the MANIC STREET PREACHERS, started out in BLACKWOOD, near Pontypool.

ASLEF, the largest of the railway unions, was formed at Griffithstown, in Pontypool, in 1880.

The SEVERN RAILWAY TUNNEL, linking Monmouthshire in Wales with Gloucestershire in England, is over 4¼ miles (6.9 km) long , making it THE LONGEST MAINLINE RAILWAY TUNNEL WHOLLY WITHIN BRITAIN. Lined with 76,400,000 bricks, it was opened in 1886 and comes ashore in Wales underneath the village of SUDBROOK. Here there is a vast pumping station that removes 60 million gallons of water from the tunnel every day.

Near the village of TINTERN, in the Wye valley, a brass plaque, erected by the National Brass Foundry Association, commemorates the fact that BRASS WAS FIRST MADE HERE BY ALLOYING COPPER WITH ZINC IN 1566.

PENHOW CASTLE, in delightful countryside between Newport and Chepstow, is THE OLDEST INHABITED CASTLE IN WALES. The core of the castle was built in 1129 by the Norman knight Sir Roger de St Maur, ancestor of Henry VIII's third wife Jane Seymour, mother of Edward VI. The castle was extended in the 15th century and has a wonderful Great Hall with a Minstrel's Gallery. It is now a private home and, unfortunately, not open to the public.

MONTGOMERYSHIRE

(SIR TREFALDWYN)

COUNTY TOWN: MONTGOMERY

Machynlleth Clock Tower, built in 1873 to mark the coming of age of Viscount Castlereagh

Montgomery
(Trefaldwyn)

Smallest County Town

There is not much to say about MONTGOMERY, and that is its joy. It bears a proud name, that of the most powerful of the Marcher Lords, Roger de Montgomery. It is THE SMALLEST COUNTY TOWN IN ENGLAND OR WALES. It has the loveliest town square in Wales. It has played its part in history and is content.

There is no urgent reason to go to Montgomery. That is why it is ignored by railways and motorways. Instead it enjoys peace, fine architecture and glorious views. It is, quite simply, a nice place to be. Sitting up on the hill by the castle you can almost feel as if you are flying. The world is spread out before you, the rich, flat vale, roads striking out dead straight into the distance, the hills of England on the horizon and the mountains of Wales at your back.

Time and cares fade away in Montgomery. May it stay that way for ever.

Machynlleth

The Last Parliament

Small and friendly, the most Welsh of towns, MACHYNLLETH radiates out from its distinctive Baroque clock tower, built in 1873 to mark the coming of age of Viscount Castlereagh, heir to the 5th Marquess of Londonderry. The Marquess lived, from time to time, at elegant Plas Machynlleth, just on the edge of town, which now houses a museum. The attractive gardens are open to the public.

Machynlleth can claim to be the ancient capital of Wales, for THE LAST NATIVE WELSH PARLIAMENT was held here, in 1404, summoned by OWAIN GLYNDWR, the last great Welsh hero and the last, unofficial, Prince of Wales of Welsh blood.

Glyndwr was probably born around 1354, to a wealthy family descended from Welsh princes, with estates in Glyndyfrdwy in the Dee valley, from where he took his name.

Upset by a land dispute with an English lord that went against him, Glyndwr took advantage of the absence of Henry IV in Scotland to raise an army of Welshmen, who were disaffected by English rule, and then sack a number of English-held towns in North Wales, such as Welshpool, Ruthin, Flint and Denbigh.

All this simply provoked Henry into greater persecution of the Welsh, which in turn hardened support for Glyndwr, and the rebellion spread south. Glyndwr's forces captured castle after castle: Harlech, Aberystwyth, Cardiff. Between 1400 and 1404, the English were almost driven out of Wales, clinging on to a thin coastal strip and a few isolated castles. No longer just a rebel leader, Glyndwr began to gain recognition from countries such as France and Spain. In July 1404, he summoned a parliament to Machynlleth, proclaimed himself Prince of Wales, and made a formal alliance with France.

After that, for no apparent reason, things started to go wrong for Glyndwr. His English allies were defeated in their own battles against Henry, the French proved unreliable, and Harlech and Aberystwyth castles were recaptured. Glyndwr became a fugitive and disappeared into the mountains, never to be seen again. He is thought to have died around 1417, but no one knows where he is buried, in spite of many efforts to find his grave.

Parliament House in Machynlleth occupies the site of Glyndwr's parliament of 1404. Although one of the oldest halls in Wales, Parliament House was built in the 15th century, after Glyndwr's time, probably using stone from the original parliament building.

The Machynlleth Sign

In October 2005, a pastiche of the famous Hollywood sign, in the hills above Los Angeles, was put up on a hillside overlooking Machynlleth, to promote the town's film festival. It was very cleverly done, with white lettering spelling out Machynlleth, perfectly recreating the instantly recognisable shape and proportions of the original. The sign was erected again in 2006 and may become a regular sight – Hollywood comes to Mid Wales.

Powis Castle

Balustrade and Balconies

Magnificent POWIS CASTLE, Y Castell Coch, glows red and towers dizzyingly into the sky above its bluff in the hills near Welshpool, THE MOST VISITED NATIONAL TRUST HOUSE IN WALES. The present building dates from the 13th century but is wrapped around the core of an earlier castle built by Welsh princes.

Inside, the STATE BEDROOM, which dates from 1660, has an ornate balustrade that separates the bed alcove from the rest of the room, a reminder of the days when royalty or the aristocracy would give audiences while in bed. Only persons above a certain rank were allowed beyond the balustrade. This is THE ONLY ROOM OF THIS KIND LEFT IN BRITAIN and it is thought to have been created for a visit by Charles II.

The formal gardens consist of four superb hanging terraces, each 600 ft (180 m) long and festooned with flowers, topiary and statues. They were laid out between 1688 and 1720 and are THE OLDEST UNALTERED GARDENS OF THEIR KIND IN BRITAIN.

In Tudor days Powis was acquired by the Herberts and later passed by marriage to the family of CLIVE OF INDIA, creator of the British Raj. Treasures from India are displayed in the Clive Museum, set out across the old billiard room in a detached wing of the castle.

Clive's descendants, the Earls of Powis, suffered mixed fortunes. In 1848, the 2nd Earl, Clive's grandson, was shot dead by one of his sons, mistaken for a woodcock while out on a shoot. The unfortunate son gained the nickname 'Bag Dad'. The 3rd Earl turned down the post of Viceroy of India. The 4th Earl lost one son in the First World War, another son in the Second World War, and his wife in a car crash in 1929. He bequeathed Powis to the National Trust in 1952, but the family maintain private apartments in the castle.

Newtown
(Y Drenewydd)

Men of Vision

NEWTOWN was new in 973, but much has happened since then in this textile town, once the centre of the Welsh flannel industry, known as 'the Leeds of Wales'.

Two great men, distant cousins, one socialist, one capitalist, both of whom helped to shape the world in different ways, were born and buried in Newtown.

Robert Owen

Down by the river, in the churchyard of the old abandoned St Mary's, is the much visited grave, surrounded by magnificent art nouveau wrought-iron railings, of BRITAIN'S FIRST SOCIALIST, ROBERT OWEN (1771–1858). He was born over a saddler's shop in Broad Street, now a bank, and at the age of ten took himself off to work in the textile trade. In his twenties he married the daughter of a Glasgow banker called David Dale, who owned the biggest mills in Britain at New Lanark, Scotland's largest industrial site. Dale handed New Lanark over to Owen, who immediately introduced untested 'socialist' measures to 'commence the most important experiment for the happiness of the human race'.

He built houses, shops, churches, nurseries, schools, health facilities – everything that his workers could possibly want throughout their lives. He also proposed the first co-operative movement and headed one of the first trade unions, the Grand National Consolidated Trades Union, which collapsed after the Tolpuddle Martyrs were convicted. He didn't live to see all his hopes for mankind realised, but he did sow the seeds of socialism long before Karl Marx. The epitaph on his gravestone sums up his belief: 'It is the one great and universal interest of the human race to be cordially united and to aid each other to the full extent of their capacities'.

Sir Pryce Pryce-Jones

Just across the river in the churchyard in Llanllwchaiarn, an obelisk marks the grave of SIR PRYCE PRYCE-JONES (1834–1920) – so good at what he did they named him twice. Born in Llanllwchaiarn, he worked from the age of 12 in a draper's shop in Broad Street, near where Robert Owen was born.

At 21 he set up his own shop nearby, selling the local Welsh flannel. Being a natural entrepreneur, he was always keen to advertise his wares to a wider market, and two things arrived in Newtown together to provide him with the means to do just that: the railways and the post office. He hit upon the idea of sending out catalogues to potential customers, and then dispatching the required goods to them by post and rail. Thus he could reach people in remote locations who were too busy or too far away to visit the shop. As the rail network expanded, so did his catchment area, and he was also able to ship in a whole new variety of goods from around the country, to bolster his catalogue. Pryce Pryce-Jones had invented THE WORLD'S FIRST MAIL ORDER BUSINESS, an innovation that was to change the world of retailing for ever.

He did not rest on his laurels. When Florence Nightingale sent in an order, Pryce-Jones shamelessly plastered her name all over his publicity material, in the first-ever celebrity endorsement. He sent catalogues to Queen Victoria and all the royal houses of Europe, and when they responded he placed their warrants on his company letterheads. By 1875, he had customers in America, in Australia, all over the world. In 1879, he built the tall red-brick ROYAL WELSH WAREHOUSE opposite the station in Newtown, and had three liveried railway wagons made for transporting his goods by train to London.

A particularly sought-after item for which he became known was the EUKLISIA RUG, a combination of rug, shawl, blanket and pillow, much used by German soldiers in the Franco-Prussian War. We know it today as a sleeping bag.

Pryce-Jones was THE FIRST PERSON IN WALES TO HAVE A TELEPHONE INSTALLED between his warehouse and his home across the river, Dolerw House.

Dolerw House is now owned by Montgomery County Council and run as a resource centre, while the Royal Welsh Warehouse is now part of the Kays catalogue company.

David Davies

Wales's First Tycoon

Buried in the churchyard at LLANDINAM, near Llandiloes, under the epitaph 'Whatever thy hand findeth to do, do it with thy might', is DAVID DAVIES (1818–90), son of a tenant farmer and WALES'S FIRST TYCOON. He began his career sawing wood, and then became a road and bridge builder. In 1846, he helped Thomas Penson to construct the first iron bridge in Montgomeryshire, over the River Severn in Llandinam. Next he pioneered the railways in Wales, laying some 145 miles (233 km) of track throughout North and Mid Wales. including the 6-mile (10 km) link from the main line at Caerwys to what was then THE BIGGEST LEAD-MINE IN BRITAIN, at VAN, just north of Llandiloes.

He then moved on to coal, sinking THE FIRST DEEP-PIT MINE IN THE RHONDDA VALLEY, and constructing the docks at Barry as an outlet for his coal. Liberal MP for the Cardigan Boroughs, he was a strict Nonconformist and believer in self-help, never shy of proclaiming himself as a self-made man, and once causing Disraeli to comment, 'I am glad to hear the Honourable Member praising his creator.'

There is a statue of Davies holding the plans of Barry docks on the quayside in Barry and a replica bronze statue in Llandinam, close to the iron bridge, by Sir Alfred Gilbert, creator of the Eros statue in Piccadilly Circus.

Gregynog

Cradle of Concrete

Davies's granddaughters, Gwendoline and Margaret, used some of their inheritance to buy GREGYNOG, a mock black-and-white timber pile near Newtown, which they developed into a Welsh arts and crafts centre. Here they built up THE LARGEST COLLECTION OF FRENCH IMPRESSIONIST WORKS IN BRITAIN, founded the Gregynog press to produce limited edition books, and established the Gregynog Music Festival, which is still held annually and, over the years, has attracted musicians of the calibre of Gustav Holst, Edward Elgar, Ralph Vaughan Williams and Benjamin Britten.

In deference to their grandfather's dislike of alcohol, the sisters ran the place on strictly teetotal lines, much to the dismay of Prime Minister Stanley Baldwin, who stayed there in 1932 and had to do without his Scotch. Gregynog is still an arts and conference centre, now run by the University of Wales.

Gwendoline and Margaret's brother, Lord Davies of Llandinam, a member of Lloyd George's 'kitchen cabinet', endowed THE WORLD'S FIRST DEPARTMENT OF INTERNATIONAL POLITICS at the University of Wales in Aberystwyth.

Gregynog was built in 1860 by Henry Hanbury Tracy, as something of an experiment, THE FIRST LARGE HOUSE IN BRITAIN MADE OF CONCRETE. It comes

as quite a shock to realise that the black-and-white timbers are merely painted on. Gregynog could be called 'the cradle of concrete', for all around the estate there are cottages and outbuildings made entirely of this material.

Well, I never knew this ABOUT MONTGOMERYSHIRE

Montgomeryshire is THE ONLY WELSH COUNTY TO SPAN WALES FROM EAST TO WEST – from Offas's Dyke to the Dovey estuary on Cardigan Bay.

The extraordinary six-sided, brick cock-pit in WELSHPOOL, built in the early 18th century, was in continual use for cock-fighting until the practice was outlawed in 1849. This is THE ONLY UNALTERED COCKPIT PRESERVED ON ITS ORIGINAL SITE IN BRITAIN.

Welshpool's livestock market is THE LARGEST ONE-DAY SHEEP MARKET IN EUROPE.

Welshpool was originally Poole. The 'Welsh' was added to distinguish it from Poole in Dorset.

Standing alone in hilly country a few miles west of Welshpool is the small brick DOLOBRAN MEETING HOUSE, THE FIRST QUAKER MEETING HOUSE IN WALES, built in 1701 by CHARLES LLOYD of Dolobran Hall. The Lloyds, successful farmers who also ran an iron-works in the nearby hills, had lived at Dolobran since the 14th century. Their ancestor, Evan Teg, adopted the name Lloyd from his grandfather's seat of Llwydiarth. The first Lloyd to become a Quaker was Charles Lloyd (1637–98), in 1662. A descendant of his, Sampson Lloyd, set up a private bank in Birmingham to invest in and prosper from the Industrial Revolution, and this grew to become what we know as the modern LLOYDS BANK.

Wales can boast of two iconic fashion designers from the 1960s, Swansea girl MARY QUANT, designer of the miniskirt, and LAURA ASHLEY, whose name has entered the language. Born in Dowlais, Glamorgan, in 1925, Laura Ashley settled in the village of CARNO, north-east of Newtown, in 1963, and established her textile factory there. It remained the headquarters of her world-wide empire until closing in 2004. She was buried in the churchyard of St John the Baptist, after a fall at her daughter's Cotswold home in 1985.

All roads meet at the picturesque 16th-century half-timbered market hall in LLANIDLOES, for it stands, on wooden pillars, at THE EXACT CENTRE OF WALES. It is also THE ONLY REMAINING MARKET HALL OF ITS KIND IN WALES. Nearby is a stone from where John Wesley preached. In Great Oak Street is THE OLDEST SURVIVING LAURA ASHLEY SHOP IN THE WORLD. The church of St Idloes in the town centre incorporates some of the pure Early English archways from nearby Cwmhir Abbey, dissolved in 1542 (see Radnorshire).

The LEIGHTON estate is indicated by a grove of impressive giant California redwoods, planted in the mid-19th century by Liverpool banker JOHN NAYLOR (1813–89), who was given the estate as a wedding present by his uncle. He built the great Gothic hall in the park and Holy Trinity Church with its landmark spire, but his proudest achievement was growing the VERY FIRST LEYLAND CYPRESS here, named after his bank in Liverpool. He rests peacefully in the family mausoleum inside the church, unaware of the nightmare he had unleashed upon suburban gardens.

The TALERDDIG CUTTING, between Carno and Llanbrynmair stations on the Newtown to Machynlleth railway line, was THE DEEPEST CUTTING IN THE WORLD when it was completed in 1863.

The squat little church of ST MELANGELL sits right at the end of a narrow road to nowhere on the edge of the Berwyn mountains. It is a detour worth taking, though, for here, behind the main altar, is possibly THE OLDEST ROMANESQUE SHRINE IN BRITAIN, dating from the early 1100s. It is a beautiful place, made more lovely still by the story of St Melangell, who hid a hare in the folds of her cloak to save it from the hounds of Prince Brochwel. So bewitched was he by the beauty and courage of this young girl, who had fled from Ireland to avoid a forced marriage, that he gave her the land in the valley where her church now stands.

Llanidloes

LAKE VYRNWY, created in 1881 to provide drinking water for Liverpool, covers an area of 3.18 sq. miles (8.23 sq. km) and is THE BIGGEST LAKE IN WALES. The distinctive Gothic water-tower jutting out into the water gives the scene a Transylvanian feel and, indeed, the lake and environs are a favourite location for filming. Lake Vyrnwy was the first of the massive reservoirs to be constructed in North and Mid Wales.

St Melangell

PEMBROKESHIRE

(SIR PENFRO)

COUNTY TOWN: HAVERFORDWEST

St David's Cathedral, slumbering in Britain's smallest cathedral city

St David's

(Tyddewi)

Small Wonder

THE MOST WESTERLY VILLAGE IN WALES, ST DAVID'S has a population of some 2,000 and was granted city status by Queen Elizabeth II in 1995. It is THE SMALLEST CATHEDRAL CITY IN BRITAIN, possibly in the world. It is also THE ONLY CITY IN BRITAIN TO LIE WHOLLY WITHIN A NATIONAL PARK, in this instance the Pembrokeshire Coast National Park.

As you approach from the east the first question that presents itself is, 'Where is the cathedral?' There appears to be nothing here except a pretty village grouped around a square with a preaching cross in the middle. Beyond is but grassy hummocks and sand dunes, sky and sea.

Your first sight of ST DAVID'S CATHEDRAL is one of those moments that stays with you for ever. Nothing has quite prepared you for the vista that unfolds as you step through the impressive 13th-century gatehouse, on the edge of the village, known as Porth y Twr. Tucked in a hollow, away from the wind and the Vikings, set lightly in a field of waving grass, mauve and honey-coloured from locally hewn stone flecked with green lichens, is the loveliest cathedral in the world. Others may be bigger or more beautiful or more spectacular, but none is more satisfying, or blends so effortlessly into the landscape, or is so redolent of the simple faith that built it. This wild and windswept corner of Britain has been a place of worship since St David founded a monastery on the site in the 6th century, and the atmosphere is powerful still.

The present cathedral was begun 1181, after St David had been canonised in 1120. It quickly became a place of pilgrimage, with people from all over Christendom coming to worship at his shrine. Pope Calixtus II decreed two pilgrimages to St David's to be worth one to Rome – '*Roma semel quantum: bis dat Menevia tantum*'.

An elegant flight of 39 steps leads down to the cathedral. The exterior of the building is rough and plain, dominated by its four-square tower, which replaced one that collapsed in 1220. The cathedral bells are housed in the tower of the gatehouse, Porth y Twr, moved there in 1730 in case their weight should cause the main cathedral tower to fall in once more.

Inside, the floor is uneven, and some of the pillars seem to lean outwards, the legacy of an earthquake of 1248 that caused considerable damage. The interior is a wonderful jumble of different periods, the earliest being the 12th-century nave. Perhaps the greatest glory is the woodwork – a gorgeously ornate and solid 16th-century roof of Irish oak, mischievously carved misericords, and a rich 14th-century choir screen – all sensitively restored by Sir George Gilbert Scott between 1862 and 1877.

A feature unique to St David's, and found in no other cathedral, is a STALL THAT BEARS THE ROYAL COAT OF ARMS – the reigning monarch is a member of the Cathedral's Chapter.

Buried in St David's Cathedral

It was during Scott's restoration that the bones of St David, thrown out by staunch Protestant Bishop Barlow in 1538, were rediscovered, and they are now preserved in an oak casket in the Sanctuary. In the south choir is the splendid stone tomb of the Welsh Prince, RHYS AP GRUFFUDD (1132–97), ruler of the kingdom of Deheubarth, who convened Wales's first National Eisteddfod at his castle in Cardigan in 1176. Next to him is GERALD CAMBRENSIS (1146–1223), one of the founders of the cathedral and celebrated for his chronicles of Welsh life, *Journey through Wales* and *A Description of Wales*. Before the High Altar lies EDMUND TUDOR, son of Henry V's widow Catherine de Valois, husband of Margaret Beaufort, and father of Henry VII. His remains were brought here by his grandson, Henry VIII.

Bishop's Palace

Right next to the cathedral, and somewhat overshadowed by it, are the impressive remains of the BISHOP'S

PALACE, once the most sumptuous in Wales, built around a spacious courtyard in the 14th century, to reflect the majesty and power of the Bishops. Alas, in the 16th century, the incumbent Bishop of St David's had five daughters, and felt obliged to strip the lead from the roof to pay for all their dowries. The palace was abandoned shortly afterwards in favour of the palace at Abergwili near Carmarthen.

St Non

Not far from St David's, in a field overlooking the sea, are the ruins of a chapel dedicated to Non, St David's mother. St David was born here, sometime around AD 500, at the height of a great storm, and at the moment of his birth a spring appeared at his mother's feet to wash the baby clean. Now watched over by a statue of St Non, the well is reputed to have healing properties, particularly for the eyesight, and pilgrims to St David's Cathedral would often pay a visit here. Inside the chapel, there used to be an altar made from part of the stone on which St Non was lying when she gave birth to David. So violent was the birth that the stone broke, and the imprint of her hand was left upon it. St Non's Chapel is possibly THE OLDEST CHRISTIAN FOUNDATION IN WALES, and a remarkably beautiful place.

Haverfordwest

(Hwlffordd)

On Line

Foley House

HAVERFORDWEST means 'ford of the heifer, or buck', with 'west' tacked on, to distinguish it from Hereford in England. The local pronunciation is 'Harford', which is the same as the proper pronunciation for the English town of Hertford.

All roads in Pembrokeshire meet at Haverfordwest, which sits almost in the middle of the county, making it the perfect choice as county town. Encircled by three rivers, it is virtually an island, situated on a strong defensive site at the tidal limit of the Western Cleddau River. The Bristol Trader Inn on Quay Street is a reminder that Haverfordwest was once an important trading port, perhaps the most important in Wales before the railways took the trade away in the 1850s. The steep High Street leading up to the old Norman castle on the hill is one of the most handsome streets in Wales, lined with buildings of every age,

St David

ST DAVID, Dewi Sant in Welsh, was descended from the Welsh kings of old. He was well educated at Whitland Abbey and travelled widely as a missionary, founding a number of abbeys, including Glastonbury. His legendary status was confirmed when the ground rose beneath his feet while he was preaching at Llanddewi Brefi (see *Cardiganshire). He lived mainly on a diet of cress and water, becoming known as 'Aquaticus', and followed a simple, austere lifestyle as an example to others. He died on 1 March (now St David's Day), in 589, at the monastery he had founded in a sleepy hollow in the far west of Wales, and was chosen as the patron saint of Wales when, in 1120, he became THE ONLY WELSHMAN EVER TO BE CANONISED. He is also THE ONLY NATIVE-BORN PATRON SAINT amongst all the patron saints of Wales, Scotland, Ireland and England.*

St David is held responsible for the adoption of the leek as a Welsh emblem. On the eve of a battle against the Saxons, he is said to have advised the Welsh soldiers to wear a leek in their caps so that they could distinguish friend from foe, and this led to a great victory. Welsh longbowmen, wearing white and green, sported leeks at the Battle of Crecy in 1346, and again at Agincourt in 1415. The Welsh word for leek is cenhinen, *which is almost identical to the Welsh for daffodil,* cenhinen pedr, *and this similarity could explain why the daffodil is also a Welsh national emblem.*

including a fine Shire Hall of 1837. In Goat Street is one of John Nash's earliest works, Foley House, built around 1790 for Richard Foley, brother of Admiral Thomas Foley who fought with Nelson at Cape St Vincent.

The castle is home to the town museum, where pride of place goes to THE OLDEST POSTBOX IN WALES, which dates from 1857 and was taken there after being rescued from being used as a gatepost in a garden on Merlin's Hill.

The artist GWEN JOHN (1876–1939) was born in Victoria Place, Haverfordwest. She eventually settled in Paris, where as well as being a fine portrait painter, she became model and mistress to the sculptor Auguste Rodin.

GRUFF RHYS, lead singer with pop group the SUPER FURRY ANIMALS, was born in Haverfordwest in 1970. The Super Furry Animals are noted for

having the longest ever title for a single record – LLANFAIRPWLLGWYNGYLL-GOGERYCHYNDROBWLLANTYSILIOGOGOGOCHYNYGOFOD.

RHYS IFANS, the unkempt flatmate from the romantic comedy film *Notting Hill*, was born in Haverfordwest in 1968. He was briefly a member of the The Super Furry Animals (*see* above).

It has been said that on market day in Haverfordwest you can hear Welsh spoken on one side of the High Street, English on the other and a mixture of both in the middle. Haverfordwest sits right on an invisible but very real boundary line called the LANDSKER, which divides Welsh-speaking North Pembrokeshire from the English-speaking South – the latter long known as 'Little England beyond Wales'.

The Landsker, which is Norse for divide, dates from the 11th century, when the Normans took control of the vast natural harbour of Milford Haven and built a chain of castles against the Welsh, from Amroth in the east to Newgale in the west. A separate Flemish, Viking and Norman culture developed in the south, and although the line was never drawn on a map, it exerted a powerful influence – marriage to someone on the other side of the line was utterly taboo. The Landsker has long since ceased to be of any real significance, but it is far from forgotten. There is still a very different feel between north and south in Pembrokeshire, and local people instinctively know when they have crossed the line . . .

Milford Haven

(*Aberdaugleddau*)

'The Finest Port in Christendom'

LORD NELSON

Lord Nelson was describing Sir William Hamilton's fine harbour at MILFORD HAVEN when he used these words, not the long-suffering diplomat's wife, his own paramour, Emma Hamilton. Nelson came here to Milford Haven in 1802 to help publicise the docks, and his visit is commemorated in Nelson Quay and the Lord Nelson Hotel. Hamilton Terrace, the smart street in which the hotel resides, remembers Sir William Hamilton, on whose land Milford Haven was built.

Milford Haven is one of the biggest natural harbours in the world, a drowned river valley, 12 miles (19 km) long and in some places 2 miles (3 km) wide, and was originally made use of by scavenging Vikings. Henry II sailed from here in 1171 to consolidate the Norman invasion of Ireland, as later did King John for the same purpose. In 1782, Sir William Hamilton, who had inherited the land from his first wife Catherine Barlow, appointed his nephew Charles Greville to develop the harbour. The first clients Greville attracted were a group of Quaker whalers from Nantucket who built up a very successful whaling fleet, supplying whale oil for street lighting. The need for new ships during the French Revolution and Napoleonic Wars gave a boost to shipbuilding at Milford Haven, although in 1814 Greville put up his charges to such an extent that the Royal Navy decided to build its own yard across the water at Pembroke Dock.

Milford Haven went on to become one of Britain's leading fishing ports, and a base for Atlantic convoys in both World Wars. Later on, the deep-water channel proved perfect for handling the new supertankers of the 1960s, and Milford Haven grew into THE SECOND LARGEST OIL PORT IN EUROPE, after Rotterdam. In 1973 THE LARGEST OIL-FIRED POWER STATION IN EUROPE opened at Milford Haven.

In 1996, a double blow hit the town when plans to burn an industrial fuel from Venezuela called orimulsion fell through, and the oil tanker *Sea Empress* ran aground at the entrance to the harbour, spilling 70,000 tons of crude oil into the sea and polluting 120 miles (193 km) of the Pembrokeshire coastline. This sparked a major debate about the risks of placing huge oil terminals in such an environmentally sensitive region, and Milford Haven's oil business declined. Plans to build two massive Liquid Natural Gas (LNG) terminals at Milford Haven, to process gas brought in liquid form from the Middle East in vast gas tankers, have re-ignited the debate on the subject.

The founder of Milford Haven, Sir William Hamilton (1730–1803), is buried in the graveyard of St Katharine's Church – inside the church are a prayer-book and Bible given by Lord Nelson.

Pembroke

(Penfro)

Birth of a Dynasty

The historic town of PEMBROKE, tucked in behind unbroken medieval walls, is a handsome place, bustling streets lined with Tudor and Georgian buildings, all under the watchful eye of its mighty castle. Pembroke Castle occupies an almost impregnable site, a rocky promontory surrounded on three sides by water, and defended from the land approach to the east by a huge gatehouse with three portcullises. It remains astonishingly intact, with miles of passageways to explore and an outstanding cylindrical keep, 60 ft (18 m) high with walls 18 ft (5.5 m) thick, and topped by a stone dome. It is THE ONLY CASTLE IN BRITAIN TO BE CONSTRUCTED OVER A NATURAL CAVERN, a huge cave known as the Wogan, which used to give the castle access from the water.

Stronghold of the Norman earls, it was from here that the Earl of Pembroke, Richard de Clare, known as 'Strongbow', departed to invade Ireland in 1170.

Harry Tudor

The present monarch Queen Elizabeth II can trace her family back in a direct line to 28 January 1457 at Pembroke Castle, for here, on that day, was born HARRY TUDOR, FATHER OF THE ROYAL HOUSE OF TUDOR, the dynasty that laid the foundations of modern Britain. The Tudors hailed originally from Anglesey, where Harri's grandfather Owen Tudor was born in 1385 (*see* Angelsey). In 1457, with the Wars of the Roses going badly for the Lancastrian side, Harri's mother Margaret Beaufort, 13 years old and heavily pregnant, had been brought to Pembroke by her brother-in-law Jasper Tudor, the Earl of Pembroke, for safekeeping. Her husband, Edmund Tudor, Earl of Richmond, had been incarcerated by the House of York in Carmarthen Castle, where he died before his son was born.

As civil war raged on, Harry grew up safe inside the castle walls as Earl of Richmond, until the death of Henry VI and his son Edward made Harri head of the House of Lancaster, through his mother, the great-granddaughter of John of Gaunt, Duke of Lancaster. The Yorkists seized the throne and Harri Tudor had to flee to France. After 14 years he returned, landing at Mill Bay on the tip of the Dale peninsula, west of Pembroke, and marched through Wales under the banner of the Red Dragon, picking up support as he went. In 1485, he defeated Richard III at Bosworth Field and took the throne as Henry VII.

Tenby
(Dinbych-y-Pysgod)

'You may travel the world over but you will find nowhere more beautiful: it is so restful, so colourful and so unspoilt'

AUGUSTUS JOHN

TENBY, called by the Welsh 'Denbigh of the Fish' to differentiate it from the Denbigh in North Wales, is the most obvious seaside resort in Pembrokeshire. Wide sandy beaches, a picturesque harbour ringed with Georgian houses, a ruined Norman castle and pale-painted, cliff-top Victorian guest-houses – all go to make up a popular holiday destination. Even Lord Nelson visited Tenby, accompanying Sir William Hamilton and his wife Emma to East Rock House in 1802.

Many writers have found inspiration in Tenby. In 1856, Mary Ann Evans began drafting her first novel, *The Sad Fortunes of the Reverend Amos Barton*, while holidaying here. It was published the following year under her pen-name GEORGE ELIOT. BEATRIX POTTER came in 1900 and stayed at Croft Terrace, where she sketched the garden pond that would feature in the soon-to-be-published *The Tale of Peter Rabbit*.

There is history in Tenby too. Narrow, winding streets and ancient buildings huddle within well-preserved 13th-century town walls. The mighty FIVE ARCHES fortified barbican gate is THE ONLY ONE OF ITS KIND IN BRITAIN. The 15th-century TUDOR MERCHANT'S HOUSE, owned by the National Trust, is

The Welsh Dragon

The Welsh emblem of the Red Dragon is derived from the days of the Celtic King Vortigern. He sought advice from Merlin the Wizard on his continuing struggles against the Saxons, and Merlin counselled the King to dig up the earth around the fortress where he was making his stand. Vortigern did so and came across two dragons, one red and one white. The dragons were having a fight, which the red dragon won, and Merlin explained that this meant that the Celts would defeat the Saxons. And, indeed, the Saxons never did prevail in Wales. From that time on the Red Dragon has been the symbol of Wales.

Tudor Merchant's House

one of the oldest surviving townhouses in Wales, with a Flemish chimney (*see* St Florence, below) and some interesting early floral murals inside. St Mary's Church is THE LARGEST PARISH CHURCH IN WALES and contains a memorial to the brilliant ROBERT RECORDE (1510–58), who was born in Tenby, the son of a merchant. He was the leading mathematician of Tudor times, THE FIRST PERSON IN BRITAIN TO ACCEPT COPERNICUS'S THEORY that the earth revolved around the sun. He invented the equals sign (=), was the first man to use plus and minus signs, discovered the square root and, to his eternal shame, introduced algebra to Britain.

The painter AUGUSTUS JOHN (1878–1961) was born in what is now the Belgrave Hotel. He grew up in Tenby with his elder sister Gwen, who was born up the road in Haverfordwest and also became a painter. The scenery around Tenby was the subject of their first pictures, and they shared their first studio together in the town, before being sent off to the Slade School of Art in London. Augustus became the most

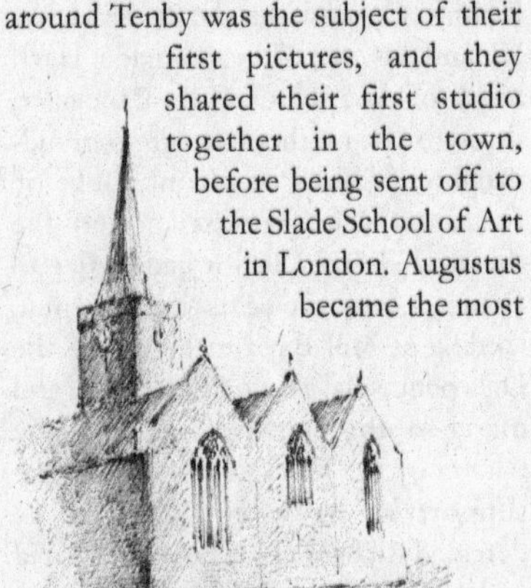

famous artist of his day, while Gwen's reputation is only now emerging from her brother's shadow. Neither returned to Tenby, but there is a permanent exhibition of their works at the Tenby Museum and Art Gallery on Castle Street.

Fishguard
(Abergwaun)

The Last Invasion

In February 1797, a force of 1,400 French troops landed on the rocky CARREG WASTAD POINT near Strumble Head, north of Fishguard, under the command of a 70-year-old Irish American called Colonel Tate. This was the time of the French Revolution, and the idea was to encourage a similar kind of 'Peasants' Revolt' in Wales, in order to cause a diversion while the main French army invaded Ireland. The French force, however, consisted mainly of prisoners pressed into service, and rather than advancing on Fishguard with military precision, they decided to lay siege to a farmhouse about a mile inland at Tre-Howel. After a fierce struggle the farmhouse was overrun and Colonel Tate set up his headquarters in the kitchen. Scarcely had the Colonel sat down when one of his men rushed in and informed him that a large force of redcoats was approaching. Tate then decided that it might be wise to retreat to the beach at Goodwick, where they were easily subdued by the local militia under Lord Cawdor, and forced to surrender. The LAST FOREIGN INVASION OF BRITAIN was over.

It wasn't until later that the French discovered that the army of redcoats they had seen advancing on the farm had in fact been a regiment of ladies from Fishguard, dressed in red petticoats and tall black hats. One of them, JEMIMA NICOLAS, single-handedly rounded up a dozen French stragglers with her pitchfork, for which she was rewarded an annual pension of £50 by an awe-struck government. She died in 1832 and is buried in St Mary's churchyard, where a stone near the church door commemorates 'the Welsh heroine who boldly marched to meet the French invaders who landed on our shores in February 1797'.

There is a memorial at Carreg Wastad Point, where the French landed, and relics of the battle, including captured weapons and the table on which the surrender was signed, are preserved at the Royal Oak pub in Fishguard's main square.

In 1997, a 100-ft (30 m) long Last Invasion Tapestry, embroidered in the style of the Bayeux Tapestry, was unveiled in Fishguard to mark the bicentenary of the invasion. It has been housed since then in St Mary's church hall in the square, but a new home is to be found for it in the Town Hall.

Fishguard consists of three parts. GOODWICK, where in the early 20th century a new harbour and breakwater were created by the Great Western Railway, is where ferries depart for Rosslare in Ireland. It was originally hoped that Goodwick might become a major terminal for transatlantic liners from New York. Indeed, in 1909, the luxury liner *Mauretania* called here, but the trade eventually went to Southampton, and Goodwick had to settle for the Irish ferry business.

South across the bay is picturesque LOWER FISHGUARD, which looks like the archetypal small fishing village. Brightly coloured houses tumble down the wooded hillside, yachts and fishing boats bob up and down on the blue sea, and the little port's film-set looks have attracted plenty of stars. The 1971 film of Dylan Thomas's *Under Milk Wood*, starring Richard Burton and Elizabeth Taylor, was filmed in Lower Fishguard, as was the 1956 film of *Moby Dick*, starring Gregory Peck.

The main town of FISHGUARD sits up on the hill between Goodwick and Lower Fishguard and is grouped around the main square, where the Royal Oak can be found.

Preseli Hills

(Mynydd Preseli)

Timeless

MYNYDD PRESELI, an expanse of mysterious bare moorland and hill south-east of Fishguard, is the only substantial inland area within the Pembrokeshire Coast National Park. At 1,760 ft (536 m), Foel Cwmcerwyn is the highest point both of the Preseli Hills and of the National Park. The views from here are stupendous, stretching as far as Snowdonia to the north and as far as the Wicklow Mountains in Ireland to the west.

In 1922, a visiting geologist discovered, on the slopes of a Preseli peak called Carnmenyn, the source of the massive bluestones that make up Stonehenge in Wiltshire. This is the only place in Britain where the white-spotted volcanic dolerite from which the bluestones were quarried is to be found. To this day no one is quite sure how the stones were transported to the middle of Salisbury Plain. Some think they might have been carried east by great ice sheets during the last Ice Age, others prefer the notion that they were spirited there by Merlin the Wizard. In 1995, a bluestone, already cut, was found at the bottom of the river near Milford Haven, suggesting that they might have been floated down the East Cleddau River to Milford Haven, sailed around the South Wales coast, up the Severn and the Avon, finally to be placed on sledges and rollered on tree trunks across Salisbury Plain, and into position.

Mynydd Preseli is an ancient and sacred place. Everywhere there are stone circles, megalithic graves, menhirs, hill forts, hut circles – all the trappings of prehistoric existence. The most striking of these, set majestically on the hills overlooking Newport, is PENTRE IFAN, a Neolithic burial chamber consisting of a huge capstone resting on the points of three tall pillars made of the same bluestone as those at Stonehenge.

Many of the tales from the MABINOGION are associated with Mynydd Preseli. The *MABINOGION* is a collection of fantastical stories, myths and romantic legends from the Welsh Dark Ages, about princes and warriors and love, passed on by mouth and written down in medieval times. The stories were given the name *Mabinogion* by LADY CHARLOTTE GUEST, who translated them in the 1840s.

One legendary king who, according to some local people may have been connected to Mynydd Preseli, was *the* King, Elvis Presley. Now follow closely. St David was baptised by a Bishop of Munster called St Elvis, and there is a small chapel dedicated to him just to the east of St David's, close to a St Elvis farm and a St Elvis cromlech. The theory goes that a family from Preseli emigrated to North America, became known as the 'people from Preseli', or Presleys, and named one of their descendants after their local Welsh saint, Saint Elvis. Elvis Presley. It doesn't stretch the imagination all that far . . .

After all, the people of this timeless place do live by different rules. For instance, the inhabitants of the tranquil, secluded GWAUN VALLEY, which runs from the Preseli Hills down to Fishguard, still adhere to the old pre-1752 Julian calendar, which means that they celebrate New Year on 13 January.

Buried in the cemetery at Mynachlog-Ddu, a hamlet on the southern edge of Mynydd Preseli, is THOMAS REES (1806–76), the leader of the first Rebecca Riots in 1839 (*see* Carmarthenshire).

Nearby is a rather incongruous sign of civilisation: a fine Georgian house called Temple Druid, one of the few major works of the architect John Nash to survive in Wales.

Cilgerran Castle

A Welsh First

High above the wooded Teifi valley on the border with Cardiganshire stands CILGERRAN CASTLE. This was THE FIRST STONE CASTLE BUILT BY THE WELSH, although the dramatic ruins we see today are Norman. The atmospheric paintings of Cilgerran by Richard Wilson and J.M.W. Turner lured

Victorian visitors here in droves, making Cilgerran one of Wales's first tourist attractions.

Buried somewhere in the church at Cilgerran is the original Dr Spock, THOMAS PHAER (1510–60), author of the first English book on childcare, *The Boke of Children*, published in 1544. A memorial plaque to him was unveiled in the church on Mothering Sunday in 1986, in the presence of the Bishop of St David's, the President of the British Paediatric Society.

In August, coracle races are held on the Teifi at Cilgerran, and in the porch of the little church at MANORDEIFI nearby, a coracle and paddle are kept propped up against the wall for the use of stranded worshippers in the event of the Teifi overflowing. Not that such a hardship would have bothered the adventurous Charles Colby, who lies beneath a splendid monument in the church having had the misfortune, we are informed, to be killed by a tiger in India, in 1852. Manordeifi dates from the 13th century and is delightfully untouched.

The Teifi was THE LAST RIVER IN BRITAIN WHERE BEAVERS WERE SEEN, way back in the Middle Ages.

Nevern

Cuckoo

The tree-embowered church of ST BRYNACH'S, in the lovely NEVERN valley between Mynydd Preseli and the sea, is a wondrous museum of early Christian monuments. Set into the window sill of the nave inside is the 5th-century MAGLOCUNUS STONE, which is inscribed in both Latin and Ogham, and proved helpful in deciphering Ogham, a type of ancient script found mostly in Ireland. Nearby is the CROSS STONE, dating from the 10th century and bearing a Viking cross.

Outside, near the porch, are the VITIALANUS STONE, which has more Latin and Ogham writing, and the jewel of the collection, ST BRYNACH'S CROSS, THE FINEST CELTIC CROSS IN WALES. It is 10th-century, 13 ft (4 m) high and exquisitely carved with intricate knotwork. Every year, they say, on St Brynach's birthday, 7 April, the first cuckoo in Wales sings from the top of the cross.

Bordering the path leading up to the church are a line of ancient yew trees, one of which bleeds a dark red resin from its trunk and is known as the 'bleeding yew'. They say it bleeds for the sins of Wales. Or possibly for a monk who was hanged from its branches for a crime he did not commit and bid the tree bleed to proclaim his innocence.

Black Bart

Seafaring Folk

On the village green of LITTLE NEWCASTLE, south of Fishguard, there is a memorial to the original 'Pirate of the Caribbean', Bartholomew Roberts, known as Barti Dhu or BLACK BART, who was born here in 1682. He was second mate on a boat called the *Princess* when it was captured by a fellow Welshman, the pirate Hywel Davies. Rather than be thrown overboard, Roberts joined the pirate crew and quickly earned their admiration, being elected captain when Davies was killed a few weeks later.

Over the next four or five years Black Bart sailed the Spanish Main, and as far north as Newfoundland, running down and boarding treasure ships of all nations and stripping them of their cargoes. He even captured a 52-gun French man-of-war, which became his flagship, the *Royal Fortune*.

He was a flamboyant and hearty character, known as much for his laugh as his cruelty. He more or less ruled the Caribbean and struck fear into the hearts of the authorities there – in 1720 he even hanged the Governor of Martinique from the mainmast of the *Royal Fortune*.

He finally met his end in a battle with the British Royal Navy off the coast of West Africa, being killed in the first exchange of fire. His crew threw his body into the sea so that the Royal Navy wouldn't be able to take it back to put on display in London.

Black Bart was THE FIRST PIRATE TO FLY THE SKULL AND CROSS-BONES, the flag that he himself designed.

Trecwn

Secret Valley

A few miles south of Fishguard, the mysterious Preseli Hills overlook an equally secluded and unfathomable place, the secretive valley of TRECWN. Here, at the end of a long, well-monitored private road, safe behind tall steel fences topped with barbed wire, and protected by guard-houses, is the old top-secret Royal Naval Armaments Depot, established in 1938. An 18-mile (29 km) narrow-gauge railway, linked to the main Fishguard to Carmarthen line, runs along the valley, branching off, herring-bone style, into 58 separate storage tunnels, each stretching back 200 ft (60 m) into the hillside and sealed with heavy steel doors.

Employing many of those made redundant when Pembroke Dock closed in 1926, the depot was used throughout the Second World War and the Cold War to store munitions and missiles that could be taken by rail to Goodwick for loading on to ships. It closed in 1998, and was bought by an Anglo-Irish company called Omega Pacific, who wanted to service jet engines in the above-ground complex and store low-grade radioactive waste in the tunnels. This plan was rejected by local people, and the site, which covers some 750 acres (304 ha), is now being turned into an industrial estate and distribution centre.

Like all secret government lairs,

Trecwn has a distinctly sinister air to it. You feel all the time as though you are being watched, which you probably are, and as you drive along the narrow valley road, you almost expect to be followed by a black Mercedes, or surrounded by hard men with guns in Land Rovers. Who knows what really goes on in those tunnels deep inside the hills? Or what was left behind there.

St Govan's Chapel

Different Steps

Pembrokeshire abounds with Celtic shrines, but there is none more evocative of simple Celtic faith than ST GOVAN'S CHAPEL, tucked into the cliffs at St Govan's Head, south of Pembroke. The tiny chapel, 20 ft (6 m) long and 12 ft (3.6 m) wide, sits on the beach in a fold of the cliffs, and is reached by a flight of steps that counts differently when descended from when ascended – after going up and down several times, my average was 52.

St Govan may well have been Sir Gawain, one of the Knights of the Round Table, who retired to become a monk after the quest for the Holy Grail (*see* Cardiganshire). He was hiding in the ravine to escape from pursuers, and the rocks closed over his head until the danger had passed. In gratitude, he built the chapel on the very same spot, and it blends in so well to the cliffs that the story rings true.

The tiny bell-cote above the entrance used to hold a silver bell. The story goes that it was taken away by pirates, then rescued by mermaids and placed on a nearby rock, which now rings sweetly when struck. There is a well, reached by more steps down on to the beach below the chapel, no longer running but still with its stone hood. The chapel inside is bare except for another, smaller well.

Out of the wind, set back from the waves in its own cleft, St Govan's remains peaceful and undisturbed – except by people trying to count the stairs . . .

Well, I never knew this
ABOUT
PEMBROKESHIRE

The PEMBROKESHIRE COAST NATIONAL PARK is THE SMALLEST NATIONAL PARK IN BRITAIN and also BRITAIN'S ONLY COASTAL BASED NATIONAL PARK. Created in 1952, it covers an area of 225 sq. miles (583 sq. km) and is 180 miles (290 km) long, running from near Cardigan in the north to Tenby in the south.

SKOKHOLM ISLAND, off the Pembrokeshire coast, was BRITAIN'S FIRST OFFICIALLY DESIGNATED BIRD RESERVE. Naturalist Ronald Lockley (1903–2000) lived on the island for 12 years and established THE FIRST BIRD OBSERVATORY IN BRITAIN there, in 1933. He wrote an account of his life on Skokholm called *Dream Island*. Guests can stay in Lockley's former farmhouse.

SKOMER ISLAND is THE LARGEST SEA-BIRD COLONY IN SOUTHERN BRITAIN and can be visited by boat from Martin's Haven.

Nine miles (14.5 km) west of Skomer, 30,000 pairs of gannets make GRASSHOLM the FOURTH LARGEST GANNETRY IN THE WORLD.

ST MARGARET'S ISLAND, off the tip of Caldey Island, has THE LARGEST COLONY OF CORMORANTS IN BRITAIN.

ROSEBUSH, 8 miles (13 km) south-east of Fishguard, was THE FIRST VILLAGE IN WALES TO HAVE PIPED WATER.

PENRHOS COTTAGE, near Llangolman, 12 miles (19 km) south-east of Fishguard, is a wonderfully preserved 19th-century example of a 'ONE-NIGHT HOUSE'. Any man who could build himself a house on his chosen spot, between sunset and dawn, was entitled to all the land that lay within a stone's throw of the door. The cottage can be viewed by appointment.

HMS DUKE OF WELLINGTON, the LARGEST THREE-DECK MAN-OF-WAR EVER BUILT, was launched from PEMBROKE DOCK in 1852. It saw duty during the Crimean War as the flagship of Admiral Napier.

Five Royal Yachts were built at Pembroke Dock, THE ONLY ROYAL DOCKYARD IN WALES. During the Second World War, Pembroke Dock was home to THE LARGEST OPERATIONAL FLYING-BOAT BASE IN THE WORLD. Over 100 aircraft, mostly Sutherlands, were based there.

CAREW MILL, near Pembroke, is THE ONLY SURVIVING TIDAL MILL IN WALES, and one of only three remaining in Britain. There are records of a mill here in 1542, although the present mill is early 19th-century, one of the mill-wheels has been dated to 1801.

The controversial artist GRAHAM SUTHERLAND (1903–80), creator of Britain's

Carew Mill

biggest tapestry, *Christ in his Glory*, in Coventry Cathedral, found inspiration in the dramatic landscapes and light of Pembrokeshire. He returned many times, particularly to the Milford Haven area, to paint some of his most famous works – his pictures of Pembrokeshire proved much more popular than his celebrated portrait of Winston Churchill, which Churchill detested so much that his wife had it burned. In 1976, a Graham Sutherland Gallery was opened in Picton Castle, the collection moving to the National Museum Wales in Cardiff for the new millennium.

PICTON CASTLE was built in the 13th century for Sir John Wogan. His descendants, now called Philips, still live there today, making it one of the oldest castles in Wales to be inhabited by the same family. The castle was remodelled in the 18th century, although it retains some of the unusual plan, with no internal courtyard. Originally, seven circular towers projected from the main body of the castle, the two at the east end being connected to form a gatehouse entrance, that led under a portcullis straight through to the undercroft of the hall.

On of the Philippses, the 2nd Lord Millford, became THE ONLY COMMUNIST TO SIT IN THE BRITISH PARLIAMENT, when he took his seat in the House of Lords in 1962.

MANORBIER CASTLE is 'the most pleasant spot in Wales' according to the man born there in 1146, Gerald de Barri, the revered 'GIRALDUS CAMBRENSIS'. He was the author of the definitive chronicles of late 12th-century Wales, *Journey through Wales* and *A Description of Wales* – both written in Latin. He gathered the material when he accompanied the Archbishop of Canterbury through Wales in 1188, drumming up support for the Third Crusade, and jotting down his observations. He is buried in St David's Cathedral.

The little village of ST FLORENCE, inland from Tenby, is noted for its first-class examples of a local architectural feature called a FLEMISH CHIMNEY – a huge, tall, conical chimney often built on to the end of a small cottage or farmhouse, and probably dating from the 15th century. Although such chimneys are called Flemish, no evidence has been found of them in Flanders.

Norman feudal Lord Adam de la Roche built ROCH CASTLE high up on the top of an inaccessible volcanic outcrop, east of St David's, in an attempt to thwart a prophecy that he would die that year by the bite of an adder. He barricaded himself in on the top floor, content to stay there until the year was out. On the last day of the fateful year he summoned a servant to bring some firewood, and as he was reaching into the basket he was bitten by an adder which had been sleeping amongst the logs.

The next morning he was found dead in front of the dying embers. The Duke of Monmouth's mother, Charles II's mistress LUCY WALTER, was born here. Roch Castle, still basically 13th-century, is now a hotel.

WYNFORD VAUGHAN-THOMAS (1908–87), BBC commentator and founder of Harlech Television, and baritone SIR GERAINT EVANS (1922–92) were both cremated in the crematorium at Narberth.

OAKWOOD THEME PARK, near Narbeth, is THE BIGGEST THEME PARK IN WALES. It claims BRITAIN'S FIRST 'BEYOND VERTICAL' FIRST DROP as well as THE FASTEST ROLLER-COASTER IN EUROPE and EUROPE'S BIGGEST WOODEN ROLLER-COASTER.

The pleasantly sheltered harbour at SOLVA, east of St David's, is situated at the head of a deep inlet. In the 19th century many Welsh emigrants said goodbye to the Land of their Fathers here, as they sailed on a one-way trip to America for ten shillings.

DALE, a busy waterside village not far from where Harri Tudor landed at the start of his march to become Henry VII, is known as THE WINDIEST PLACE IN WALES. However, it is also THE SUNNIEST PLACE IN WALES.

In 1933, King George VI bought his daughter Elizabeth a PEMBROKESHIRE CORGI called Dookie, and corgis have now become synonymous with Queen Elizabeth II. They are thought to have been introduced to Pembrokeshire by Flemings in the 12th century, originally to herd cattle and horses.

Radnorshire

(SIR FAESYFED)

County Town: Presteigne

Old Radnor Church, home of the oldest font in Britain

Presteigne
(Llanandras)

'Neither in Wales nor in England, but simply in Radnorshire'

George Borrow

With a population of some 2500, Presteigne is the second smallest county town in England and Wales. And one of the most attractive. It perches sleepily on the west bank of the River Lugg, which here forms the border with England, and for those travelling along the coach road from London to Aberystwyth it was for a long time known as the first town in Wales.

Although Presteigne was bypassed long ago, there are several inns in the town that survive from the days of horse and coach. Perhaps the most eye-catching is the superb black and white Radnorshire Arms, which dates from 1616 and is said to have a number of secret passages and priest's holes. The house is thought to have been built originally for one of Queen Elizabeth I's favourite courtiers, Sir Christopher Hatton, Captain of the Queen's Bodyguard and Lord Chancellor, after whom Hatton Garden, London's diamond centre, is named. The house eventually passed on to the Bradshaw family, one of whom, John Bradshaw, was the Lord President of the High Court of Justice that presided over the trial of Charles I. His was the first signature on the King's death warrant.

The galleried Duke's Arms is RADNORSHIRE'S OLDEST INN. It replaced one that was burned down by Owain Glyndwr in 1401.

The jewel in Presteigne's crown is the former Shire Hall, an impressive Georgian building now known as 'THE JUDGE'S LODGINGS'. It was built in 1829 and described by Lord Chief Justice Campbell in 1855 as 'the most commodious and elegant apartments for a judge in all England and Wales'. Now a museum, it has been restored inside to look as it would have appeared in the 1870s and proudly shows off THE ONLY WORKING EXAMPLE OF A GAS-POWERED CHANDELIER IN BRITAIN.

Also on display is the original headstone of 17-year-old Mary Morgan, who was sentenced to death in 1805 for killing her new-born baby with a kitchen knife. She was THE LAST WOMAN IN WALES TO BE PUBLICLY EXECUTED, and this headstone tells of her 'sin and shame'. However, some thought that Mary had been seduced by a local squire who was sitting on the jury that condemned her, and the people of Presteigne erected a second headstone to her which bears the inscription 'He that is without sin among you, let him cast a stone at her'.

This headstone is in the churchyard of St Andrew's, a Saxon foundation and the church which gives the town its Welsh name of Llanandras. The church's finest treasure is a 16th-century Flemish tapestry, ONE OF ONLY TWO PRE-REFORMATION TAPESTRIES TO BE FOUND IN A CHURCH IN BRITAIN.

A prominent member of the jury who condemned Mary Morgan was ADMIRAL SIR PETER PUGET, whose family lived at the Red House, a red-brick house in Broad Street. As a commander, Admiral Puget had sailed with Captain Vancouver to survey the west coast of America. Puget Sound and Puget Island are named after him.

Battle of Pilleth

'. . . the noble Mortimer,
Leading the men of
Herfordshire to fight,
Against the wild and
irregular Glendower,
Was by the rude hand of
that Welshman taken,
A thousand of his
people butchered'

WILLIAM SHAKESPEARE
Henry IV Part I

Deep in the countryside west of Presteigne, approached along a grassy track, is the gorgeous little church of OUR LADY OF PILLETH. Six hundred years ago, in 1402, the church found itself in the middle of the Battle of Pilleth, when the forces of Owain Glyndwr defeated those of Edmund Mortimer, inflicting heavy casualties. Many are buried in the churchyard or on the steep hillside above, and bones are still regularly turned up. In the 19th century, the local MP Sir Richard Green-Price planted four tall Wellingtonia fir trees to mark where the Welsh soldiers were buried, and placed a stone monument in the churchyard in memory of the English dead. The church was also a casualty of the fighting, being badly damaged. In 1894 a fire almost completed the destruction, but the church is now almost fully restored. Despite its violent history, or maybe because of it, the little white church on the side of the hill is today a heavenly, peaceful place.

Knighton
(Tref-y-Clawdd)

The Town on the Dyke

Knighton is the only town that stands right on Offa's Dyke, BRITAIN'S LONGEST ARCHAEOLOGICAL MONUMENT. The Dyke was built toward the end of the 8th century by the Saxon King Offa, to separate Mercia from the kingdoms of the Welsh. It was THE FIRST OFFICIAL BORDER BETWEEN ENGLAND AND WALES, and the line of the modern boundary of today is not substantially different.

According to the 19th-century writer of *Wild Wales*, George Borrow, 'It was customary for the English to cut off the ears of every Welshman who was found to the east of the dyke, and for the Welsh to hang every Englishman found to the west of it.'

The Dyke ran for 149 miles (240 km) from the River Severn near Chepstow to the sea at Prestatyn. For most of the way it consisted of a ditch and rampart, some 89 ft (27 m) wide and 26 ft (8 m) high, from the bottom of the ditch to the top of the bank. The ditch was on the Welsh side. Some 80 miles (129 km) of the Dyke is still traceable, with the best-preserved sections being found near Knighton, home of the Offa's Dyke Centre, which gives information about the 170-mile (274 km) long-distance footpath which broadly follows the line of the Dyke along the Welsh Marches.

Just outside Knighton, the Heart of Wales railway line, running from Shrewsbury to Swansea, crosses the Teme valley on the 13 arches of one of the engineering marvels of the Victorian age, the 70-ft (21 m) high neo-Gothic Knucklas Viaduct, built in 1863.

King Arthur is believed to have lived in a castle at Knucklas with his wife Guinevere. The Norman castle was destroyed by Llywelyn ap Gruffudd in 1262.

Clyro

Of Diaries and Dogs

The peaceful village of CLYRO, set in low rolling hills and looking out over the Wye valley to the Black Mountains, has found fame through the lyrical diaries of the REVD FRANCIS KILVERT (1840–79), curate here from 1865 to 1872. His affectionate and perceptive descriptions of Victorian life in this small village, and the surrounding Radnorshire countryside, have become a minor classic. Opposite the Baskerville Arms there is a memorial plaque to Kilvert on the wall of Ashbrook House, where he lived and wrote. Although the gentle world that Kilvert observed is now lost, there is still something in Clyro of the wistful atmosphere that his diaries evoke.

CLYRO COURT, a Jacobean-style manor house just outside the village, was built for the local landowner Thomas Baskerville. Sir Arthur Conan Doyle stayed here while writing his most famous Sherlock Holmes tale, *The*

Hound of the Baskervilles. Although he set the story on Dartmoor, it is possible that he based the plot on the local legend of evil squire Sir Thomas Vaughan of Hergest Court, across the border in Herefordshire. Black Vaughan and his ghostly hound The Black Dog of Hergest are said to haunt the Marcher lands hereabouts.

Llandrindod Wells

(Llandrindod)

'Let England boast Bath's crowded springs, Llandrindod happier Cambria sings'

GENTLEMEN'S MAGAZINE, 1748

Llandrindod Wells is Radnorshire's largest town, and the only one of a string of famous 19th-century Welsh spa towns, the others being Builth Wells, Llanwrtyd Wells and Llangamarch Wells, that still offer spa facilities. You can take the sulphur and magnesium spring waters at the spa room, and there are tea-rooms, rock gardens and ravishing scenery. Visitors have been coming here since the 17th century, but it was the arrival of the railway that really launched Llandrindod Wells as a fashionable health resort and holiday destination. It remains an almost perfect model of an unspoilt Victorian town with elegant villas, comfortable hotels and attractive wrought-iron canopies across the pavements. A Victorian Festival is held every summer, when traffic is banned from the town centre and the local people dress up in Victorian garb.

Buried in the old parish churchyard is TOM NORTON (1870–1955), friend of Henry Ford and WALES'S FIRST TRANSPORT SUPREMO. In 1912, he opened THE FIRST FORD AGENCY IN WALES and introduced WALES'S FIRST BUS SERVICE, from Llandrindod to Newtown. Both were based in the exotic art deco Automobile Palace which is now home to the National Cycle Exhibition. Tom Norton was President of the Fellowship of Old Time Cyclists, whose membership was restricted to those who were born before 1873 and had ridden a penny farthing before they reached the age of 17.

Elan Valley

'Rocks piled on each other to tremendous heights, rivers formed into cataracts by their projections, and valleys clothed with woods, present an appearance of enchantment.'

PERCY BYSSHE SHELLEY

When the water is low in the Caban Coch reservoir, the haunting remains of a fine mansion can be seen emerging from the icy water, a place that once echoed with laughter and poetry, a house once filled with parties and gaiety and fun. For this was NANTGWYLLT HOUSE, where the poet Shelley and his child bride Harriet came to live in 1812, and dreamed of setting up a community of friends and poets and philosophers.

Shelley had fallen in love with the beautiful and remote Elan Valley the previous year, when he had walked here from his home in Sussex to stay with his uncle Thomas Grove at Cwm Elan, a big house just across the hills from Nantgwyllt. He spent his time exploring and sailing his cat down the river in a paper boat, using his only five-pound note as a sail. After eloping to Edinburgh to get married, Shelley brought Harriet back to Nantgwyllt, which they were both desperate to buy for their new home.

It was not to be. They could not raise the money, and at the end of the summer of 1812 they left, never to return. As Harriet wrote, 'you may imagine our sorrow at leaving so desirable a spot, where every beauty seems centred.' Two years later Shelley abandoned his young wife for Mary Godwin (who would later write the Gothic horror novel *Frankenstein*), and the unhappy Harriet drowned herself in the Serpentine in London's Hyde Park. Shelley himself drowned in the sea off Tuscany in 1822. And Nantgwyllt House drowned beneath the rising waters of the Caban Coch reservoir in 1904.

There was a long-held belief that Nantgwyllt was still intact when it was engulfed, which may have inspired Francis Brett Young to write his 1932 novel *The House Beneath the Water*. This tale was disproved, however, when the demolished remains were first sighted again during a drought in 1937.

A celebrated daughter of Nantgwyllt House was EMMELINE LEWIS LLOYD who, in the mid 19th century, became the eighth woman to climb Europe's highest mountain, Mont Blanc. There is a memorial to her in St Bride's church in Cwmdeuddwr.

The Elan Valley was drowned at the end of the 19th century to provide drinking water for the rapidly expanding industrial city of Birmingham. In THE BIGGEST CONSTRUCTION PROJECT OF THE VICTORIAN ERA, involving a series of large dams, 100 inhabitants of the valley were moved, while three manor houses (including Nantgwyllt and Cwm Elan), 18 farms, a school and a church were all lost. Because the area is relatively high, the water is transported the 73 miles (117 km) to Birmingham by gravity, obviating the need for pumps.

The newest and largest of the dams is

the Claerwen Dam, which was opened in 1952 by the Queen in one of her first official engagements as the monarch. It is one of the highest gravity dams in Britain, 184 ft (56 m) high and 1,165 ft (355 m) across. It is also the only one of the dams to be made of concrete and is dressed with stone to harmonize with the earlier dams. A working farmhouse sits right underneath the colossal looming wall, seemingly quite unconcerned by the huge mass of water held back just yards away.

The five man-made lakes stretch for almost 9 miles (14 km) and are surrounded by glorious scenery which attracts walkers and cyclists, while bird-watchers come to see once rare red kites wheeling majestically in the skies. When the reservoirs are full, water cascades in sparkling silver sheets down the face of the dams, creating a spectacular show.

Doldowlod

Hidden Treasure

Hard to believe, but papers, personal effects, doodlings, musings and mementoes of one of the great geniuses of all time, a man who did more than almost any other to create the modern world, were hidden away in a quiet Radnorshire valley for over 100 years. In 1785, James Watt, the engineer, inventor and pioneer of steam engines, whose name is immortalised on every light bulb, bought DOLDOWLOD HALL, 1 mile (1.6 km) south of Llanwrthwl, near Rhayader, as a retirement home. Watt himself designed and built a portion of the hall, and after his death in 1819, his descendants continued to live there. In 1899, Watt's papers, personal possessions and many of the contents of his workshop in Heathfield, Birmingham, were all brought to Doldowlod, where they remained until the death of his great-great-great-grandson, Lord Gibson-Watt, in 2002.

David Gibson-Watt was Conservative MP for Hereford from 1956 until 1974, Minister of State at the Welsh Office, and proud guardian of his ancestor's secret treasure trove at Doldowlod. After Gibson-Watt died, a number of James Watt's personal items, such as his spectacles, watch and walking stick, were sold at auction at Sotheby's, raising almost £2 million. Perhaps the most intriguing lot was a personal account by Watt's cousin, Jane Campbell, of the 'kettle incident', that seminal moment when the teenage Watt realised the possibilities of steam power while playing with a steaming kettle.

Abbeycwmhir

'Alas! Alas! poor Radnorsheere
Never a park, nor never a deere
Never a man with five
hundred a year
Save Richard Fowler of
Abbey Cwm Hir'

This old Radnorshire rhyme could be said to hold true today, for there are still few big houses or large towns in this most rural of counties. The lands of Abbeycwmhir passed to the Fowler family of the rhyme at the Dissolution of the Monasteries, but by then there was little left of the abbey itself. It had been sacked by Owain Glyndwr, who suspected the monks of supporting the English.

The name, meaning 'abbey in the long valley', is all that now points to the historic importance of this tiny hamlet, set in a tranquil valley amongst the high, forested hills east of Rhayader. A church, a big house with gables, a farm and the Happy Union Inn are left to

stand sentinel over one of the most evocative places in Welsh history. A gate opposite the farm gives access to the scant remains of what was once THE LARGEST ABBEY IN WALES, a Cistercian house, founded in 1143, that boasted a nave 242 ft (74 m) in length – longer than any church in Britain save Durham or Winchester.

A hawthorn tree now grows in place of the high altar, and a modern stone slab marks the spot where the headless body of LLYWELYN AP GRUFFUDD, THE LAST NATIVE PRINCE OF WALES, was secretly laid to rest by the monks, after he was slain at Cilmeri (*see* Breconshire) in 1282. His head had been sent to London to be paraded through the streets as a symbol of Edward I's domination of Wales.

Llywelyn ap Gruffudd, Prince of Gwynedd, also known as Llywelyn Ein Llyw Olaf or Llywelyn the Last, is one of the greatest Welsh heroes, and even today his grave at lonely Abbeycwmhir is a place of pilgrimage. Grandson of Llywelyn Fawr, or Llywelyn the Great, he ruthlessly united many of the old Welsh kingdoms under his rule and took advantage of the weakness of Henry III to gain recognition from the English king as the true Prince of Wales, by the Treaty of Montgomery in 1267. When Edward I came to the throne in 1272, Llywelyn misjudged the new King's strength and refused to pay due tribute or swear his allegiance. Edward determined to deal with the troublesome Welsh Prince and a ten-year struggle ensued, ending at Cilmeri in 1282, when Llywelyn died – and with him all hopes of an independent Wales. As one Welsh poet put it, 'Oh God! That the sea might engulf the land! Oh, why are we left to our long weary darkness?'

Well, I never knew this ABOUT RADNORSHIRE

RADNORSHIRE is THE MOST SPARSELY POPULATED COUNTY IN ENGLAND OR WALES.

The ancient hilltop settlement of OLD RADNOR is now not much more than a church – but what a church. Sublimely beautiful, 15th-century, set 840 ft (256 m) up on a hill in a prehistoric circular enclosure, and THE ONLY CHURCH IN WALES DEDICATED TO ST STEPHEN. The font is THE OLDEST FONT IN BRITAIN, a scooped-out igneous boulder used as an altar stone in the Bronze Age, and somehow connected to the numerous standing stones that run north to south past Old Radnor. It was a font in a church on this site as far back as the 6th or 7th century. Even more precious, and a remarkable find in such a remote country church, is the matchless, early 16th-century organ case, THE OLDEST OF ITS KIND IN BRITAIN, a treasure beyond compare and one that would grace the grandest cathedral. Hidden away, high up and hard to find, amongst the rocks above the village of ABEREDW is a small cave where Llywelyn the Last hid on the night before he was killed in 1282 (*see above*). Legend has it that he went to the blacksmith in Aberedw to have the shoes of his horse reversed, so as to confuse the English who were tracking him.

The doors of the lonely 13th-century church at CREGINA once sported the paws of a wolf, said to be those of THE LAST WOLF KILLED IN WALES, during the reign of Elizabeth I.

Erected in 1717, PALES MEETING HOUSE in Llandegley is THE OLDEST CONTINUOUSLY USED QUAKER MEETING HOUSE IN WALES.

HERGEST RIDGE is a ridge of hills that straddles the border of England and Radnorshire, south of Presteigne. MIKE OLDFIELD, the composer of the classic album *Tubular Bells* (the record which set Virgin Records founder Sir Richard Branson on the road to fortune) called his second album *Hergest Ridge*, having moved to the area to escape media attention brought about by the success of the first. *The Red Book of Hergest* is one of the sources for the *Mabinogion* (*see* Pembrokeshire).

Radnorshire has THE LOWEST LEVELS OF LIGHT POLLUTION IN ENGLAND AND WALES, a quality that attracted former Army officer Jay Tate to set up BRITAIN'S FIRST SPACEGUARD CENTRE, at an observatory on top of a hill 2 miles (3.2 km) south of Knighton. The aim of the centre is to gather information on Near Earth Objects such as comets and asteroids, and to monitor their threat to Earth. The centre, the observatory and a planetarium can all be visited by appointment.

Gazetteer

NT National Trust

CADW Welsh Heritage

Anglesey

Marquess of Anglesey's Column
Llanfair PG
Tel: 01248 714393
Open all year round 9am – 5pm daily

Plas Newydd (NT)
3m south of Llanfair PG on A4080
Tel: 01248 714795

Beaumaris Gaol
Buntiers Hill,Beaumaris
Tel:: 01248 724444
www.anglesey.gov.uk/english/culture/gaol.htm

Beaumaris Old Courthouse Museum
Beaumaris Courthouse, Castle Street, Beaumaris,
Tel: 01248 811691

Beaumaris Castle CADW
Castle Street Beaumaris
Tel: 01443 336000
www.cadw.wales.gov.uk

Penmon Priory
4m north of Beaumaris off B5109
Open daily

South Stack
3m west of Holyhead on minor roads
www.southstack.co.uk

Penmynnyd
2m west Menai Bridge on B5420

Llangadwaladr Church
16m west of Menai Bridge on A4080

Breconshire

Cilmery
2m west of Builth Wells on A483

Trefeca
Aberhonddu
18m north west of Abergavenny on B4560 in Trefeca Village
Tel: 01874 711423

Craig-y-Nos
15m west of Merthyr Tydfil on A4067
Tel: 01639 731167
www.craigynoscastle.co.uk

Dan-yr-Ogof
1m north of Craig-y-Nos on A4067
Tel: 01639 730284
www.showcaves.co.uk

Ogof Fynnon Ddu
www.ogof.net

Maen Madoc Stone
On track 1m north west of Ysradfellte
12m north west of Merthyr Tydfil
Map ref SN91822 15771
Porth-yr-Ogof
South of Ystradfellte on minor roads
www.brecon-beacons.com
car park open daily
Chartist Cave
On moors west of B4560
between Ebbw Vale and Llangynidr
Map ref SO 12771 15230
Mynydd Llangatwg
On hills above Llangattock
South of Crickhowell
Map ref SO190145
Shakespeare's Cave
In Clydach Gorge, 6m west of Abergavenny
Off A465
Llangoed Hall
Llyswen
10m north east of Brecon on A470
Tel: 01874754525
www.llangoedhall.com
Capel-y-Ffin
14m north of Abergavenny
minor road between Llanthony Priory and Hay-on-Wye
Brecon Mountain Railway
3m north of Merthyr Tydfil
Tel: 01685 722988
www.breconmountainrailway.co.uk
Castell Dinas
33m south of Talgarth off A479

CAERNARFONSHIRE

Caernarfon Castle CADW
Tel: 01443 336000
www.cadw.wales.gov.uk
Conwy Castle CADW
Tel: 01443 336000
www.cadw.wales.gov.uk
Aberconwy House NT
Castle Street Conwy
Tel: *01492 592246*
Plas Mawr CADW
Conwy
Tel: 01443 336000
www.cadw.wales.gov.uk
Penrhyn Castle NT
Bangor
Tel: 01248 353084
Porth Oer (Whistling Sands)
3m north of Aberdaron on minor roads
Plas yn Rhiw NT
Tel: *01758 780219*
Lloyd George Museum
Llanystumdwy
2m west of Criccieth
Tel: 01766 522 071
Gwydir Castle
1m south west Llanrwst off B5106
Tel: 01492 641687
www.gwydircastle.co.uk
open 1 March to 31 October
Snowdon Mountain Railway
Llanberis
www.snowdonrailway.co.uk
Tel: 0870 458 0033
Aber Falls
2m south of Abergwyngregyn
On minor roads
Ty Mawr NT
1m west of Penmachno on minor road
(signposted)
Tel: *01690 760213*
St Cian's Llangian
1m west of Abersoch on B road

Cardiganshire

Aberystwyth Cliff Railway
Tel. 01970 617642
www.aberystwythcliffrailway.com
Vale of Rheidol Railway
Adjacent Aberystwyth station
Telephone 01970 625819
www.rheidolrailway.co.uk
Strata Florida CADW
Tel: 01443 336000
10m south of Devils Bridge
Minor road off B4343
www.cadw.wales.gov.uk
Nanteos
2m south of Aberystwyth at Rhydyfelin
Tel: 01970 624363
www.nanteos.co.uk
Llanerchaeron NT
2m south east of Aberaeron on A482
Telephone: 01545 570200
Soar-y-Mynydd
7m south east of Tregaron
on minor road to Abergwesyn

Carmarthenshire

Dolaucothi Gold Mine NT
10m north east of Llandovery
Tel: 01558 650177
Laugharne Boat House
Tel: 01994 427420
www.dylanthomasboathouse.com
Open May to October
Paxton's Tower NT
6m east of Carmarthen off B4300
Tel: 01558 650359
Open Daily Admission free
Aberglasney Gardens
10m east of Carmarthen on A40
Tel: 01558 668 998
www.aberglasney.org
Open every day
Dolauhirion Bridge
5m north of Llandovery
1m north of Rhandirmwyn
on minor roads

Denbighshire

Nantclwyd Hall
3m south of Ruthin on A494
Plas Newydd
Hill Street Llangollen
Tel: 01824 708223
Pontcysyllte Aqueduct
4m east of Llangollen off A5
Chirk Castle NT
3m south east of Llangollen on B4500
Tel: 01691 777701
Erddig NT
1m south of Wrexham (signposted)
Tel: 01978 355314

Flintshire

Hawarden Castle
5m north east of Mold on A5104-B5125.
The Tower, Nercwys
Nercwys, 2m south of Mold
Tel: +44 (0) 1352 700220
www.towerwales.co.uk
Plas Teg
3m south of Mold on A541
Tel: 01352 771 335
www.plasteg.co.uk
Rhuddlan Castle CADW
Village Centre
Tel: 01443 336000
www.cadw.wales.gov.uk

Glamorgan

Castell Coch CADW
2m north west of Cardiff on A470
Tel: 01443 336000
www.cadw.wales.gov.uk

Cardiff Castle
Tel: 0292 087 8100
www.cardiffcastle.com
Caerphilly Castle CADW
Village Centre
Tel: 01443 336000
www.cadw.wales.gov.uk
Aberdulais Falls NT
1m north east of Neath off A465
Tel: 01639 636674

Merioneth

Ffestiniog Railway
Porthmadog
Tel: 01766 516000
www.festrail.co.uk
Bala Lake Railway
Bala
www.bala-lake-railway.co.uk
Tel: 01678 540666
Harlech Castle CADW
Harlech
Tel: 01443 336000
www.cadw.wales.gov.uk
Portmeirion
2m south east of Porthmadog
Tel: (0)1766 770000
www.portmeirion-village.com
Fairbourne Steam Railway
Fairbourne, south of Barmouth
Tel: 01341 250362
www.fairbournerailway.com
Talyllyn Railway
Tywyn
www.talyllyn.co.uk

Monmouthshire

Tintern Abbey CADW
6 miles north of Chepstow on A466
Tel: 01443 336000
Blaenavon
6m south west of Abergavenny
www.world-heritage-bleanavon.org.uk
Gelligroes Mill Museum
Gelligroes Pontllanfraith
5m west of Cwmbran
Tel: *01495 222322*
Caerleon Roman City
Tel: 01633 423134
www.caerleon.net
Tredegar House
1m north of Newport
Tel: 01633 815 880
Chepstow Castle CADW
Chepstow Town Centre
Tel: 01443 336000
www.cadw.wales.gov.uk

Montgomeryshire

Powis Castle NT
2m south of Welshpool
minor road off A490
Tel: 01938 551929
St Melangell Church
Pennant Melangell
Minor road from Llangynog on B4391
www.st-melangell.org.uk

Pembrokeshire

Pembroke Castle
Pembroke Town Centre
Tel: 01646 684585
www.pembroke-castle.co.uk
Tudor Merchant's House NT
Tenby
Tel: 01834 842279
St Govan's Chapel
6m south of Pembroke
minor road S off B4319
Carew Mill
6m east of Tenby off A477
Tel: 01646 651782
www.carewcastle.com

Picton Castle
3m east of Haverfordwest
minor road S off A40
Tel: 01437 751326
www.pictoncastle.co.uk

Manorbier Castle
4m south west of Tenby off A4139
Tel: 01834 871394
www.manorbiercastle.co.uk

Oakwood Theme Park
8m east of haverfordwest signposted off A40
www.oakwoodthemepark.co.uk

Radnorshire

The Judge's Lodgings, Presteigne
Town Centre
Tel: 01544 260650
www.judgeslodging.org.uk

Abbeycwmhir
8m north of Llandrindod Wells
minor road NW off A483
`www. abbeycwmhir.org

Index of People

Aaron 130
Abercrombie, Sir Patrick 14
Abergavenny 1st Earl of 127
Addison, Joseph 60
Alexandra, Princess 51
Allgood, Thomas 129
Amundsen, Roald 96
Anglesey, 1st Marquess 3
Anglesey, 6th Marquess 35
Arnodin, Ferdinand 132
Arthur, King 72, 98, 129, 130, 167
Ashley, Laura 144
Ashley, Sir Bernard 25

Baker, Stanley 18, 110
Baldwin, Stanley 143
Barlow, Bishop 148
Barlow, Catherine 151
Barri, Gerald de 162
Baskerville, Thomas 167
Bassey, Dame Shirley 97
Beatles, The 35
Beatty, Warren 65
Beaufort, Margaret 10, 85, 87, 148, 153
Bennett, Hywel 65
Bestall, Alfred 46
Betjeman, Sir John 37
Black Bart 159
Blackmore, R.D. 111
Booth, Richard 26
Borrow, George 81, 164, 166
Bowdler, Thomas 104
Bowen, Jeremy 98
Boyce, Max 110
Bradshaw, John 165
Brangwyn, Frank 103
Branson, Sir Richard 173
Briggs, Sir 133
Britten, Sir Benjamin 143
Brown, Sir Samuel 107
Buckland, Jonny 89
Burges, William 94, 95
Burke, Edmund 76
Burne-Jones, Edward 9, 86
Burrows, Stewart 107
Burton, Philip 101
Burton, Richard 101, 156
Bute, 1st Marquess of 95
Butler, Eleanor 76

Cadfan 11
Cadwaladr 11
Caine, Michael 18
Cambrensis, Gerald 148
Campbell, Jane 170
Campbell, Lord Chief Justice 165
Campbell, Sir Malcolm 61, 62
Cardigan, 7th Earl of 48
Carnegie, Andrew 128
Carnegie, Lady Katharine 134
Carter, Isaac 58
Carter, Jimmy 103
Caryll, Mary 76
Castlereagh, Viscount 138, 139
Cawdor, Lord 155
Cayo-Evans, Julian 58
Chantrey, Sir Francis 54
Chaplin, Charlie 109
Charles I 50, 165
Charles II 133, 140, 163
Charles VI 10
Charles, Prince of Wales 31, 35, 44, 58, 82, 83
Charles, Thomas 117

Christie, Sir Archibald 25
Church, Charlotte 98
Churchill, Winston 42, 62, 109, 162
Cighill, Lieutenant 17
Clare, Gilbert de 49, 110
Clare, Richard de 152
Clemenceau, Georges 42
Clinton, Bill 27, 108
Clive of India 141
Clough, Richard 81
Coburn, Alvin 43
Colby, Charles 158
Coleridge, Samuel Taylor 53
Collins, Michael 119
Colton, James 65
Columbus, Christopher 78
Conan Doyle, Sir Arthur 167, 109
Constable, John 88
Constantine 31
Cooper, Tommy 110
Corbett, Judy 44
Cornwall, Duchess of 115
Cothi, Lewis Glyn 67
Coward, Noel 121
Crawshay, Richard 105, 106
Crawshay, Robert Thompson 106
Crawshay, William 105
Cromwell, Oliver 24, 50, 110
Cruise, Tom 86
Cyngen, Prince 75

Dahl, Roald 96
Dale, David 141
Dalton, Timothy 81
David, Bishop of Bangor 34
Davies, David 142, 143
Davies, Glyn 57
Davies, Gwendoline 143
Davies, Hywel 159
Davies, Jonathan 65
Davies, Lord 143
Davies, Margaret 143
Davies, Marion 109
Davies, Revd. D.M. 19
Davies, Rupert 39, 40, 71
Davies, Russell T 103
Davies, W.H. 130, 132
Davies, Walter 64
Diana, Princess of Wales 115
Douglas, Michael 104, 115
Drevacus 23
Dudley, Robert, Earl of Leicester 70
Duff, Lady Caroline 35
Duff, Sir Michael 35
Dwight, Geoff 72
Dylan, Bob 64

Earhart, Amelia 68
Edward I 4, 5, 11, 12, 30, 31, 50, 54, 60, 69, 72, 80, 85, 86, 91, 171
Edward III 19
Edward VI 137
Edward VII 22, 51, 95
Edward VIII 28
Edwards, Gareth 64, 65
Edwards, Thomas 70
Edwards, William 67, 107
Eisenhower, General 62
Elgar, Sir Edward 56, 143
Eliot, George 153
Elizabeth I 69, 81, 164, 172
Elizabeth II 31, 35, 92, 115, 147, 152, 163, 169
Elizabeth, Queen Mother 35
Ellis, Ruth 91
Epstein, Brian 35
Epstein, Jacob 97
Evans, Edgar 111
Evans, Ellis Humphrey 124
Evans, Gwynfor 47, 60
Evans, Mary Ann 153
Evans, Richard 7
Evans, Sir Geraint 56, 57, 107, 163
Evans, Theophilus 19
Evans, William 108
Everest, Sir George 24
Everett, Robert 14

Fairlie, Robert 116
Ferain, Catrin O 81
Fleming, Ian 61
Foley, Admiral Thomas 150
Foley, Richard 150
Follett, Ken 98
Fonda, Jane 13
Foot, Michael 135
Ford, John 111
Foster, Sir Norman 66
French, Dawn 14
Frost, John 131, 135
Fychan, Ednyfed 10

Gaunt, John of 126
Geldof, Bob 81
Gelert 46
George III 93
George IV 9
George V 115
George VI 163
Gibson-Watt, Lord 170
Gilbert, Sir Alfred 143
Gilchrist, Percy Carlyle 128
Gill, Eric 26
Gladstone, William 51, 86
Gloucester, Robert of 99
Glyndwr, Owain 50, 139, 165, 166, 170
Glynne, Catherine 86
Godwin, Mary 169
Goldman, Emma 65, 66
Goodman, Dr Gabriel 71
Greene, Hughie 82
Green-Price, Sir Richard 166
Greville, Charles 151, 152
Gruffudd, Llywelyn ap 18, 167, 171
Gruffudd, Rhys ap 148
Gruffydd, Ioan 79
Gruffydd, Lord Rhys ap 49, 54
Guest, Josiah John 105
Guest, Lady Charlotte 105, 136, 157
Guinevere, Queen 167
Gwilym, Dafydd ap 54, 55
Gwynedd, Owain 34, 78

Hahn, Kurt 109
Hall, Sir Benjamin 136
Hamilton, Emma 127, 151, 153
Hamilton, Sir William 127, 151, 152, 153
Hanbury, John 129
Hanratty, James 91
Hansom, Joseph 4
Hardie, Keir 106
Harlech, Lord David Ormsby-Gore 123
Harris, Howell 20
Harrison, Rex 65
Hatton, Sir Christopher 165
Havard, Rt. Revd. W.T. 28
Healey, Denis 101
Hearst, William Randolph 44, 109
Hemans, Felicia 84
Hemmings, David 13
Henry II 151, 171
Henry IV 81, 85, 139
Henry V 10, 84, 126, 148
Henry VI 153
Henry VII 10, 11, 85, 87, 131, 148, 153, 163
Henry VIII 54, 55, 64, 148
Henry, Lenny 14
Heseltine, Michael 101,103
Heslop, Thomas 58
Hildred, Falcon D. 116
Hill, Thomas 127
Hillary, Sir Edmund 45
Hill-Johnes, Sir James 66
Homfray, Samuel 106
Hoover, J. Edgar 65
Hope, Bob 109
Hopkins, Gerald Manley 85
Hopkins, Sir Anthony 101
Hopkins, Thomas 127
Hopper, Thomas 35, 99
Howe, Lord 101, 103
Hughes, Henry 54
Hughes, Nerys 91
Hughes, Richard 64, 123

Humphrys, John 97
Hutchence, Michael 81

Iddon, Prince 25
Ifans, Rhys 151

Jack 103
Jackson, Colin 98
Jaffreys, Judge George 74
James of St George 5, 86, 91
James, James 107
Janes, Evan 107
Jenkins, Arthur 135
Jenkins, Katherine 101, 108
Jenkins, Roy 135
Joan, Princess 5
John, Augustus 153, 154
John, Barry 64, 65
John, Gwen 150, 154, 155
John, King 5, 34, 151
John, Sir Goscombe 107
Johnes, Judge John 66
Johnes, Marianne 54
Johnes, Thomas 53, 54
Johnson, Amy 62
Johnson, Dr 79
Jones, Aled 14
Jones, Arwel 82
Jones, Elizabeth 92
Jones, Inigo 81, 90
Jones, John 80
Jones, Lewis 118
Jones, Mary 117
Jones, Michael D. 117, 118
Jones, Sir Tom 108
Jones, Terry 81
Jones, William 135
Jones-Parry, Sir Love 118
Jones-Parry, Sir Thomas 40
Joyce, William 116
Julius 130

Keck, Anthony 99
Kemble, Charles 18
Kennedy, J.F. 109
Kilvert, Revd. Francis 167
Kinnock, Glenys 14
Kinnock, Neil 14, 135
Koestler, Arthur 116

Lancaster, Duke of 10
Lancelot, Sir 98
Lawrence, T.E. 45
Leland, John 100
Lennon, Cynthia 72
Lennon, John 72
Lennon, Julian 72
Leopold II 71
Leverhulme, 1st Viscount 121
Lewis, Richard 106
Lewis, Saunders 51
Lewis, St David 136
Liddell, Alice 37
Liddell, Very Revd. Dr Henry 37
Lincoln, Abraham 21
Livingstone, David 71
Llewellyn, Richard 111
Lloyd George, David 37, 42, 43, 44
Lloyd George, Mair 43
Lloyd George, Margaret 43
Lloyd Jones, Anna 57
Lloyd Price, Richard John 118
Lloyd Wright, Frank 57
Lloyd, Charles 144
Lloyd, Emmeline Lewis 169
Lloyd, Richard 42
Llwyd, Humphrey 70
Llywelyn the Great 5, 46, 54
Llywelyn, the Last 172
Lockley, Ronald 161
Lowe, Howard 79
Lyne, Joseph Leycester 25
Lyttelton, Lord 88

Macdonald, Flora 88
Mackworth, Sir Humphrey 100
Macmillan, Harold 35
Macnamara, John 25

MacSweeney, Terence 119
Madoc, Prince 78
Maelgwn, King 33
Malory, Sir Thomas 55, 126
Mandela, Nelson 109
Manic Street Preachers 136
Marconi, Guglielmo 111, 129
Margaret, Princess 35
Marx, Karl 141
Mary, Queen 115
Masefield, John 132
Matthews, Cerys 98
Maximus, Magnus 31
Maybery, John 110
McCartney, Sir Paul 72
McDougall, Sir Arthur 122
McGoohan, Patrick 121
Meadow, James 9
Melus, The Doctor 46
Melville, Lieutenant 17
Mendelssohn, Felix 89
Merlin 59, 156
Milland, Ray 101
Mills, Hayley 96
Mollison, Jim 62
Monmouth, Duke of 163
Monmouth, Geoffrey of 126, 130
Montgomery, Field-Marshal 62
Montgomery, Roger de 138
Moore, Arthur 129
Morgan, Bishop William 46, 81, 83
Morgan, Capt. Godfrey 133
Morgan, Captain Sir Henry 134
Morgan, John 57
Morgan, Mary 165
Morgan, Sir Charles Gould 133
Morris, William 9
Mortimer, Edmund 166
Mortimer, Roger de 80
Mostyn, 3rd Lord 38
Myddelton, Richard 70
Myddelton, Sir Hugh 70
Myddelton, Sir Thomas 70

Nash, Beau 103
Nash, David 116
Nash, John 50, 54, 57, 60, 150, 157
Nation, Terry 97
Naylor, John 145
Naylor-Leyland, family 72
Nelson, Lord 105, 126, 127, 151, 152, 153
Neufmarche, Bernard de 16, 17
Newcastle under Lyme, 4th Duke 53
Nicolas, Jemima 155
Nicolini, Ernesto 21
Norton, Tom 168
Nott, Sir William 60
Novello, Ivor 97

Oates, Titus 136
O'Connell, J.J. 119
Oldfield, Mike 173
O'Toole, Peter 65, 111
Owen, Daniel 88, 89
Owen, David 135
Owen, Robert 141, 142
Owen, Sian 121

Pantycelyn, William Williams 66
Parry Thomas, John 61, 62, 74
Parry, Elizabeth 71
Parry, Joseph 106, 108
Patti, Adelina 21, 22, 102, 103
Paxton, Sir Joseph 80
Paxton, William 66
Peck, Gregory 156
Penrhyn, 2nd Lord 36
Penson, Thomas 142
Perrins, Mrs 119
Perrot, Sir John 64
Peters, Mike 93
Petty, Sir William 15
Phaer, Thomas 158
Philby, Kim 116
Philby, Sir John 116
Phillips, Sian 65
Plaid Cymru 46, 47

Ponsonby, Sarah 76
Pope Calixtus II 148
Pope Paul VI 136
Potter, Beatrix 79, 153
Powell, Annie 111
Powell, George Paul 55, 56
Powell, Howell 18
Powell, Thomas 55
Powis, Earls of 141
Powys, John Cowper 116
Pratt, Benjamin 127
Prescott, John 91
Presley, Elvis 157
Price, Dr Hugh 18
Price, Dr William 107, 108
Price, Sir John 18
Pryce, Jonathan 85
Pryce, Tom 72
Pryce-Jones, Sir Pryce 142
Puget, Admiral Sir Peter 165

Quant, Mary 144
Queen Elizabeth, Queen Mother 115

Recorde, Robert 154
Rees, Thomas 157
Rennie, John 134, 135
Repton, Humphry 124
Reuter, Julius 22
Rhys Jones, Griff 98
Rhys, Gruff 150
Richard ap Meryk ix
Richard II 85
Richard III 153
Richards, Brinley 60
Richards, Ebeneezer 57
Rinvolucri, G 9
Roberts, Rachel 65
Robertson, Henry 77
Roche, Lord Adam de la 162
Rodgers, William 135
Rodin, Augustus 150
Rolls, Charles Stewart 126, 135, 136
Rowlands, John 71
Rowlands, Richard 4
Royce, Henry 136
Rudd, Anthony 67
Rush, Ian 84
Russell, Bertrand 123

Salusbury, Colonel William 124
Savin, Thomas 50
Scott, Ridley 99
Scott, Robert Falcon 98, 111
Scott, Sir George Gilbert 9, 34, 148
Scott, Sir Walter 76, 77
Scott-Lee, Lisa 84
Scurlock, Mary 60
Secombe, Sir Harry 103
Seymour, Jane 137
Shakespeare, William 23, 85, 126, 166
Shelley, Harriet 168, 169
Shelley, Percy Bysshe 168, 169
Siddons, Sarah 18, 76
Siemens, William 102
Simenon, Georges 39
Sinclair, Sir Clive 112
Smith, Janie 79
Snowdon, Lord 35
Somerset, Duke of 10
St Alban 130
St Asaph 83
St Augustine 90
St Beuno 38, 84
St Cadfan 40
St Cybi 9
St David 55, 58, 148, 150, 157
St Dwynwen 12
St Elvis 157
St Govan 160
St Kentigern 83
St Maur, Sir Roger de 137
St Melangell 145
St Non 149
St Nywyn 41
St Seiriol 6
St Trillo 78
St Tysilio 2

St Winefride 84
Stanley, Henry Morton 71, 92
Stapleton, Maureen 66
Steele, Sir Richard 60
Stephens, Adrian 105
Stephenson, Robert 2
Stereophonics, The 112
Stevenson, Frances 43
Super Furry Animals 150
Sutherland, Graham 161
Sweyne, King 102

Talbot, Christopher 99
Talbot, Fanny 119
Talbot, Thomas Mansel 99
Tate, Colonel 155
Tate, Jay 173
Taylor, A.J.P. 63
Taylor, Elizabeth 156
Taylor, George 82
Taylor, Mrs A.J.P 63
Teg, Evan 144
Telford, Thomas 1, 2, 9, 31, 77
Tennyson, Lord 129
Thatcher, Margaret 101, 103
Thomas, Caitlin 63
Thomas, Colm 63
Thomas, Dylan 57, 62, 63, 102, 103, 133, 156
Thomas, Sidney Gilchrist 128
Thomas, Sir Rhys ap 60
Thomas, William 57
Tolkien, Professor 120, 126
Tolpuddle Martyrs 141
Tracy, Henry Hanbury 143
Tredegar, Viscount Evan 133
Tremble, Harry 66
Trevithick, Richard 106
Trevor, John 75
Trevor, Sir John 89
Tudor, Edmund 10, 148, 153
Tudor, Henry (Harry) 60, 119, 163, 153
Tudor, Jasper 10, 131, 153
Tudor, Owen 10, 153
Tudur, Fychan ap 11
Tudur, Owain 10
Turner, JMW 53, 64, 68, 88, 157
Tyler, Bonnie 101

Valois, Catherine de 148
Vancouver, Captain 165
Varney, Reg 91
Vaughan Williams, Ralph 143
Vaughan, Sir Thomas 168
Vaughan-Thomas, Wynford 163
Victoria, Queen 21, 36, 38, 86, 142
Vorderman, Carol 91
Vortigern, King 39, 154
Vosper, Sydney Curnow 121

Waddington, Augusta 136
Wagner, Richard 56
Wales, Don 62
Walter, Lucy 163
Watt, James 75, 170
Waugh, Andrew 24
Webb, Captain Matthew 82
Welford, Peter 44
Welles, Orson 44
Wellington, Duke of 76
Wen, Dafydd y Garreg 45
Wesley, John 112, 145
Whistler, Rex 3
Whitehead, Tatham 34
Wiiliams-Ellis, Sir Clough 118
Wilkinson, Ann 74
Wilkinson, John 'Iron Mad' 74, 75
Williams, Dr Rowan 103
Williams, Evan 28
Williams, JPR 64
Williams, Shirley 135
Williams, Talog 19
Williams, Zephaniah 135
Williams-Ellis, Sir Clough 25, 43, 72, 81, 121, 124
Williams-Ellis, Susan 121
Williams-Wynn family 81

Williams-Wynn, Sir Watkin 88
Willoughby de Broke, Lady 92
Wilson, Richard 88, 157
Wilson, Woodrow 42
Wingfield, Major Walter 72
Wogan, Sir John 162
Wordsworth, William 76
Wright, Wilbur 136
Wyatt, James 3
Wyatt, Thomas 21
Wynn, Sir John 44
Wynne, Robert 33

Yale, Elihu 73, 74
Yates, Jess 82
Yates, Paula 81, 82
Yogi, Maharishi Mahesh 35
Yorke, Philip 80
Young, Francis Brett 169

Zborowski, Count 61
Zeta-Jones, Catherine 104, 115

Index of Places

Aberystwyth Castle 50
Abbeycwmhir, Radnorshire 170, 171
Aber Falls, Caernarfonshire 45
Aberath, Cardiganshire 56, 57
Aberconwy House, Conwy 32
Abercynon, Glamorgan 106
Aberdaron, Caernarfonshire 38, 41
Aberdulais Falls, Glamorgan 112
Aberedw, Radnorshire 172
Aberfan, Glamorgan 110
Aberffraw, Anglesey 11, 15
Abergavenny Sugar Loaf 24
Abergavenny, Monmouthshire 128, 134, 136
Aberglasney, Carmarthenshire 67
Abergwili, Carmarthenshire 149
Abergynolwyn. Merioneth 122
Abersoch, Caernarfonshire 39
Abersychan, Monmouthshire 135
Aberystwyth Castle 56
Aberystwyth, Montgomeryshire 143
Aberystwyth, Cardiganshire 49, 50, 51, 52
Acton Hall, Wrexham 74
Adpar, Cardiganshire 58
All Saints, Gresford 79
All Saints, Oystermouth 104
Amlwch, Anglesey 8
Ammanford, Carmarthenshire 65

Bala Lake 116, 122
Bala, Merioneth 116, 117, 118
Bangor Cathedral 33, 34
Bangor, Caernarfonshire 33, 34, 35, 84
Bangor-is-y-Coed 90
Barclodiad-y-Gawres, Anglesey 14
Bardsey Island, Caernarfonshire 38, 39, 40, 41, 90
Barmouth Railway Bridge 119
Barmouth, Merioneth 119, 120, 122
Beaumaris Castle 5, 6, 86
Beaumaris Courthouse, Anglesey 4
Beaumaris Gaol, Anglesey 4
Beaumaris, Anglesey 1, 3
Beaumaris, St Mary's Church 4
Beaumaris, Ye Old Bull's Head 5
Beddgelert, Caernarfonshire 46
Bedwellty House, Monmouthshire 136
Bersham, Denbighshire 74, 75, 80
Bethesda, Caernarfonshire 36
Bethlehem, Carmarthenshire 67
Betws, Carmarthenshire 65
Betws-y-Coed, Caernarfonshire 46
Big Pit Mine 127
Bird Rock, Merioneth 124
Black Mountain 65
Black Mountains 167
Black Point, Anglesey 7
Blackwood, Monmouthshire 136
Blaenallyddu 57
Blaenau Ffestiniog, Merioneth 115, 116
Blaenavon, Monmouthshire 127, 128
Boat House, Laugharne 63
Bodelwyddan Hall, Flintshire 92
Bodnant gardens, Denbighshire 69
Bodrhyddan Hall, Flintshire 93
Bontddu, Merioneth 114
Boston, Massachusetts 73, 22, 128
Brangwyn Hall, Swansea 103
Brecon and Abergavenny Canal 127
Brecon Beacons 105, 106
Brecon Beacons National Park 22, 28
Brecon Cathedral 16, 17

Brecon Mountain Railway 28, 29
Brecon, Breconshire 16, 17, 18, 25
Brecon-y-Gaer, Breconshire 16
Britannia Bridge 2, 6, 32
Brymbo Hall, Denbighshire 75
Bryn Celli Ddu, Anglesey 14
Brynmawr, Breconshire 28
Builth Wells, Breconshire 25, 28
Bull bay, Anglesey 9
Burry Port, Carmarthenshire 68
Bwlch Iccyn, Merioneth 116
Bwlch-y-Groes, Merioneth 123

Cader Idris 88, 117
Caeo, Carmarthenshire 66
Caerleon, Monmouthshire 129, 130, 131
Caernarfon Castle 30, 31, 58, 82, 83, 86, 88
Caernarfon, Caernarfonshire 30, 31, 38, 43
Caerphilly, Glamorgan 110
Caerphilly, Castle 110
Caerwent, Monmouthshire 130
Caerwys, Montgomeryshire 143
Caerwys, Flintshire 49
Caldey Island, Pembrokeshire 162
Camddwr, River 57
Candleston Castle 111
Capel Lon Swan, Denbigh 70
Capel Pendref, Denbigh 70
Capel Ystrad Ffin, Carm. 68
Capel-y-Ffin, Breconshire 25, 26
Cardiff Bay 96
Cardiff Castle 94, 95
Cardiff, Glamorgan 94, 95, 96, 97, 98, 131
Cardigan Bay 40, 49, 122, 144
Cardigan Castle 49
Cardigan, Cardiganshire 48, 56, 148
Carew Mill, Pembrokeshire 161
Carmarthen Bay 61
Carmarthen Castle 153
Carmarthen, Carmarthenshire 59, 60
Carn Coch, Carmarthenshire 67
Carno, Montgomeryshire 144, 145
Carreg Cennen Castle 68
Carreg Wastad, Pembrokeshire 155
Castell Dinas, Dale, Breconshire 29
Castle Coch, Glamorgan 94
Castle Hotel, Neath 58, 100
Cefn Sidan Sands, Carm. 68
Cefncymerau, Merioneth 121
Cefneithin, Carmarthenshire 65
Celtic Manor Resort 136
Chartist Cave, Breconshire 23
Chepstow Castle 134
Chepstow, Monmouthshire 90, 134, 135, 166
Chirk Castle, Denbighshire 74, 80
Cilfyndd, Glamorgan 107
Cilgerran Castle 88, 157, 158
Cilmery, Breconshire 18, 19, 171
Claerwen Dam 169
Cleddau River, East 156
Clogau Gold Mine 114, 115
Clwyd, River 91
Clwydian Hills 92, 93
Clydach Gorge, Breconshire 23
Clyro Court 167
Clyro, Radnorshire 167, 168
Coed -y-Bleiddiau, Merioneth 116
Colwyn Bay, Denbighshire 81, 82
Constitution Hill, Aberystwyth 51, 52
Conwy Bay 7
Conwy Castle 31, 32, 86
Conwy, Caernarfonshire 31, 33
Conwy, River 37
Cors Caron 57
Craig-y-Nos, Breconshire 21, 22, 103
Cregina, Radnorshire 172
Creunant, Glamorgan 111
Criccieth, Caernarfonshire 42
Crickhowell Bridge 24
Crickhowell, Breconshire 23, 24
Croes Foel Farm, Denbighshire 74
Cwm Elan, Elan Valley 169
Cwmaman, Glamorgan 112

Cwmdonkin park, Swansea 103
Cwmhir Abbey, Radnorshire 145
Cyfartfha Castle 105, 106
Cyfarthfa, Glamorgan 105

Dale Peninsula, Pembrokeshire 153
Dale, Pembrokeshire 28, 163
Dan-y-Ogof, Breconshire 22
Dee, River 77, 85, 123
Denbigh Castle 69
Denbigh, Denbighshire 69, 70, 71, 139
Devil's Bridge, Cardiganshire 52, 53
Dinorwig Power Station 46
Dolauchirion, Bridge, Carm. 67
Dolaucothi, Carmarthenshire 61
Doldowlod Hale, Radnorshire 170
Dolgellau, Merioneth 114, 115, 124
Dolobran Meeting House 144
Dolwyddelan Castle 78
Dovey, River 144
Dowlais, Glamorgan 105, 144
Dublin 15, 87
Dwyfor, River 42, 43
Dynevor Park, Carmarthenshire 59

Ecliptic Observatory, Swansea 102
Efailwen, Carmarthenshire 65
Eisteddfod 49, 60
Elan Valley, Radnorshire 168, 169, 170
Eliseg's Pillar, Denbighshire 75
Erddig Hall, Denbighshire 80
Ewyas, Vale of 25

Fairbourne Railway, Merioneth 122
Ferndale, Glamorgan 110
Ffestiniog Railway 36, 115
Fishguard, Lower 156
Fishguard, Pembrokeshire 155, 156
Flint Castle 85, 86
Flint, Flintshire 85, 86, 139
Foel Cwmcerwyn, Preseli Hills 156
Fron Goch, Merioneth 118, 119

Garnant, Carmarthenshire 65
Gelligroes Mill, Monmouthshire 129
Gilfach Goch, Glamorgan 111
Glanaman, Carmarthenshire 65, 66
Glodffa Ganol, Merioneth 116
Glynneath, Glamorgan 110, 111
Glyntaf, Glamorgan 108
Goodwick, Pembrokeshire 155, 156
Gower Peninsula 111, 112
Great Orme, Caernarfonshire 36, 37, 38
Greenwood Forest Park 45
Gregynog, Montgomeryshire 143, 144
Gresford, Denbighshire 79
Griffithstown, Monmouthshire 137
Grwyne Fawr, Breconshire 24
Guildhall, Carmarthen 60
Gwaenynog Hall, Denbighshire 79
Gwaun Valley, Pembrokeshire 157
Gwaun-cae-gurwen, Carm. 65
Gwerndall, Crickhowell 24
Gwydir Castle, Caernarfonshire 44

Hafod House, Cardiganshire 53, 54
Harlech Castle 86, 120, 121
Harlech, Merioneth 120, 121
Haverfordwest, Pembrokeshire 147, 149, 150, 151
Hawarden Castle, Flintshire 86, 87
Hay-on-Wye, Breconshire 25, 26, 27
Hendre, The, Monmouthshire 126, 135
Heol Senni, Breconshire 28
Hergest Ridge 173
Hirwaun, Glamorgan 110
Holyhead Mountain, Anglesey 9
Holyhead, Anglesey 8, 9, 14, 15
Holywell, Flintshire 84, 85, 92
Honddu, River 16

Ivy Bush Hotel, Carmarthen 60

Jubilee Tower, Moel Famau 93

Knighton, Radnorshire 166, 173
Knucklas Viaduct 167

Lampeter, Cardiganshire 58
Landsker, The 151
Laugharne, Carmarthenshire 62, 63, 64
Lavan Sandbank, Caernarfonshire 4
Lavernock Point, Glamorgan 111
Leighton Estate, Mont. 145
Little Newcastle, Pembrokeshire 159
Little Orme, Caernarfonshire 37
Liverpool 7, 8, 34, 118, 145
Llanallgo, Anglesey 7
Llanberis, Caernarfonshire 45
Llandaff Cathedral 97
Llandaff, Glamorgan 96, 97
Llanddewi Brefi, Cardiganshire 58
Llanddona, Anglesey 14
Llandegfan, Anglesey 14
Llandegley, Radnorshire 172
Llandeilo Talybont, Glamorgan 112, 113
Llandeilo, Carmarthenshire 68
Llandewi Brefi, Cardiganshire 150
Llandinam, Montgomeryshire 142, 143
Llandovery, Carmarthenshire 28
Llandrillo-yn-Rhos, Denbighshire 78
Llandrindod Wells, Radnorshire 168
Llandudno, Caernarfonshire 37, 38, 91
Llandwrog, RAF 45
Llandyfriog, Cardiganshire 58
Llanelli, Carmarthenshire 64, 65
Llanelly House, Llanelli 64
Llanerchaeron, Cardiganshire 57
Llanfaes Priory, Anglesey 5
Llanfaes,Anglesey 4, 12
Llanfair PG, Anglesey 12, 13, 15, 122
Llanfair Talhaearn, Denbighshire 80
Llanfair-ar-y-bryn, Carm. 66
Llanfihangel -y-Pennant, Merioneth 117
Llanfihangel-y-traethau 123
Llanfoist, Monmouthshire 128
Llanfor, Merioneth 118
Llangadwaladr, Anglesey 11
Llangamarch Wells, Breconshire 168
Llangar Church, Merioneth 124
Llangattock, Breconshire 23
Llangattock-vibon-Avel, Mon. 135, 136
Llangefni, Anglesey 15
Llangernyw, Caernarfonshire 47
Llangoed Hall, Breconshire 25
Llangollen, Denbighshire 75, 76
Llangors Lake, Breconshire 29
Llangranog, Cardiganshire 56
Llangunnor, Carmarthenshire 60
Llanidloes, Montgomeryshire 145
Llanllwchaiarn, Montgomeryshire 142
Llannefydd, Denbighshire 81
Llanover Court, Monmouthshire 136
Llanover, Monmouthshire 136
Llanrwst, Denbighshire 81
Llanthony Priory, Monmouthshire 25
Llantrisant, Glamorgan 108, 109
Llantwit Major, Glamorgan 112
Llanwrtyd Wells, Breconshire 19
Llanwrtyd, Breconshire 168
Llanystumdwy, Caernarfonshire 42, 43, 44
Llechwedd Slate caverns 116
Lleyn Peninsula 3, 38, 39, 40, 41, 42, 120
Lloyd George Museum 42
Llwyd, River 127
Llyn Brianne 68
Llys Rhosyr Palace, Anglesey 12
Lochtyn, Cardiganshire 56
Lookout Mountain, Alabama 78
Lugg, River 164

Machynlleth, Montgomeryshire 138, 139, 140
Madrid 21
Madryn Castle, Caernarfonshire 39, 40
Maen Achwyfaen, Flintshire 92
Maen Madoc, Breconshire 22
Maenan Abbey 81
Maerdy, Glamorgan 111
Man, Isle of 9
Manchester 42
Manod Quarry, Merioneth 116

Manorbier Castle 162
Manordeifi, Pembrokeshire 158
Margam Abbey 99
Margam Castle 99
Margam Country Park 99
Margam Orangery 99, 100
Margam, Glamorgan 99, 100
Mawddach Valley, Merioneth 119
Menai Bridge 1, 2, 3, 6, 31, 32
Menai Strait 1, 2, 3, 5, 34, 35, 36
Merlin's Hill, Carmarthenshire 59, 150
Merlin's Oak, Carmarthen 59, 60
Merthyr Mawr, Glamorgan 111, 112
Merthyr Tydfil, Glamorgan 28, 104, 105, 106, 112, 127
Middleton on Gower, Glamorgan 111
Milford Haven, Pembrokeshire 127, 151, 152, 162
Millenium Stadium, Cardiff 98
Mobile Bay, Alabama 78
Moel Famau, Flintshire 93
Moelfre, Anglesey 7
Mold, Flintshire 87, 88, 89
Monmouth Castle 126
Monmouth, Monmouthshire 124, 126, 127
Monnow Bridge 125
Monnow, River 125
Montgomery, Montgomeryshire 138
Mt Snowdon 45, 88, 119, 120
Mumbles, The, Glamorgan 103, 104
Mynachlog-Ddu, Pembrokeshire 157
Mynydd Enlii, Bardsey 40
Mynydd Llangatwg, Breconshire 23, 28
Mynydd Mawr, Caernarfonshire 40
Mynydd Preseli, Pembrokeshire 157, 158

Nant Gwrtheyrn, Caernarfonshire 39
Nantclwyd Hall, Denbighshire 72
Nantclwyd House, Ruthin 71
Nanteos, Cardiganshire 55, 56
Nantgwyllt House, Elan Valley 168, 169
Narberth, Pembrokeshire 163
National Botanical Gardens 66
National Library, Aberystwyth 52
National Slate Museum, Llanberis 46
Neath Abbey 100
Neath, Glamorgan 100, 101
Neath, River 100
Nefyn, Caernarfonshire 39
Nelson Museum, Monmouth 127
Nercwys, Flintshire 89
Nevern, Pembrokeshire 158
New Haven, Connecticut 73
New Quay, Cardiganshire 57
Newborough, Anglesey 12, 15
Newport Cathedral 131
Newport, Monmouthshire 84, 130, 131, 132, 133, 136
Newton House, Dynevor Park 59
Newtown, Montgomeryshire 142, 168, 141
Norwegian Church, Cardiff 96
Nott Square, Carmarthen 60
NottageCourt 112

Oakwood Theme Park 163
Offa's Dyke 144, 166, 167
Ogof Fynnon Ddu, Breconshire 22
Old Cilgwyn Gardens, Cardiganshire 58
Old Radnor, Radnorshire 172
Our Lady Star of the Sea, Anglesey 9
Overton, Flintshire 92
Oystermouth, Glamorgan 104

Pales Meeting House 172
Pantymwyn, Flintshire 89
Parys Mountain, Anglesey 8
Patrishow, Breconshire 24, 25
Patti Pavilion, Swansea 102
Paxton's Tower, Carmarthenshire 66
Pembroke Castle 10, 152
Pembroke Dock, Pembrokeshire 159, 161
Pembroke, Pembrokeshire 152, 153
Pembrokeshire Coast Nat Park 147, 156, 161

Pen-y-Fan, Breconshire 28
Penderyn, Breconshire 28
Pendine Sands, Carmarthenshire 61, 62
Penegoes, Montgomeryshire 88
Penhow Castle 137
Penmon, Anglesey 6, 7
Penmorfa, Llandudno 37
Penmynnyd, Anglesey 10, 11
Penrhos Cottage, Llangolmen 161
Penrhyn Castle, Caernarfonshire 35, 36, 99
Penrhyn Point, Merioneth 122
Penrhyn Quarry, Caernarfonshire 36
Penrhyndeudraeth, Merioneth 123
Pentre Ifan, Preseli Hills 157
Pentrefelin, Caernarfonshire 45
Pen-y-Crug, Breconshire 16
Pere Lachaise 22
Picton Castle, Pembrokeshire 162
Pierhead Building, Cardiff 96
Pilleth, Radnorshire 166
Pirbright, Surrey 71
Pistyll Rhaeadr, Denbighshire 81
Pistyll, Caernarfonshire 39
Plas Mawr, Conwy 33
Plas Brondanw, Merioneth 124
Plas Grono, Wrexham 73
Plas Machynlleth 139
Plas Mynach, Barmouth 119
Plas Newydd, Anglesey 3, 14, 35
Plas Penmynnyd, Anglesey 10
Plas Teg, Flintshire 44, 89
Plas yn Rhiw, Caernarfonshire 41, 42
Plynlimmon, Cardiganshire 56
Poermeirion, Merioneth 114
Pontcycyllte, Denbighshire 77
Pontrhydyfen, Glamorgan 101
Pontrhydygroes, Cardiganshire 53
Pontypool, Monmouthshire 128, 129, 136
Pontypridd, Glamorgan 107, 108
Port Lynas, Anglesey 8
Port Penrhyn, Caernarfonshire 36
Port Talbot, Glamorgan 99, 101
Porth Madryn 40
Porth, Glamorgan 108
Porthmadog, Merioneth 115, 116, 121
Porth-y-Ogof, Breconshire 23
Portmeirion, Merioneth 121, 122
Powis Castle 140, 141
Preseli Hills, Pembrokeshire 156, 157
Prestatyn, Flintshire 93, 166
Presteigne, Radnorshire 164, 165
Prior's House, Penmon 6
Puerto Madryn 40
Puffin Island, Anglesey 7
Pwllheli, Caernarfonshire 46

Rheidol, River 52
Rheidol, Vale of 52, 53
Rhiwlas, Merioneth 118
Rhondda Valley, Glamorgan 107, 143
Rhoose Point, Glamorgan 111
Rhoscolyn, Anglesey 14
Rhos-on-Sea, Denbighshire 78, 79
Rhossili, Glamorgan 111
Rhuddlan 91
Rhuddlan Castle 86, 91
Rhydowen, Cardiganshire 57
Rhyl, Flintshire 91
Roch Castle, Pembrokeshire 162, 163
Rock Mile Woollen Mill 57
Rosebush, Pembrokeshire 161
Royal Welsh Warehouse 142
Ruthin Castle 72
Ruthin, Denbighshire 71, 72, 88, 139

Salem Chapel, Merioneth 121
Saugus, River 128
Segontium 30, 31
Senghenydd, Glamorgan 110
Severn Railway Tunnel 137
Severn, River 166
Sgwd y Eira, Breconshire 23
Shakespeare's Cave, Clydach Gorge 23
Sker House, Glamorgan 112
Skerries, The 15
Skewen, Glamorgan 101

Skirrid Inn, Monmouthshire 136
Skokholm Island, Pembrokeshire 161
Skomer Island, Pembrokeshire 161
Snowdon Mountain Railway 45
Snowdonia 2, 3, 9, 35, 43, 46, 101, 156
Soar-y-Mynydd, Cardiganshire 57
Sodom, Flintshire 92
Solva, Pembrokeshire 163
South Stack, Anglesey 9, 10
Spaceguard Centre, Radnorshire 173
Spillers Records, Cardiff 98
St Asaph Cathedral 83, 84
St Asaph, Flintshire 83, 84, 92
St Bartholomew's, Llanover 136
St Bride's, Cwmdeuddwr 169
St Brynach's, Nevern 158
St Bueno's, Caernarfonshire 38
St Bueno's, Holywell 84
St Bueno's, Pistyll 39
St Cadfan's Monastery, Bardsey 40
St Cadfan's, Tywyn 123
St Cian's, Llangian 46
St Cybi's, Holyhead 9
St Cynog's-y-stradgynlais 22
St David's Cathedral 84, 147, 148, 149, 162
St David's, Pembrokeshire 147, 148, 149
St Deiniol's Church, Hawarden 86
St Donat's Castle, Glamorgan 109
St Florence, Pembrokeshire 162
St Giles, Wrexham 73
St Govan's Chapel, Pembrokeshire 160
St Gwendoline's Talgarth 20
St Katharine's, Milford Haven 152
St Lawrence, Lavernock Point 111
St Marcella's Denbigh 70
St Margaret's Island, Pemb. 161
St Martin's, Laugharne 62
St Mary's Brecon 17
St Mary's Church, Tenby 154
St Mary's Overton 92
St Mary's, Aberavon 106
St Mary's, Dolgellau 114
St Mary's, Fishguard 155
St Mary's, Llanfair 121
St Mary's, Mold 87
St Mary's, Monmouth 125, 135
St Mary's, Newtown 141
St Melagell's, Montgomeryshire 145
St Michael's, Abergele 82
St Non's Chapel, Pembrokeshire 149
St Peter's Ruthin 71
St Tegai's, Llandygai 36
St Trillo's Chapel, Rhos-on-Sea 78
St Tysilio's Chapel, Anglesey 1, 2
St Winefride's Well, Flintshire 85
Stradey Park, Llanelli 64
Strata Florida, Cardiganshire 48, 53, 54, 55
Strumble Head, Pembrokeshire 155
Swallow Falls, Betws-y-Coed 44, 46
Swansea Museum 102
Swansea, Glamorgan 101, 102, 103, 144, 167

Table Mountain 24
Taff Railway 96
Taff, River 97
Talerddig Cutting, Mont. 145
Talley Abbey, Carmarthenshire 67
Tallylyn Railway, Merioneth 122, 123
Tan-y-Bwlch 116
Tarrell, River 16
Tawe, River 102
Teifi, River 54, 58, 157, 158
Tenby, Pembrokeshire 153, 154, 155
The Tower, Flintshire 89
Theatre Royal, Drury lane 22
Three Loggerheads Inn, Flint. 88
Tiger Bay, Cardiff 96, 97
Tintern Abbey, Monmouthshire 125
Tintern, Monmouthshire 137
Trawsfynydd, Merioneth 124
Trebarriad House, Breconshire 23
Trecastle, Breconshire 28
Trecwn, Pembrokeshire 159, 160
Tredegar House, Monmouthshire 133, 134

Tredegar, Monmouthshire 135
Trefeca, Breconshire 20
Trefechan Bridge, Aberystwyth 51
Tregaron, Cardiganshire 57
Tre-Howel, Pembrokeshire 155
Tremadog Bay 122
Tremadog, Caernarfonshire 45
Tremeirchion, Flintshire 92
Tre'r Ceiri, Caernarfonshire 39
Trimsaran, Carmarthenshire 65
Twyi Bridge 68
Twyi, River 67
Ty Gwyn, Barmouth 119
Ty Mawr, Caernarfonshire 46
Ty'n Dwr Hall, Denbighshire 80
Tywyn, Merioneth 122, 123

University of Wales 51
Usk, River 16, 131

Valle Crucis Abbey, Denbighshire 75
Van, Montgomeryshire 143
Vaynol Park, Caernarfonshire 35
Vyrnwy, Lake 145, 146

Welsh National Museum 95
Welshpool, Montgomeryshire 139, 144
West Bute Dock, Cardiff 96
Whiteford Lighthouse 112
Wiseman's Bridge, Carm. 62
Wrexham, Denbighshire 73, 74
Wye, River 25, 56, 125, 134
Wylfa Nuclear Power Station 15

Y Rug, Merioneth 124
Ynys Llanddwyn, Anglesey 12
Ynys Seiriol, Anglesey 7

Acknowledgements

My thanks to Alun Roberts, whose marvellously informative and entertaining book, *Discovering Welsh Graves*, was an inspiration.

I would like to thank, as always, Hugh Montgomery-Massingberd, a true gentleman. Also my agent Ros for her friendship and advice. And the ever patient home team at Ebury, Carey Smith, Vicky Orchard and Caroline Newbury. Thanks too, to Steve Dobell for his fine editing.

I would like to offer special thanks to Simon and Gayle for all their generous hospitality and kindness in letting us stay in the Old Church Hall. We could not have done this book without them.

And my love and gratitude to Mai – you just get better and better.